Hearing Gesture

Susan Goldin-Meadow

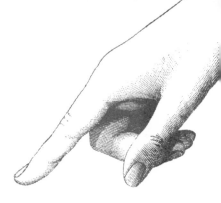

HEARING GESTURE

How Our Hands Help Us Think

The Belknap Press of Harvard University Press

Cambridge, Massachusetts, and London, England 2003

Library of Congress Cataloging-in-Publication Data

Goldin, Susan.
Hearing gesture : how our hands help us think /
Susan Goldin-Meadow.
    p.   cm.
Includes bibliographical references and index.
ISBN 0-674-01072-8 (alk. paper)
1. Gesture.   2. Thought and thinking.
3. Cognition in children.   4. Communication.
I. Title.

P117.G65 2003
302.2'22—dc21   2003050333

Illustrated by Linda K. Huff
Designed by Gwen Nefsky Frankfeldt

To Xander, Shmug, Beanie, and Bill

Contents

Preface

Much to my embarrassment, I had never heard of Jean Piaget when I left for my junior year abroad from Smith College to study psychology in Geneva, Switzerland (in my defense, it was quite some time ago and before Piaget's name had become synonymous with developmental psychology). I went because Smith had an excellent study-abroad program in Geneva and because French was the only foreign language I knew. The Genevan program was not, in fact, designed for students of psychology, but rather for students of international relations. There were three of us in psychology that year and the psychology faculty at the Piagetian Institute very graciously selected a set of courses that we were able to take and arranged for our own private (and oral) exams. I found myself in courses taught by Piaget himself, by Barbel Inhelder, and by Hermine Sinclair (my eventual advisor in Geneva) and, at exam time, responding to questions about Piaget and his theory posed by the experts themselves.

This experience was, to say the least, intimidating, but as many intimidating experiences are, it was also life-changing. I became hooked on psychology and developed a deep appreciation for Piaget's methods. In addition to learning the nuts and bolts of Piagetian theory (including an in-depth introduction to conservation that turned out to play an important role in our early studies of gesture), I learned how to observe. Piaget was an incredible observer of children. He noticed things that others didn't, and those things always offered unique insight into how children think. Moreover, he considered what children *said* about their thoughts to be only part of the story, and probably not even the most interesting part of the story for early thinking. I learned to consider what children *do* as learners in their own worlds to be an important source of information about their thoughts.

This focus on children as learners in naturalistic contexts was reinforced for me in graduate school at the University of Pennsylvania. My advisor, Rochel Gelman, had become famous for her challenges to Piaget's theory. But what was compelling about Rochel's approach was that her goal was not to pick away at the Piagetian edifice but to think constructively about what it is that children do know. I have always been impressed with Rochel's ability to observe children in their worlds and then design just the right study to figure out what they know about those worlds. I learned from my mentors how important it is to watch children as they learn, and I chose to watch their hands.

My studies of gesture began serendipitously, as many studies do. Rochel had lent me a videotape to use in the Introduction to Developmental Psychology class I was teaching at the University of Chicago. The tape was one-inch reel-to-reel, which gives those of you who know the history of video recorders some idea of how long ago this happened (Rochel was the experimenter on the tape and was wearing a miniskirt, which also dates the event). The tape showed a series of children participating in Piagetian conservation tasks, to be described in Chapters 1 and 3. I used the tape in my developmental class every year. Over time I became less fascinated with the children's verbal responses on the tasks, and I began to *look* at the tape as well as listen to it. I finally noticed that the children couldn't keep their hands still when they talked—they gestured constantly. Even the children who had already mastered conservation gestured throughout the task.

I asked Breckie Church, one of my graduate students, to take a look at children's hand movements. We collected our own videotapes of children participating in conservation tasks and, after hours of careful study, Breckie was convinced that these movements were not just hand waving. Rather, the children were using their hands to convey substantive information about the task.

Not wanting the way we described the gestures to be influenced by the speech we heard during transcription, we next went through the tapes coding speech without gesture (with the picture turned off) and gesture without speech (with the sound turned off). And here we made our most interesting discovery—the observation that underlies all others I will describe in this book. Many times, a child would produce a gesture that conveyed the same information he or she had just articulated in speech. At other times, however, a child would give one explanation in speech and a completely different explanation in gesture, producing what we called a gesture-speech "mismatch."

Our second discovery was that these gesture-speech mismatches have cognitive significance. When we gave children who had initially given incorrect answers on the conservation task instruction in the task, only some of the children profited from our instruction—those who had produced many gesture-speech mismatches in their previous explanations. We thus concluded that gesture not only reveals a child's unspoken thoughts, but also can give us notice that the child may be ready to learn new things.

The goal of the research program that grew out of these discoveries, and the goal of this book, is to understand and convey the importance of gestures of this sort. When does gesture reveal thoughts that are not expressed in speech? What kind of thoughts does it reveal? Does gesture play an active role in the conversations we have or, even more fundamentally, the thoughts we think? In the chapters that follow, I will try to make the case that gesture can indeed shape both our conversations and our thoughts. In this way, gesture can reveal, and propel, cognitive change.

My research program was born in collaboration and has continued in collaboration. The list of students and colleagues with whom I've had the good fortune to work is large. The studies of the gestures children and adults use when solving problems were done in collaboration with Breckie Church, Michelle Perry, Martha Alibali, Philip Garber, Miriam Bassok, Sharon Syc, and Theresa Graham. The studies of the gestures young children use when learning language were done in collaboration with Marolyn Morford and Cynthia Butcher. The studies of the gestures congenitally blind children use when solving problems and learning language were done in collaboration with Jana Iverson, Heather Tencer, and Jill Lany. The studies of how adults get meaning from children's gestures were done in collaboration with Melissa Singer, Cathy Sandhofer, Deborah Wein, Cecilia Chang, Janna Hicks, San Kim, and Lucia Flevares. The studies of the cognitive processes underlying the gestures that children and adults produce were done in collaboration with Susan Wagner, Howard Nusbaum, Spencer Kelly, Jessica Somerville, and Stella Lourenco. The study of how gesture is used in interview situations was done in collaboration with Sara Broaders. The studies of the gestures that deaf children produce when they can't learn spoken language and haven't yet learned sign language were done in collaboration with Lila Gleitman, Heidi Feldman, Carolyn Mylander, Jill Morford, Xiao-lei Wang, Ming-yu Zheng, Jody Saltzman, Amy Franklin, Bari Wieselman Schulman, Sarah van Deusen Phillips, Rachel Mayberry, Peggy Miller, and Susan Gelman. And finally, the studies of the gestures that hearing adults produce when they are forced to use their hands to talk were done in collaboration with Jenny Singleton, Lisa Gershkoff-Stowe, Elif Yalabik, Amy Hammond, and David McNeill, the father of gesture studies at the University of Chicago. I thank all of my collaborators for making the process of discovery so thoroughly enjoyable. Needless to say, this book would not exist were it not for them.

I also thank Carolyn Mylander for running my lab for over twenty years, ably assisted by Martha Scott. In addition to making everything in the lab run smoothly, Carolyn and Martha work hard to make sure that people respect one another and have fun together. The weekly meetings that we hold in the lab are to me the heart of the research and educational process. I thank all of the students and colleagues who attend for the hard and constructive thinking they do every Wednesday afternoon.

My research program has received generous support from a number of sources: the National Institute of Child Health and Human Development (RO1 HD18617, 1984–1990; RO1 HD31185, 1994–1996), the National Institute on Deafness and Other Communication Disorders (RO1 DC00491, 1988–2006), the National Science Foundation (BNS 8810769, 1977–1992), the March of Dimes (1993–2000), and the Spencer Foundation (1980–1983, 1995–2000). I would also like to thank Irving B. Harris, whose chair I hold in the Department of Psychology and Committee on Human Development at the University of Chicago. He has done much over his long career to better the lives of children in our society, and I am grateful for his support and honored to hold a professorship bearing his name. The actual writing of the book took place while I was supported by a John Simon Guggenheim Fellowship and a James McKeen Cattell Fellowship. I spent my sabbatical year at home at the University of Chicago, avoiding all discussions of departmental matters and talking only about gesture—it was a wonderfully satisfying year.

At Harvard University Press, I thank Elizabeth Gilbert for her graceful edits, and Elizabeth Knoll for helping me put together a readable book with all of the pictures that a book on gesture ought to have. I thank Linda Huff for transforming the videotapes I sent her into beautiful line drawings that capture the essence of gesturing. I found it remarkably difficult to tell Linda how to segment the gestures that accompany speech—far more difficult than it had been to tell her how to isolate gestures for the book I had just completed on deaf children using gesture as their sole means of communication (Goldin-Meadow 2003). This difficulty, in a sense, captures an important aspect of the phenomenon I describe in this book—the gestures that accompany speech are not easily described as segmented, stable lexical units strung together to form larger sentential units (but the deaf children's gestures are—see Chapter 14). The gestures that accompany speech make use of a distinctly different representational format than speech (or sign, or the deaf children's gestures) and, as a result, may be naturally suited to convey different notions from those typically conveyed in speech. Getting the pictures ready for Linda, whose skill as an artist led to superb drawings of both kinds of gestures, brought home this fundamental difference as forcefully as any study.

The manuscript improved immensely as a result of careful readings by many colleagues and friends. I thank them all for their comments and suggestions: Martha Alibali, Rochel Gelman, Mildred Goldin, Annette Karmiloff-Smith, Sotaro Kita, David McNeill, Howard Nusbaum, Asli Özyürek, and Jim Stigler. I thank Dario Maestripieri for encouraging me to use a draft of the book in the course we taught together on the communicative uses of nonverbal behavior. The comments from the class, and particularly from Dario, were very helpful. I thank Dedre Gentner for our monthly sustaining dinners that often turned to gesture. I thank Kathy and Kevin Clougherty and the Gibson family for their friendship and support while I worked on revisions on Washington Island. I heartily recommend an island for book writing.

And most of all, I thank my family. All three of my children, perhaps not surprisingly, are big gesturers and have contributed to my studies of gesture. Alexander ("Xander") as a youngster was the only child in all of our studies to produce no interpretable words, only gestures. Jacqueline ("Beanie") was a key participant in our cognitive-load studies (although she still complains that, as the daughter of the person in charge, she had to forfeit her yo-yo when there weren't enough to go around). And Nathaniel ("Shmug") came up with the title—*Hearing Gesture*—which nicely captures the important role that the hands play in communication (and thinking). I thank them for bringing immeasurable joy to our household and to my life. Finally, I thank my husband, Bill Meadow. He has, over the years, read every word I have ever written, often more than once. His feedback has made me a better writer and his companionship, love, and friendship have made me a better person. I owe him more than I can say.

Hearing Gesture

part one

A Window on the Mind

Gesture Is Everywhere

A student walks into a class wearing a tie. The male professor is not. Both are making a statement about their attitude toward the class, whether or not they mean to. Such acts are part of what is called "nonverbal communication." A wide-ranging array of behaviors count as nonverbal communication—the home and work environments we create, the distance we establish between ourselves and our listeners, whether we move our bodies, make eye contact, or raise our voices, all collaborate to send messages about us (Knapp 1978). But these messages, while important in framing a conversation, are not the conversation itself.

We might be tempted to restrict what we take to be the conversation to the words that come out of the speaker's mouth. Indeed, the traditional view of communication divides it into its verbal and nonverbal components, with little attention to the way the two interact to convey meaning. Adam Kendon (1980) was among the first to challenge this view, arguing that at least one form of nonverbal behavior—gesture— cannot be separated from the conversation itself. As David McNeill (1992) has shown in his groundbreaking studies of gesture and speech, the hand movements we produce as we talk are tightly intertwined with that talk in timing, meaning, and function. To ignore gesture is to ignore part of the conversation.

The focus of this book is the way we move our hands, not the way we wear our hats. I further restrict my focus to the way we move our hands when we speak. These movements are what I mean when I use the term *gesture* in this book. It is obvious that how we position our bodies, wear our clothing, and hold our possessions are nonverbal cues that occur everywhere—they are pervasive and inescapable (see, for example, Goffman 1976). It is less obvious that *gesture,* as I am using the term, is also everywhere. But it is. We have not yet discovered a culture in which speakers do not move their hands as they talk (Feyereisen and de Lannoy 1991). Indeed, even individuals who are blind from birth and have never seen others gesture purposefully move their hands as they talk (Iverson and Goldin-Meadow 1998). Whenever there is talk, there is gesture.

What Is Gesture?

Gesture is a term that encompasses a great deal. We have already narrowed our focus to the hand movements that co-occur with speech, yet even this set of behaviors does not form a single category. In 1969 Ekman and Friesen proposed a scheme for classifying nonverbal behavior and identified five types—illustrators, adaptors, emblems, affect displays, and regulators.[1] Our focus is on one of these five—illustrators, called "gesticulation" by Kendon (1980) and "gesture" by McNeill (1992). These terms refer to hand movements that are directly tied to speech. They can beat the tempo of speech, point out referents of speech, or exploit imagery to elaborate the contents of speech. For example, a child says that the way to get to her classroom is to go upstairs, and she illustrates the path by simultaneously arcing her hand upward.

The gestures that I will focus on in the first three parts of this book are almost always produced along with speech. They consequently take on the intentionality of speech. Although speakers may not be completely aware of having produced hand movements, they are very aware of having spoken. Their gestures are in the service of communication and, in this sense, are deliberate.

Gestures, as I am using the term, contrast with *adaptors,* fragments or reductions of previously learned adaptive hand movements that are maintained by habit—smoothing your hair, pushing your glasses up on

---

1. Two of the five categories do not involve hand movements at all: "affect displays," whose primary site is the face, and "regulators," which typically involve head movements or slight changes in body position. Regulators maintain the give-and-take between speaker and listener. Like gestures, they are related to the conversation; unlike gestures, however, which are interlaced with moment-to-moment fluctuations in speech, regulators are involved in the pacing of the exchange.

your nose even when they are perfectly positioned, holding or rubbing your chin. Adaptors are performed with little awareness and no intent to communicate (Ekman and Friesen 1969).

At the other end of the awareness spectrum, we find *emblems*. Emblems are what people first think of when I tell them I'm writing a book about gesture—the "thumbs up," the "okay," the "shush," and a host of other hand movements, many of which have unprintable meanings. Speakers are always aware of having produced an emblem and produce it to communicate with others, often to control their behavior.[2]

Emblems differ from gestures in a number of respects (McNeill 1992). Most important, they do not depend on speech. They convey their meanings perfectly well when produced without any speech at all. Moreover, unlike gestures whose meanings are constructed in an ad hoc fashion in the context of the speech stream, emblems have a constant form–meaning relation that does not depend on the vagaries of the conversation. In the above example, the arcing-upward gesture referred to taking the stairs. If that same movement were produced in the context of the sentence "their dispute seems to be escalating," it would refer instead to mounting tensions. In contrast, the "okay" emblem means "things are fine" independent of the particular sentence it accompanies, and even if it is not accompanied by any sentence whatsoever.

Emblems are held to standards of form. Imagine making the "okay" sign with the middle finger, rather than the index finger, forming a circle with the thumb—it just doesn't work. But producing the arcing-upward gesture with either a pointing hand, an open palm, or even an O-shaped hand seems perfectly acceptable. In this sense, emblems (but not gestures) are like words, with established forms that can be understood by members of the community in the absence of context or explanation.

It is precisely because gestures are produced as part of an intentional communicative act (unlike adaptors) and are constructed at the moment of speaking (unlike emblems) that they are of interest to us. They participate in communication, yet they are not part of a codified system. As such, they are free to take on forms that speech cannot assume and are consequently free to reveal meanings that speech cannot accommodate.

2. Many cultures, particularly in Africa, have developed relatively elaborate systems of emblems that are used for counting. These gestures can be used in place of spoken number words or for emphasis (Zaslavsky [1973] 1999).

Types of Gestures That Accompany Speech

There are almost as many schemes for classifying the gestures that accompany speech as there are gesture researchers. The differences, however, lie mainly in the size and number of slices, not in where the major cuts are made. McNeill (1992) identifies four different types of gestures. Efron ([1942] 1972) and Ekman and Friesen (1969) divide the pie into smaller slices, whereas Krauss, Chen, and Gottesman (2000) divide it into bigger slices. I use McNeill's terms here; Table 1 displays the relation between this categorical system and the others.

ICONIC GESTURES

A child makes a twisting motion in the air while saying, "I can't open this jar." The form of this gesture bears a close relation to the semantic content of speech. It is consequently considered an *iconic* gesture (McNeill 1992). Iconic gestures come in all forms:

- A spreading-apart motion produced when a child says of a row of checkers, "All you did was spread them out" (an example of Ekman and Friesen's [1969] *kinetographic* gesture depicting bodily action).

- An arcing-upward motion produced while saying, "I had to go upstairs to find my slippers" (an example of Ekman and Friesen's *spatial movement* gesture depicting a spatial relation).

- Tracing a circle in the air with the index finger while saying, "It

Table 1.   Schemes for classifying types of gestures

Krauss, Chen, and Gottesman (2000)	McNeill (1992)	Ekman and Friesen (1969)
		Kinetographic gestures
Lexical gestures	Iconic gestures	Spatial movement gestures
		Pictographic gestures
	Metaphoric gestures	Ideographic gestures
Deictic gestures	Deictic gestures	Deictic gestures
Motor gestures	Beat gestures	Baton gestures

was a round ornament" (an example of Ekman and Friesen's *picto-graphic* gesture depicting a drawing in the air).

In general, iconic gestures represent body movements, movements of objects or people in space, and shapes of objects or people. They do so concretely and relatively transparently. But they are constructed in the act of speaking, and as a result, their "transparency" depends on the speech they accompany. For example, consider a rotating gesture made with a pointing hand. The gesture refers to a ballerina's movements when the speaker says, "She does lovely pirouettes." However, the same gesture refers to a hand twisting off a jar lid when the speaker says, "Which direction shall I turn this?" Iconic gestures are, by their nature, opportunistic and improvisational (Bavelas 1994).

METAPHORIC GESTURES

When adults are asked to solve algebra word problems, they gesture. For example, consider an adult asked to solve the following problem (Alibali et al. 1999):

> After a seven-day harvest, a potato farmer notices that his rate of gathering potatoes increased steadily from 35 bushels/day to 77 bushels/day. How many bushels of potatoes total did the farmer collect during the seven-day harvest?

Adults produce two types of gestures when explaining problems of this sort: (1) gestures containing smooth, continuous motions (such as sweeping, arcing, dragging) that represent change over a single non-partitioned event, that is, a continuous representation; and (2) gestures containing a set of discrete movements (such as a sequence of three or more taps or zigzags) that represent change over a series of steps, that is, a discrete representation. The form of these gestures indicates whether the adult conceptualizes the problem as one of continuous change or discrete change, and thus presents an abstract idea rather than a concrete object. Gestures of this type are consequently considered to be *metaphoric* gestures (McNeill 1992).

DEICTIC GESTURES

A speaker points at his sister while saying, "I gave it to her yesterday." This is a *deictic* gesture—gestures used to indicate objects, people, and locations in the real world (McNeill 1992). Deictic gestures always indicate, but they do not always indicate visible objects or people. For example, the speaker could have produced precisely the same sentence while pointing toward the chair where his sister sat earlier that day but no longer sits—the speaker would be pointing at the chair but using that pointing gesture to refer to his sister. More abstract still, the speaker could have pointed at a space that, earlier in the conversation, had been established as standing for his sister. Even the simple pointing gesture can be quite abstract.

BEAT GESTURES

Beat gestures do just that—they beat musical time. The hand moves along with the rhythmical pulsation of speech (McNeill 1992). Beat gestures assume the same form regardless of content. They are typically made with short, quick movements in the periphery of the gesture space. Unlike iconic, metaphoric, and deictic gestures, which carry information about the plot line, beat gestures reflect the structure within which the plot line unfolds. By putting stress on a word, beat gestures index that word as significant, not for its content, but for its role in the discourse (McNeill 1992).

In the chapters that follow, I will focus primarily on gestures that tell the story—iconics, metaphorics, and deictics—for these are the gestures that have the potential to reveal, and perhaps shape, speakers' thoughts.

Studying Gesture

The first task in studying gesture is to identify it in the stream of motor behavior. Gesture occurs during the act of speaking, but not all acts performed by a speaker count as gesture. If I twist off the lid of the jelly jar while asking you to give me the peanut butter, my jar-twisting action would not be considered a gesture, despite the fact that it occurs with speech (and despite the fact that the jelly-jar twist gives you a good sense of what I intend to do with the peanut butter once I get it). My jar twisting is a functional act on an object and therefore is not a gesture. It opens the jar—it does not symbolize opening the jar. The criteria for a gesture thus stipulate that the hand motion (1) be produced during the communicative act of speaking (although it itself need not communicate information to a listener—more on this later) and (2) not be a functional act on an object or person.

Our next task is to describe the form of the gestures. My approach has been to borrow a descriptive system from the sign language literature. I and my fellow investigators describe the shape of the hand as it moves, using the set of symbols developed to describe handshapes in American Sign Language. We also describe the trajectory of the motion, the location of the hand relative to the body, and the orientation of the hand in relation to the motion and body.

The final task, attributing meaning to the gestures, is the most difficult. We get some idea of a gesture's meaning from its form. For example, movements that rotate in a circle typically refer to acts that rotate, objects that have a circular shape, or abstract ideas that have circularity at their core. However, context is equally important in identifying a gesture's meaning. A pointing finger rotating in space can refer to a ballerina's pirouetting movements in one context, and a rotating hand in another, as we have seen. In general, gesture meaning has to be coded in relation to the task at hand. We use speech and other aspects of the communication context to provide a framework for the gestures that the speaker produces, and we then interpret the gestures within that framework. For example, in our conservation studies, where children are asked whether the transfer of a liquid (or other medium) moved from one container to a differently shaped container has affected the quantity, the appropriate unit of analysis for the task is the conservation rationale—the type of explanation the child gives to justify his or her beliefs about a quantity (children before age seven or eight are convinced that the amount of liquid does change when it changes containers, and can give reasoned explanations for their beliefs). There is a large literature describing and cataloguing the rationales children produce in speech on this task. When we code the gestures that children produce, we first ask whether the children convey information in gesture that is relevant to a conservation rationale; if so, we attempt to code the children's gestures in terms of rationales. To the extent that this is possible, we can then compare the rationales children convey in their speech with the rationales they convey in their gestures.

Note, however, that gesture and speech never convey exactly the same information, as we will discover in Chapter 3. The extent to which gesture and speech convey diverging information is always one of degree, and depends crucially on the level at which we are analyzing the task. For example, saying "the glass is tall" does not convey exactly the same thing as gesturing "tall" (a flat palm held horizontally at the top of the glass). The speech indicates that the child is thinking generally about the height dimension, the gesture indicates a particular height. In terms of type of rationale for a conservation of water task, however, both gesture and speech are conveying the same information—the "focus on height" rationale. What we choose to focus on as the child's "meaning" depends on the question we are asking. If we want to use gesture to probe the child's understanding of conservation, we need to code speech and gesture at the level of the rationale. If, however, we want to use gesture to probe how children describe the dimensions of objects, we will want to code at a finer level of detail.

Thus the meaning codes we use for gesture can be more or less detailed—although, unfortunately, whatever system we use, gesture coding always takes time. It is a slow, painstaking process. At the end of the process, moreover, there is no guarantee that the meaning we assign a particular gesture is, in fact, the right meaning for that speaker. As in all studies that involve subjective coding, we need to establish reliability—that other coders would attribute this particular meaning to the speaker—and validity—that this meaning is, in fact, what the speaker had in mind. I tackle issues of reliability in gesture coding in Chapter 3 and validity in Chapter 5.

The typical gesture study relies on video recordings of people talking—conversing naturally, narrating a story, explaining how they solved a problem, and so on. Researchers observe the gestures that are produced in relation to speech, and use those gestures to make inferences about how the speaker talks and thinks. Often the content of talk is directed by having all of the speakers watch the same cartoon, describe the same objects, or solve the same problems. Giving all of the speakers the same stimulus to react to has the advantage of narrowing the range of responses. Speakers are likely to say the same kinds of things on such tasks, which then allows us to interpret gesture in the context of spoken sentences that are similar in content and form.

We can also be clever about which speakers we study. For example, if speakers who have been blind from birth gesture when they speak, it tells us something about how important—or in this case, how unimportant—seeing gesture is to using gesture. As another example, we can study children who are having difficulty learning language. These children, by using gesture to go beyond their linguistic limitations or not, can tell us whether gesture and speech can complement each other in children whose development has gone awry. My colleagues and I have also spent many years studying deaf children who have not learned to speak and have not been exposed to sign language. It turns out that these children use gesture to communicate. Comparing the gestures that the deaf children use with those produced by hearing speakers when

they talk can tell us whether gesture changes its form when it is not produced in the context of speech. Thus we can learn a great deal just by observing gesture in a variety of well-chosen speakers and tasks.

In addition to observing gesture as it occurs along with relatively natural talk, we can manipulate aspects of a task and look at what happens to gesture. For example, we can make a task harder and explore
whether rate or type of gesture changes as speakers increase the amount
of cognitive effort they are putting into the task. We need studies of this
type in order to better understand the causes that lead to gesturing—its
mechanism. We can also manipulate gesture itself, and observe the con-
sequences. For example, we can prevent speakers from gesturing and
explore the effect that this manipulation has on their performance of
other cognitive tasks. These types of studies are necessary to understand
the function gesture serves.

Overall, the key to any study of gesture is its coding system—isolat-
ing gesture from the stream of motor behavior, describing its form, and
assigning it meaning (and, of course, going through the steps to ensure
that the meaning codes are reliable and valid). Although time-consum-
ing, looking at gesture is essential if our goal is to fully understand what
people are thinking about as they talk.

2

Not Just Hand Waving

We all know that nonverbal behavior can "give us away." A smile, for example, can reveal our pleasure with an outcome despite verbal protestations to the contrary. What many people do not instinctively realize is that nonverbal behavior—gesture, in particular—can reveal thoughts as well as feelings.

Argyle (1975) characterizes the various roles that nonverbal behavior can play in human communication, noting that it can express emotion, convey interpersonal attitudes, present one's personality, and help manage turn-taking, feedback, and attention. But, in a striking omission, his list gives nonverbal behavior no role in conveying the message itself, only a role in conveying the speaker's attitude toward the message or in regulating the interaction between speaker and listener (Mueller 1998; Wundt [1900] 1973; see Feyereisen and de Lannoy 1991 for a review of studies focusing on gesture as a reflection of emotion and attitude).

Argyle (1975) has his finger on the folk view of gesture—that gesture can, for example, mark us as liars, but does not give away the content of our lies. And the folk view is correct in part—our hand gestures can indeed identify us as liars (Ekman and Friesen 1972, 367). But gesture can also give our lies away—and our truths, for that matter. A truth is communicated when a speaker says "I ran all the way upstairs," while spiraling her hand upward. The speaker has conveyed through her gesture, and only through her gesture, that the staircase she mounted was a spiral. Perhaps if her spiral movement were produced slowly and with little enthusiasm, it would also convey the speaker's attitude toward her climb. But at the least, the gesture provides specific information that goes beyond feelings and attitudes.

Conveying Substantive Information

The gestures that speakers produce along with their talk are symbolic acts that convey meaning. It is easy to overlook the symbolic nature of gesture simply because its encoding is iconic. A gesture looks like what it represents—for example, a twisting motion in the air resembles the action used to open a jar—but the gesture is no more the actual act of twisting than is the word "open." Or a speaker may hold her hands five inches apart while walking around the house muttering, "Now where did I put those scissors?" She has indicated with her hands that it is the small pair of scissors she seeks, not the large. Her gesture stands for the scissors but is not the scissors. If, however, she were to hold her hands in precisely the same arrangement to determine whether a length of cloth will fit a particular spot, her hand movements would be substituting for a ruler and therefore would not be symbolic at all—nor would they constitute a gesture.

Because gesture can convey substantive information, it can provide insight into a speaker's mental representation (Kendon 1980; McNeill 1985, 1987, 1992). For example, a speaker in one of McNeill's (1992, 12) studies says "and he bends it way back" while his hand appears to grip something and pull it from a space high in front of him back and down to his shoulder. The speaker is describing a scene from a comic book in which a character bends a tree back to the ground. The gesture reveals the particular point of view that the speaker takes of the event—he is gripping the tree as though he were the tree-bender, making it clear by his actions that the tree was anchored on the ground. He could, alternatively, have represented the action from the point of view of the tree, producing the same motion without the grip and perhaps in a different space (one that was not tied to his shoulder), a movement that would have conveyed the tree's trajectory but not the actions performed on it.

As another example, when asked to explain why a particular gear will rotate (or fail to rotate) when the handle attached to another gear is turned, adults frequently use their hands as they talk, and their hands can be quite informative (Perry and Elder 1997; see also Schwartz and Black 1996). The adult is shown a picture of three gears, all touching one another, and a target gear touching one of the three (but not the gear with the handle; see Figure 1). The gear with the handle (on the right in

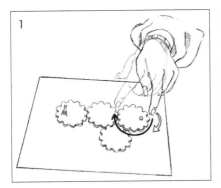

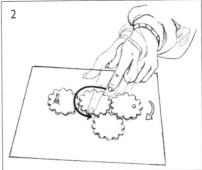

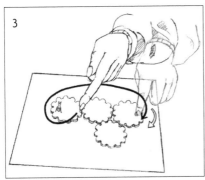

Figure 1. An adult gesturing as she explains which way the gears will turn. The adult indicates with her gestures that adjacent gears move in opposite directions.

each frame of the figure) is pictured with an arrow showing the direction in which it will be rotated (clockwise in this example). The adult is asked whether the target gear (the gear on the left in each frame of the figure) will turn if the gear with the handle is rotated and, if so, in which direction the target gear will turn. She says, "This one is turning this way, which will make this go the opposite way, which makes this one go the same as this one." At the same time, she traces a clockwise motion on the gear with the handle (frame 1), a counterclockwise motion on the adjacent gear in the middle (frame 2), and a clockwise motion on the target gear (frame 3)—this last circular motion swings around and ends in a point on the gear with the handle. This adult has, through her speech and gestures, made it clear that she understands that adjacent gears move in opposite directions (although, because she ignores the top, fourth gear, which prevents the target gears from turning at all, she answers the question incorrectly). Note that, in this instance, the speaker represents the motion from the point of view of the gears—rather than moving her hand as though she were holding the handle and rotating the gear, she traces the path of motion that the gear itself follows.

Lest you begin to think that gesture conveys substantive information only about concrete events, I offer an example of a speaker gesturing about a moral dilemma (Church et al. 1995). An adult is asked to judge whether a father has a right to ask his son to give up the money he earned to go camping so that the father can go fishing (Kohlberg 1969). For our purposes, the adult's judgment is less important than the explanation he gives to justify that judgment. Adults can be very abstract in their verbal justifications: "I think about opportunities like this where you have two interests that compete with one another. This is the point where people develop the skills of negotiation." But adults can be equally abstract in gesture (see Figure 2): here the speaker holds both hands out in front 6 to 8 inches apart, with the thumb and index finger of each hand resembling an equals sign (frame 1). He then brings his

Figure 2. An adult reasoning about the moral dilemma posed by a father's desire to use his son's money. In speech, he stresses that there are two distinct points of view that need to be reconciled. He conveys a similar message in gesture: his hands indicate two equal points of view coming into a dynamic interaction with each other.

hands in toward each other and holds them in the air (frame 2). Finally, he pivots both wrists in an alternating manner so that while one is forward, the other is back (frame 3). The hands indicate two equal points of view "negotiating" with each other. This gesture, like the speech that accompanies it, conveys the notion that there are two points of view that need to be integrated.

Children also use hand gestures as they speak (Jancovic, Devoe, and Wiener 1975), gesturing when asked to narrate a story (for example, McNeill 1992) or when asked to explain their responses to a problem (for example, Church and Goldin-Meadow 1986). The gestures children produce in a problem-solving situation provide insight into the way they represent those problems. For example, Evans and Rubin (1979) taught children between the ages of five and ten to play a simple board game and then asked them to explain the game to an adult. The children's verbal statements of the rules were routinely accompanied by gestures that conveyed information about their knowledge of the game.

Crowder and Newman (1993) found that gestures were a frequent mode of communication in a sixth-grade science lesson on the seasons, and that the gestures the students produced revealed knowledge that the children possessed about the topic. One child used both hands to produce a symmetrical gesture, laying down temperature bands on either side of the equator, and thus demonstrating, through her hands, knowledge of the symmetry of the hemispheres.

These examples from both adults and children suggest that gesture can convey meaning. The studies presented later in this book bolster this suggestion, and argue further that gesture offers a substantive view (and often a unique view) of speakers' mental representations.

One System, Not Two

Gesture not only conveys meaning but does so in a manner that is integrated with speech. Several types of evidence lend support to the view that gesture and speech form a single, unified system. First, gestures occur with speech. While emblems may be delivered in utter silence, the spontaneous gestures that speakers generate are almost always produced when the speaker is actually talking. McNeill (1992) found that 90 percent of gestures were produced during talk. Thus acts of speaking and gesturing are bound to each other.

Second, gestures and speech are semantically and pragmatically co-expressive. When people speak, they produce a variety of gesture types, as described in Chapter 1. Each type of gesture has a characteristic type of speech with which it occurs (McNeill 1992). For example, iconic gestures accompany utterances that depict concrete objects and events and fulfill a narrative function—they accompany the speech that "tells the story." The bend-back gesture described above is a concrete description of an event in the story and is a good example of an iconic gesture. In contrast, metaphoric gestures can accompany utterances that refer to the structure of the discourse rather than to a particular event in the narrative. A speaker, when announcing that what he had just seen and was about to recount was a cartoon (McNeill 1992, 14), produced a metaphoric gesture: he raised his hands as though he were offering an object to the listener. He produced this gesture as he said "it was a Sylvester and Tweety cartoon," an utterance that set up and introduced the topic of discussion rather than forming part of the story line. Other gesture types similarly have their own parallels with speech (McNeill 1992, chap. 7), suggesting a linked relation between the two modalities.

Finally, and perhaps most convincingly, gesture and speech are temporally synchronous and thus form a unified system in this sense. The gesture and the linguistic segment representing the same information as that gesture are cotemporal. Specifically, the gesture movement—the "stroke"—lines up in time with the equivalent linguistic segment. For example, in the bending-back gesture, the speaker produced the stroke of the gesture just as he said "bends it way back" (see Kita 1993, for more subtle examples of how speech and gesture adjust to each other in timing, and Nobe 2000). Typically, gesture precedes the word with which it is coexpressive, and the amount of time between the onset of the gesture and the onset of the word is quite systematic—the timing gap between word and gesture is larger for unfamiliar words than for familiar words (Morrel-Samuels and Krauss 1992). The systematicity of the relation suggests that gesture and speech are part of a single production process. Gesture and speech are systematically related in time even when the speech production process goes awry. For example, gesture production is halted during bouts of stuttering (Mayberry and Jaques 2000). Synchrony of this sort underscores once again that gesture and speech form a single integrated system.

But Not from the Beginning

Is there a time early in development when gesture is primarily used without speech, or is gesture combined with speech from the outset? If young children do produce gesture in combination with speech, are the two modalities integrated both temporally and semantically, as they are in adult systems? To explore these questions, Cynthia Butcher and I observed the relation between gesture and speech longitudinally in six children between the ages of twelve and twenty-seven months as the children made the transition from one-word speech to two-word utterances (Butcher and Goldin-Meadow 2000). We examined each child's production of gesture not only in relation to meaningful words, but also in relation to the uninterpretable sounds that the child produced in communicative contexts.

All six children produced communicative symbolic gestures and meaningful words early in our observations. But they didn't produce them together. Indeed, for five of the six children, there was no evidence at the beginning that gesture and speech formed an integrated system, either semantically or temporally (the sixth child was the most advanced linguistically and appeared to have already formed a unified gesture-speech system before we began our observations). Specifically:

- The children did not combine their gestures with meaningful words even though they did combine their gestures with uninterpretable sounds. For the most part, they produced gesture on its own, without any speech at all. In this sense, gesture and speech did not form a unified *semantic* system—all of the meaningful words the children produced were uttered without gesture.

- When the children did combine their gestures with meaningless sounds, those gesture-speech combinations were asynchronous— that is, the sounds did not occur on the stroke or the peak of the gesture. Thus gesture and speech also did not form a unified *temporal* system.

The relation between gesture and speech changed dramatically as soon as each child began to produce gesture in combination with meaningful words (between fourteen and twenty-three months). Gesture-speech combinations became frequent, accounting for at least 80 percent of each child's communications containing gesture—that is, gesture was no longer produced on its own. Moreover, because gesture was now combined with meaningful words, gesture and speech held a semantic relation to each other, with gesture typically conveying the same information as the word it accompanied; for example, point at a dog +

"dog." Finally, gesture and speech began to relate to each other temporally—the children produced their words on the stroke of the gesture in at least 80 percent of their gesture-speech combinations. Importantly, the change in synchronization was not unique to meaningful words but was also seen in gesture + meaningless sound combinations—from this moment on, whenever meaningless sounds were produced with gesture, they too were temporally synchronized.

Thus when gesture is first produced, it does not form a fully integrated system with speech. However, gesture becomes integrated with speech quite early in development—interestingly, before children begin producing words in combination with other words. At that point (and forever after), gesture and speech become unified into a single system characterized by both semantic and temporal coherence.

Gesture around the Globe

Speakers of all languages gesture. But do they gesture in the same way? Languages differ across the globe. If gesture and speech form a single system working together semantically and temporally, we might expect gesture to vary as a function of the particular language it accompanies—and it does.

Consistent with the folk theories most of us have that Italians are big gesturers, people who speak Italian attend to gesture when they listen to speech more than people who speak English (Graham and Argyle 1975). And the set of emblem gestures that Italian speakers use differs from the set found in English speakers (Kendon 1992, 1995). But for us, the important question is whether Italians gesture differently because they are speaking Italian rather than English—that is, are the differences in gesture attributable to differences in the structure of the languages that accompany those gestures?

Efron (1972) was the first to systematically explore cross-cultural differences in the spontaneous gestures that accompany speech. He studied Italian and Jewish immigrants to America, and found more kinetographic gestures (showing bodily actions) and pictographic gestures (drawing pictures) accompanying the talk of Italian immigrants than Jewish immigrants. This is a classic study, rightfully cited by all students of gesture. But what's really curious is that Efron never explicitly states what language the adults in his study were speaking. He actually studied two groups of Italian and Jewish immigrants—"traditional" and "assimilated" immigrants. Traditional immigrants had "retained the language and mores" of their original group; assimilated immigrants had "more or less broken away from the customs" of their original group (Efron 1972, 65–66), although Efron doesn't actually say that the assimilated groups were speaking English. Interestingly, the gestural differences that Efron found between the traditional Italian and Jewish immigrants disappeared when he compared the assimilated Italian and Jewish immigrants. The obvious guess is that the differences between the traditional groups stem from the fact that they were speaking different languages, and that the nondifferences between the assimilated groups reflect the fact that they were speaking the same language, English. But these findings leave us wondering—what is it about the immigrants' native languages that might lead them to use gesture differently?

More recent cross-cultural studies begin with languages that differ in some aspect of linguistic structure and then determine whether those linguistic differences are accompanied by gestural differences. In fact, there is evidence that different languages are accompanied by different gestures. Future studies will, at some point, have to ask whether these gestural differences are truly a product of linguistic differences, rather than of other differences that may exist among the cultures. But for now, we focus on the fact that both the *types* of gestures and the *timing* of gestures can vary with the language spoken. These cross-linguistic findings underscore the semantic and temporal coherence of the gesture-speech system.

Having a readily accessible linguistic expression in one language but not in another can result in different types of gestures. For example, English has an easily accessible term, "swing," to describe agentive change of location with an arc trajectory (as in "the cat swings across the street on a rope"). There is no corresponding verb, and no easy paraphrase for this meaning, in Japanese. Thus there is a gap in the expressive resources in Japanese relative to English. Predictably, when describing a scene in which Sylvester the cat flies on a rope in an arc trajectory and hits a building across the street, English speakers use the intransitive verb "swing" to encode the cat's trajectory. Japanese speakers use verbs such as "iku" (*go*) or "tobu" (*fly*) that do not encode the arc. The interesting point is that the speakers' gestures also reflect this pattern— English speakers use arced gestures to represent the cat's motion; Japanese speakers use straight gestures (Özyürek and Kita 1999).

On a more systemic level, typological differences across languages in how motion events are coded can also result in different types of gestures. For example, English and Turkish represent two classes of languages differing in how they encode path (the trajectory that an object or person takes when moving across space—down, up, into, and so on) and manner (the way the object or person moves along the path—rolling, hopping, jumping, and so on). English is a satellite-framed language, which means that path is encoded in a satellite to the verb ("rolls *down*"); manner is encoded in the verb itself ("*rolls* down"). English speakers can therefore encode manner and path within a single verbal clause, and might be expected to package both components within a single gesture. In contrast, Turkish is a verb-framed language. Path is encoded in the main verb ("*yuvarianarak iniyor*" = *descends* rolling), and manner is encoded in a subordinate verb that can be separated from the main verb ("yuvarianarak *iniyor*" = descends *rolling*). Turkish speakers therefore use two verbal clauses to express manner and path, and might find it easier to package each component in a separate gesture. This pattern is precisely what Özyürek and Kita (1999; Kita and Özyürek 2003) find—English speakers prefer manner + path gestures (for example, the hand moves down while at the same time rotating); Turkish speakers prefer separate gestures for manner (for example, the hand rotates in place without moving down) and path (for example, the hand moves down without rotating). Once again, differences in speech are mirrored by differences in gesture.

Finally, differences between the structure of two languages can result in differences in the timing between gesture and speech. For example, English is a subject-prominent language, Mandarin a topic-prominent language. Action gestures typically co-occur with the predicate in English sentences, but not in Mandarin sentences (McNeill and Duncan 2000). In the English sentence "the old lady *hit* him with a big stick," the action gesture (downward blow) waits for the predicate "hit" and is produced along with it. In contrast, in the comparable Mandarin sentence, the action gesture does not wait for the predicate "hit-down," which occurs at the end of the sentence, but is produced when the word for big stick is uttered ("old lady hold *big stick* him hit-down"). Gesture and speech together create a topic-like frame early in the sentence (the gestured "hit" with the spoken "big stick"). The timing of gesture in relation to speech therefore depends, at least in part, on structural parameters of the spoken language.

In addition to observing the effects of linguistic differences on gesture across speakers of different languages, we can also look at a single speaker learning two different languages at the same time. Nicolades,

Mayberry, and Genessee (1999) investigated the development of gestures in French-English bilingual children between the ages of 2;0 and 3;6 (years;months). Not surprisingly, the children developed their languages at different rates. The question is whether the gestures they used with each language also developed at different rates—the short answer is yes. The children used gestures differently with their two languages and, in particular, used more iconic gestures with their more developed language. Thus the same child gestured differently depending on the language he or she was speaking—as we might expect if gesture and speech form a single, unified system.

To summarize thus far, we have seen that speech-accompanying gestures can do more than convey feelings and attitudes—they can, and often do, convey substantive information. Moreover, those gestures are coordinated, both semantically and temporally, with the speech they accompany—though this system is not present from birth.

But gesture represents information in a very different way than speech does. It consequently presents opportunities for speakers to convey information not found in their speech, as we will see in the next chapter.

3

Giving Our Thoughts Away

Imagine a child explaining his beliefs about the amount of water in a glass by saying "it's skinny," while indicating the height of the glass with his hand (Church and Goldin-Meadow 1986). Now consider an adult saying "she chased him," while brandishing an imaginary umbrella in her hands (McNeill 1992). Vignettes of this type are not difficult to imagine and, in fact, are often spotted in spontaneous conversation. In both of these examples, the hands convey information that is not conveyed in the accompanying speech—the height of the glass in the first; the manner of assault during the chase in the second. Gesture can reveal thoughts that are not revealed in speech.

Different Perspectives

Why are gesture and speech so easily able to take different perspectives on the same event? I suggest that the method used by gesture for conveying meaning is fundamentally different from the method used by speech.

The most obvious difference between gesture and speech is that speech conforms to a codified, recognizable system; gesture does not. We can use words creatively ("I put the hat on the pot") and even create new words out of old (the "napkin-stealer" is a novel term which my children use to describe our dog, Kugel, who does, indeed, steal napkins from our laps while we sit at the table). But by and large, we are constrained to the words that our language offers. And sometimes those words fail us. It is difficult, for example, to rely exclusively on words to describe the coastline of the eastern seaboard of the United States (Huttenlocher 1973, 1976). A gesture, unencumbered by the standards of form that language imposes and able to take advantage of visual imagery, can convey the shape of the coastline far better than even a large number of words.

For the most part, gesture conveys information through imagery. A fist moves in a winding motion, conveying the action performed on the wind-up crank of an old car (Beattie and Shovelton 1999a). A loose palm traces an arc in the air, conveying the trajectory of a cat's flight on a rope into a wall (Özyürek and Kita 1999). A pointing finger moves back and forth between two rows of checkers, pairing the checkers and thus conveying the one-to-one correspondence between the checkers in the two rows (Church and Goldin-Meadow 1986). In each case, the hand in motion makes use of visual imagery to convey meaning.

One feature of visual imagery is that it can present simultaneously information that must be presented sequentially in speech. For example, when commenting on a spider that he sees on the kitchen counter, a speaker says (or perhaps shrieks if the speaker is Harry Potter's Ron Weasley) "there's a spider running across the counter," while moving his hand, all five fingers wiggling, over the counter. The gesture presents, in a single motion, information about the spider (it has many legs, as indicated by all five fingers moving), the manner of motion (running, as indicated by the wiggling fingers), the path (across, as indicated by the path of the hand), and location (the counter, as indicated by the place where the gesture is produced).

In contrast, the scene must be broken up into parts when it is conveyed in speech. The effect is to present what had been a single instantaneous picture in the form of a string of segments: the spider, the running, the direction, the location. These segments are organized into a hierarchically structured string of words. Speech then has the effect of segmenting and linearizing meaning. Segmentation and linearization to form a hierarchy are essential characteristics of all linguistic systems (including sign languages which are not spoken at all; see Chapter 13).

Saussure ([1916] 1959) argued that the linear-segmented character of spoken language is a property that arises because language is unidimensional but meanings are multidimensional. Language can only vary along the single dimension of time. At all levels (phonemes, words, phrases, sentences, discourse), language depends on variations along this one axis. This restriction forces language to break meaning complexes into segments and to reconstruct multidimensional meanings by combining the segments in time.

But gesture is not similarly restricted. Gestures are free to vary on dimensions of space, time, form, trajectory, and so on, and can present meaning complexes without undergoing segmentation or linearization. Unlike spoken sentences, in which lower constituents combine into higher constituents, each gesture is a complete expression of meaning unto itself (McNeill 1992). The spider gesture is a symbol whose parts gain meaning because of the meaning of the whole. The wiggling fingers mean "running" only because we know that the gesture, as a whole, depicts the spider running and not because this speaker consistently uses wiggling fingers to mean running. Indeed, in other gestures produced by this same speaker, wiggling fingers could easily have a very different meaning (for example, "indecision amid a number of possibilities"). Note that since the speaker does not use the components of the spider gesture to convey stable meanings, the gesture cannot stand on its own without speech—and this is consistent with the principle that speech and gesture form an integrated system.

Mismatches

Gesture and speech encode meaning differently. Gesture conveys meaning globally, relying on visual and mimetic imagery. Speech conveys meaning discretely, relying on codified words and grammatical devices. Because gesture and speech employ such different forms of representation, it is difficult for the two modalities to contribute identical information to a message. Indeed, even deictic pointing gestures are not completely redundant with speech. For example, when a child utters "chair" while pointing at the chair, the word labels and thus classifies (but doesn't locate) the object. Pointing, in contrast, indicates where the object is but not what it is. Word and gesture do not convey identical information, but they work together to more richly specify the same object.

But word and gesture can, at times, convey information that overlaps very little, if at all. Pointing, for example, can indicate an object that is not referred to in speech—the child says "daddy" while pointing at the chair. Word and gesture together convey a simple proposition—"the chair is daddy's"—that neither modality conveys on its own.[1]

As another example, consider a child asked whether the amount of

---

1. Like the comparable two-word combination "daddy chair," the gesture plus word combination ("daddy" + point at chair) can be ambiguous. We rely on context to tell us whether the child is referring to the chair that belongs to daddy or to the fact that daddy recently sat down in the chair.

water changed when it was poured from a tall, skinny container into a short, wide container (see Figure 3). The boy says that the amount of water has changed "'cause that's down lower than that one," while first pointing at the relatively low water level in the short, wide container (frame A1) and then at the higher water level in the tall, skinny container (frame A2). Again, word and gesture do not convey identical information—speech tells us that the water level is low, gesture tells us how low—yet they work together to more richly convey the boy's understanding. In contrast, another child gave the same response in speech, "'cause this one's lower than this one," but indicated the widths (not the heights) of the containers with her hands: two C-shaped hands held around the relatively wide diameter of the short, wide container (frame B1), followed by a left C-hand held around the narrower diameter of the tall, skinny container (frame B2). In this case, word and gesture together allow the child to convey a contrast of dimensions—this one's lower but wide, that one's higher but skinny—that neither modality conveys on its own.

We can posit a continuum based on the overlap of information conveyed in gesture and speech. At one end of the continuum, gesture elaborates on a topic that has already been introduced in speech. At the other end, gesture introduces new information that is not mentioned at all in speech. Although at times it is not clear where to draw a line to divide the continuum into two categories, the ends of the continuum are obvious and relatively easy to identify. In previous work (Church and Goldin-Meadow 1986), we have called cases in which gesture and speech convey overlapping information "gesture-speech matches," and cases in which gesture and speech convey non-overlapping information "gesture-speech mismatches."

The term "mismatch" adequately conveys the notion that gesture and speech convey different information. For many, however, "mismatch" also brings with it the notion of conflict, a notion that I do not intend. The pieces of information conveyed in gesture and in speech in a mismatch need not conflict, and in fact they rarely do. There is almost always some framework within which the information conveyed in gesture can be fitted with the information conveyed in speech. For example, it may seem as though there is a conflict between the height information conveyed in the girl's words ("lower") and the width information conveyed in her gestures. But in the context of the water conservation problem, the two dimensions actually compensate for each other. Indeed, it is essential to understand this compensation—that the water may be

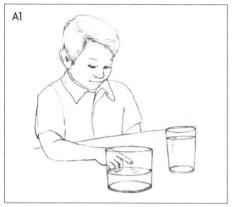

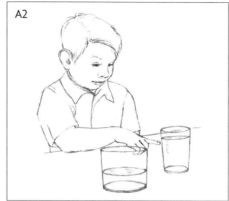

Figure 3. Two children who say that the amount of water in the two containers is different because the water level is lower in one container than the other. The boy in frames A1–A2 conveys the *same* information in gesture (he indicates the height of the water in each container)—he has produced a gesture-speech match. The girl in frames B1–B2 conveys *different* information in gesture (she indicates the width of each container)—she has produced a gesture-speech mismatch.

lower than the original dish but is also wider—in order to master conservation of liquid quantity.

Let's take another example. Consider a child asked first whether the number of checkers in two identical rows is the same, and then whether the number of checkers in one of the rows changes when the checkers are spread out (see Figure 4). The child says that the number of checkers in the two rows is the same at the beginning, but that they are different after the spreading-out transformation. When asked to explain, this particular child focuses on the experimenter's movements in both

Figure 4. Two children who say that the number of checkers in the two rows is different because the experimenter moved the checkers in one row. The child in frame A conveys the *same* information in gesture (he produces a "spreading-out" motion)—he has produced a gesture-speech match. The child in frames B1–B3 conveys *different* information in gesture (he aligns the checkers in one row with the checkers in the other row)—he has produced a gesture-speech mismatch.

speech and gesture—he says that the number of checkers is different "'cause you moved them out" while producing a spreading-out motion with his hands (frame A). The child is thus conveying a justification in speech and gesture that overlaps a great deal. In contrast, another child gives precisely the same explanation in speech—it's different "'cause you moved them"—but conveys one-to-one correspondence in gesture—he moves a pointing hand between the checkers in one row and the checkers in the other row (frames B1–B3). This child is focusing on the experimenter's movements in speech but on the checker pairs in gesture. His responses do not match and thus give the appearance of conflict. But as in the water conservation problem, the child must grasp both aspects of the task and understand the relation between them— that the pairing of checkers does not change when the checkers are moved—in order to master conservation of number.

As observers, we are often able to see the framework that would re- solve a potential conflict between the information encoded in speakers' talk and the information encoded in their gestures. The question, of course, is whether speakers themselves see that framework. I argue that speakers often do not. If, in fact, a speaker were able to grasp the rela- tion between the information conveyed in the gesture and speech of a mismatch, it is quite likely that that speaker would also be able to ex- press both pieces of information (and the relation itself) in speech. I ex- plore this issue, and the implications of gesture-speech mismatch for learning, in Chapters 4 and 5 and again in Chapter 8.

Gesture-speech mismatch may have implications, not only for learn- ing but also for speaking (see Kita 2000; McNeill 1992). Consider the ex- ample given at the beginning of Chapter 2 in which the speaker says "I ran all the way upstairs," while gesturing a spiral trajectory. The speaker is very likely to have a framework in mind that could unite the spiraling gesture and the upstairs run. However, the speaker may not have devel- oped the framework sufficiently at that point in the conversation for it to be explicitly articulated. Indeed, McNeill and Duncan (2000) argue that the interplay between gesture and speech reflects what is newsworthy in discourse, and serves as the dynamic force that propels discourse for- ward.

I thus offer the following working hypothesis that allows us to pro- ceed. A speaker who has produced a gesture-speech mismatch knows (at some level) the information conveyed in both modalities. However, the speaker has not yet developed a framework—either a knowledge framework over developmental time (the conservation examples) or a discourse framework over conversational time (the stair-climbing exam- ple)—within which those pieces can be fitted together.

The Product of a Single System

Utterances in which gesture and speech convey the same information provide rather obvious evidence for the integration between gesture and speech. In contrast, utterances in which gesture and speech convey different information might a priori be thought to reflect a lack of integration across the two modalities. Gesture-speech mismatches could be the product of two systems operating independently and in parallel, rather than the product of a single integrated system. Findings from two very different types of studies, however, suggest that this is not so: (1) a study of the very first gesture-speech productions toddlers produce (Butcher and Goldin-Meadow 2000; Goldin-Meadow and Butcher 2003), and (2) a study in which we attempted to predict the rate at which children produce gesture-speech matches and mismatches using two models—one in which gesture and speech are assumed to act independently as separate systems versus one in which gesture and speech are assumed to be part of a single system (Alibali and Goldin-Meadow 1993a).

MISMATCHES AND GESTURE-SPEECH INTEGRATION

Three aspects of a toddler's gesture-speech utterances suggest that mismatches are an outgrowth of gesture and speech working in concert (Butcher and Goldin-Meadow 2000; Goldin-Meadow and Butcher 2003).

First, the utterances that toddlers produce in which gesture and speech convey different information are all semantically coherent. Gesture refers to one semantic element in a proposition and speech refers to another element in that same proposition. For example, one child produced a *fall* gesture (a palm flipping over) while saying "mouse," thus describing both the action and the actor of a single proposition ("mouse falls").

Second, the utterances that children produce in which gesture and speech convey different information are temporally coherent. The word ("mouse") was produced in synchrony with the stroke of the gesture *(fall)*, despite the fact that the word did not have the same referent as the gesture. In fact, once gesture and speech become temporally coordinated (see Chapter 2), children are as likely to produce a synchronous utterance when their gesture and speech convey different information (that is, mismatches such as "mouse" + *fall* gesture) as when their gesture and speech convey the same or overlapping information (that is, matches such as "mouse" + point at *mouse*).

Finally, utterances in which gesture and speech convey different information (that is, mismatches such as "dada" + a point-at-hat gesture, meaning "that's dad's hat") do not appear until the two modalities are used to convey the same information (that is, matches such as "dada" + point at dad). If mismatching utterances are the product of a speech system randomly coming together with an independent gesture system, these utterances ought to occur before gesture-speech matches just as often as after. But they don't. The five children who began to produce gesture-speech matches during our observations produced mismatching utterances at the same time as (for two children) or after (for three children) matching utterances. Thus only after gesture and speech become integrated into a single system and are used to convey the same information is the child able to use the two modalities to convey different pieces of information within the same communicative act.

MODELS OF MATCHES AND MISMATCHES

How are gesture-speech matches and mismatches generated? One possible mechanism rests on the assumption that the speaker has two distinct sets of representations, one set accessible to gesture (that is, representations that can be conveyed only in gesture) and a second set accessible to speech (representations that can be articulated only in speech). The two representations are sampled independently—that is, to produce an utterance, the speaker samples a representation accessible to gesture and independently samples a representation accessible to speech. We will call this the "Independent" model.

According to this model, a speaker produces a gesture-speech match by sampling a representation from the set of representations accessible to gesture and, by chance, independently sampling that same representation from the set accessible to speech. A speaker produces a gesture-speech mismatch by sampling a representation from the set of representations accessible to gesture and, by chance, independently sampling a different representation from the set accessible to speech.

If this Independent model is correct, the probability of producing a gesture-speech match should be equal to the probability of sampling a particular representation from the set of representations accessible to speech, multiplied by the probability of sampling that same representation from the set accessible to gesture. We evaluated this model with respect to children explaining their solutions to a series of mathematical equivalence problems (for example, $4 + 5 + 3 = \_\_ + 3$; Alibali and Goldin-Meadow 1993a).

At each of three assessment points, we asked children to solve and explain six addition problems. Each explanation was coded as a gesture-speech match or mismatch. Children varied from zero to six in the number of gesture-speech matches they produced at each of the three assessment points. Using criteria developed previously (Church and Goldin-Meadow 1986), we classified children as mismatchers if they produced three or more mismatches, and as matchers if they produced fewer than three mismatches. We calculated the number of matchers and mismatchers expected at each assessment point, assuming that the children sampled representations accessible to gesture independently from sampling representations accessible to speech (see Goldin-Meadow, Alibali, and Church 1993, for the details of these calculations).

We compared the number of matchers and mismatchers predicted by the Independent model with the actual number observed (see Figure 5, top and middle graphs). The Independent model fit the data quite poorly. The model predicted a distribution that differed significantly from the observed distribution at two of the three assessment points. In addition, in a separate analysis, we found that the Independent model did not accurately predict the distribution of the precise numbers of matches the children produced (Alibali and Goldin-Meadow 1993a).

An alternative model, the "Integrated" model, assumes that gesture and speech draw upon a *single* set of representations, some of which are accessible to (can be articulated in) both gesture and speech, and some of which are accessible only to gesture (see Chapter 5 for evidence that, at least for mathematical equivalence problems, children have many representations accessible to gesture and not speech, but few accessible to speech and not gesture). If the child samples a representation that is accessible to both gesture and speech, the child will produce a gesture-speech match. If, however, the child samples a representation that is accessible to gesture but not to speech, he or she will not be able to express in speech the same information expressed in gesture. In this case, the child selects another representation to articulate in speech and thus produces a gesture-speech mismatch.

If this Integrated model is correct, the probability of producing a gesture-speech match on any given problem should be equal to the probability of sampling a representation that is accessible to both gesture and speech. To evaluate this model with respect to our data on children solving mathematical equivalence problems, we recalculated the number of matchers and mismatchers expected at each assessment point, assuming that gesture and speech form an integrated system.

Figure 5 (facing page). The distributions of children classified as matchers or mismatchers (1) predicted by the Independent model (top), (2) actually observed (middle), and (3) predicted by the Integrated model (bottom). At each assessment point, children who did not produce any strategies in gesture were excluded from the analyses.

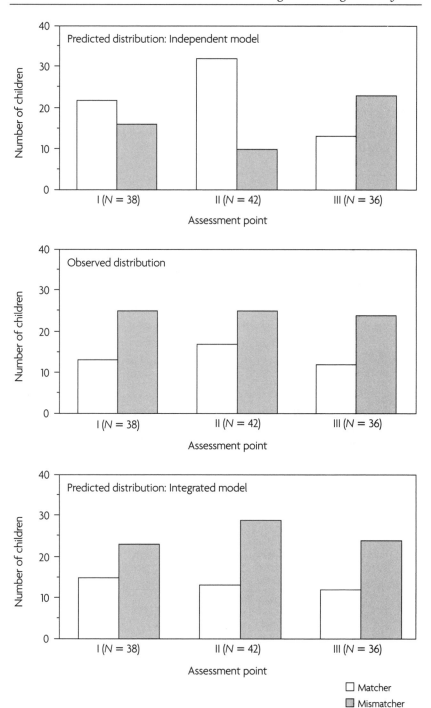

Unlike the Independent model, the Integrated model was relatively accurate in predicting the number of matchers and mismatchers actually observed (see Figure 5, middle and bottom graphs). At each of the three assessment points, the Integrated model predicted a distribution that did not differ significantly from the observed distribution. In addition, the Integrated model also accurately predicted the distribution of the precise numbers of matches the children produced at each of the three assessment points.

Thus when we attempt to estimate how many matches and mismatches a speaker is likely to produce, we find that we need a model in which gesture and speech draw upon a single set of representations. Matches and mismatches alike appear to be the product of an integrated gesture-speech system.

Who Produces Mismatches, and When

As the examples provided earlier suggest, both children and adults produce gesture-speech mismatches. Moreover, they do so in a wide variety of situations, including ordinary conversation. For example, mismatches have been observed in:

- Toddlers going through a vocabulary spurt (Gershkoff-Stowe and Smith 1997)

- Preschoolers explaining a game (Evans and Rubin 1979) or counting a set of objects (Alibali and DiRusso 1999; Graham 1999)

- Elementary school children explaining Piagetian conservation problems (Church and Goldin-Meadow 1986), mathematical equations (Perry, Church, and Goldin-Meadow 1988), and seasonal change (Crowder and Newman 1993)

- Children and adults discussing moral dilemmas (Church et al. 1995)

- Children and adults explaining how they solved Tower of Hanoi puzzles, a brain teaser in which items are moved from one location to another, one at a time, with constraints on the order in which items can be moved (Garber and Goldin-Meadow 2002)

- Adolescents explaining when rods of different materials and thicknesses will bend (Stone, Webb, and Mahootian 1991)

- Adults explaining how gears work (Perry and Elder 1997; Schwartz and Black 1996)

- Adults describing pictures of landscapes, abstract art, buildings, people, machines, and so on (Morrel-Samuels and Krauss 1992)

- Adults describing problems involving constant change (Alibali et al. 1999)

- Adults narrating cartoon stories (Beattie and Shovelton 1999a; McNeill 1992; Rauscher, Krauss, and Chen 1996)

Thus we find gesture-speech mismatches in all sorts of speakers and situations. Sometimes gesture is absolutely essential for the spoken sentence to make sense. For example, an adult narrating a cartoon story says "so the hand is now trying to start the car," an odd formulation and one that is difficult to make sense of without the accompanying gesture—a hand moving in a winding motion, which lets the listener know that the car is an old one started with a crank (Beattie and Shovelton 1999a, 5). In other instances, speech can stand on its own, but takes on a different sense when interpreted in the context of gesture. For example, Kendon (1985, 225) describes a husband sitting in the living room and talking with his wife about what the children had done that day. He says, "They made a cake, didn't they?"—a question that appears quite straightforward. While producing the word "cake," however, the speaker gestured toward the garden, thereby indicating that the activity had taken place not in the kitchen but in the garden, and implying that the cake was of the mud variety. In both cases, gesture conveys information that cannot be found in, and is not even implied by, the accompanying speech.

Studying Mismatches

It is usually easy to attribute meaning to speech simply because it's a codified system—as users of the spoken language, we know its words and rules of combination and can easily interpret sentences that we have never heard before. But gesture is not codified—that, I argue, is part of its appeal. How do we attribute meaning to gesture and, in particular, how do we attribute meaning to gesture when we're not listening to the speech that it was produced with—a necessary step if we are to code gesture in as unbiased a fashion as possible?

We routinely get meaning from gesture when we interpret it in the context of speech (more on this in Part II). If, however, our goal is to study the mismatches between gesture and speech, and to do so without reading more into gesture than we ought, we need to be able to attribute meaning to gesture when it's on its own—that is, to code gesture with the sound turned off.

My colleagues and I have developed a heuristic that allows us to code gesture without speech, and speech without gesture—a heuristic that works only because gesture and speech form a single system. The basic premise of this procedure is that, overall, speakers produce gestures that convey the same information as speech—that is, that gesture-speech matches occur more often than mismatches (and they do). We therefore use the gestures and speech that a sample of different speakers produce on a task to develop a gestural "lexicon" for that task. We note which gestures are particularly likely to occur with a given verbal utterance, and we take those gestures to be the gestural equivalent of that verbal utterance. The result is a list of gestural responses, described in terms of form and meaning, that can be used to code another set of videotapes on a different set of speakers—even when the sound is turned off.

Let's take as an example the gestural lexicon we established for conservation tasks (Church and Goldin-Meadow 1986). We began by videotaping children explaining their conservation judgments, and then using those tapes to develop a coding system. In developing such a coding system for conservation, we relied, of course, on the extensive work that had already been done documenting the kinds of explanations children produce on this task in speech. Our job was to determine whether children produce comparable explanations in gesture.

Many children produced spoken explanations that focused on the equivalence between the two quantities. For example, children were first shown two parallel sticks of equal length; one stick was rotated so that it was perpendicular to the other. Children who believed that the two sticks were still the same length after the rotation often said "turn it the other way," to indicate that all the experimenter needed to do to verify this equivalence was rotate the transformed stick back to its original position. These same children produced comparable explanations in gesture—a small C-handshape pivoted from vertical to horizontal orientation, a gesture indicating the motion needed to return the transformed stick to its original position.

Children also produced explanations that did not focus on the equivalence between the two quantities, in both speech and gesture—"you poured my glass in there," said while producing a pouring motion from the glass to the dish and then pointing at the dish. Both gesture and speech refer to the motion that the experimenter used to transform the original quantity. Neither referred to the motion that could have been used to reverse the transformation.

After establishing a set of gesture-speech equivalents for the conservation rationales that children produced, our next task was to make sure that these codes could be used reliably. We collected another set of videotapes of children performing conservation tasks and had our coders go through them. Two speech coders independently listened to the tapes with the picture turned off. Two gesture coders independently watched the tapes with the sound turned off. Our reliability was quite good—88 percent agreement between the two speech coders, and 87 percent agreement between the two gesture coders.

We were then ready to take the next step—to determine gesture-speech mismatches. For each child, we compared the speech code for a given response to the gesture code for that same response. Responses containing speech and no gesture (which happens rarely in a conservation task, 14 percent of the time) and those containing gesture and no speech (which happens even more rarely, 3 percent) were obviously not coded for match or mismatch. For responses containing both speech and gesture, the procedure was straightforward: if the speech code matched the gesture code, the response was called a "gesture-speech match." If the speech code did not match the gesture code, the response was called a "gesture-speech mismatch." Reliability was again excellent—88 percent agreement between independent coders.

Thus we take advantage of the fact that gesture and speech typically express overlapping information to construct a gestural lexicon. We can then use this lexicon to code gesture out of its natural habitat, that is, without speech. It is important to note, however, that a gestural lexicon of this sort is not a lexicon in the traditional sense. It is very unlikely that someone who had not received training in the lexicon would be able to accurately attribute meaning to the gestures on the list if those gestures were presented without speech or in a different context (see Krauss, Morrel-Samuels, and Colasante 1991, for experimental verification of this prediction). As we have seen, gesture is not a "known" system, with consistent forms associated with consistent meanings. The only reason our so-called lexicon works is because the situation is constrained—the uniformity that we find across speakers is not there because the speakers have an agreed-upon code, but because of the limited range of meanings that children express in a conservation task (see McNeill 1992, 22, for further discussion of this point).

Of course, we typically do not attempt to get meaning from gesture when it is on its own, and I am not suggesting that our coding procedure has anything to do with how we process gesture and speech in the real world. But it is a procedure that allows us to detect gesture-speech mismatches in an experimental situation. As such, it makes it possible to explore the communicative and cognitive significance of gesture in a relatively controlled way. We are now poised to discover what our hands can tell us about our minds.

4

Who Is Ready to Learn?

We have seen that gesture-speech mismatches are not restricted to a particular age or task. Importantly, they are also not restricted to particular individuals. The same speaker who produces many mismatches on one task may produce none on another. For example, children who produce many mismatches when explaining how to solve a mathematical equivalence task can produce none at all when explaining how to solve a conservation task—this pattern is particularly common if the child is in the midst of learning about mathematical equivalence but has already mastered conservation (Perry, Church, and Goldin-Meadow 1988).

Even within the same domain, a child may produce many mismatches on a hard task and few on an easy task. For example, two-year-olds produce more mismatches when counting a relatively large set of objects (four or six objects) than when counting a small set (two objects). For three-year-olds, who know more about counting, the pattern is the same but the line between easy and hard falls at a different point—they produce mismatches only when counting six-object sets and not when counting two- or four-object sets (Graham 1999).

Since the same person can produce many or few mismatches depending on the task, gesture-speech mismatch cannot be a personality trait or communicative style. But mismatch does appear to be a characteristic of individuals in a particular state. Children who produce many gesture-speech mismatches when explaining a task are likely to benefit from instruction on that task—reliably more likely than children who produce few mismatches. Mismatch marks a child as being open to instruction, and thus on the precipice of learning.

Mismatchers Learn When Taught by Experimenters

CONSERVATION

Breckie Church and I were initially surprised to find that all children gesture when they explain their judgments on conservation tasks, and even more surprised to find that sometimes those gestures reveal notions that do not appear in the accompanying speech. It seemed like an obvious next step (and a good dissertation topic for Breckie) to ask whether children who produce many of these gesture-speech mismatches differ from children who produce few. We guessed that the children might differ in their potential for learning. The mismatchers seemed to be unstable in their understanding of the task, and this instability could make them particularly open to instruction. At first, we considered waiting around until the children improved in their understanding of conservation to see who got there first. It was Tom Trabasso who suggested that this was not the best strategy for a dissertation (at least not for a dissertation Breckie hoped to finish in a finite amount of time), and that it might be better to give the children instruction to hurry their progress along. And so we did (Church and Goldin-Meadow 1986).

We first gave five- to eight-year-old children a pretest of six problems and assessed their understanding of conservation. None of the children had full understanding of conservation on the pretest (else there would have been no point in instructing them), but all did produce at least some correct judgments on it (that is, they were partial conservers). We also used the pretest to determine whether the children were gesture-speech matchers or mismatchers. We classified children as mismatchers if they produced three or more mismatching explanations on the task, and as matchers if they produced fewer than three. We then gave all of the children instruction in the task—half were given explicit instruction in conservation, and half were given experience in manipulating the task objects but no training or feedback. After the instruction session, the children were again given the six conservation problems and we assessed their improvement, if any, from pretest to post-test. We assessed progress in two ways: producing six (out of six) correct judgments on the post-test; and producing a new correct explanation on the post-test, one that the child had not produced at any point before instruction.

We found that, not surprisingly, children given explicit instruction made more progress than children given only the opportunity to manip-ulate the objects (for example, none of the manipulators ended up pro-ducing six correct judgments on the post-test). However, the important point is that, no matter what type of instruction the children received, mismatchers made significantly more progress than matchers. In both instruction groups, more mismatchers than matchers added a new cor-rect explanation to their repertoires (.86 versus .37, $p = .03$, in the explicit instruction group; .40 versus .00, $p < .05$, in the manipulation group) and, in the explicit instruction group, more mismatchers than matchers produced six correct judgments (.36 versus .06, $p = .05$). Importantly, the matchers and the mismatchers did not differ in the number of correct explanations or correct judgments they produced on the pretest—prior to instruction, the only way to tell the groups apart was by the number of gesture-speech mismatches each produced.

Thus gesture-speech mismatch in a child's explanations of conserva-tion is an excellent sign that the child is ready to learn conservation. But is gesture-speech mismatch a general index of readiness-to-learn, or is it specific to the conservation task? Or specific to five- to eight-year-olds? To address this question, we set about exploring another task—mathematical equivalence—which is typically mastered by older chil-dren (nine- to ten-year-olds).

MATHEMATICAL EQUIVALENCE

Mathematical equivalence is the notion that the two expressions on ei-ther side of an "equal" sign must be equal. We used addition problems of the following sort to tap this notion: $4 + 5 + 3 = \_\_ + 3$ (these are the same problems that we used in Chapter 3 to model the production of gesture-speech matches and mismatches in order to determine whether mismatches were a product of a single system). Fourth-grade children in the United States typically have trouble figuring out that 9 is the number that ought to go in the blank. Interestingly, the same children can easily solve problems such as $4 + 5 + 3 = \_\_$ and thus, on the surface, appear to understand that the two sides of the equation must add to the same amount. In these problems, however, children may be getting the right answer for the wrong reason. For example, a child may interpret the equal sign as an instruction to add all of the numbers in the problem, and not as an instruction to make both sides of the equation equal (see Behr, Erlwanger, and Nichols 1980; Ginsburg 1977; Kieran 1980). The fact that children cannot solve the more complex equivalence problems suggests that this is so.

Our first task, as in the conservation study, was to establish a gestural lexicon for mathematical equivalence (see Perry, Church, and Goldin-Meadow 1988). Michelle Perry videotaped children explaining how they solved the complex addition problems. Many of the children videotaped did not know how to solve the problem and gave incorrect explanations in both speech and gesture. One frequent explanation the children gave was the "add the numbers up to the equal sign" strategy (see Figure 6A). For example, for the problem $6 + 3 + 4 = \_\_ + 4$, the child puts 13 in the blank and says "6 plus 3 is 9, 9 plus 4 equals 13," while pointing at the 6 (frame A1), the 3 (frame A2), the 4 on the left side of the equation (frame A3), and the 13 in the blank (frame A4; we will consider the B and C portions of Figure 6 when we turn to the mismatches that children produce on this task). Another frequent incorrect approach was the "add all of the numbers in the problem" strategy. For example, for the same problem, the child puts 17 in the blank and says "I added 6 plus 3 plus 4 plus 4 equals 17," while pointing at the 6, the 3, the 4 on the left side of the equation, the 4 on the right side of the equation, and the 17 in the blank. In both of these examples, the child gives the same incorrect explanation in speech and in gesture.

Not surprisingly, the children who knew how to solve the problems frequently gave correct explanations and did so in both speech and gesture (see Figure 7A). For the problem $6 + 5 + 9 = \_\_ + 9$, the child puts 11 in the blank and says "this is all 20 and 11 plus 9 is 20," while first sweeping her hand from the 6 to the 9 on the left side of the equation (frame A1) and then sweeping her hand from the 9 to the 11 on the right side of the equation (frame A2). In this example, the child focuses on the fact that there are two parts to the problem that need to be treated alike—an "equalizer" strategy. Another correct approach that the children often used was the "grouping" strategy. On the same problem, the child might say "I added the 6 and the 5 and put 11 in the blank," while pointing with a "horns" hand to the 6 and 5, the two numbers that are not found on both sides of the equation and thus can be grouped and summed to get the correct answer.

As in our conservation studies, however, we found that at times the children conveyed different information with their gestures than they conveyed with their words—that is, they produced gesture-speech mismatches. These mismatches were produced with incorrect spoken strategies (Figure 6B,C) but also with correct spoken strategies (Figure 7B). As an example of the first type, for the problem $7 + 6 + 5 = \_\_ + 5$, the child puts 18 in the blank and says "7 plus 6 is 13 plus 5 more is 18 and that's all I did"—in other words, she gives an add-to-equal-sign strategy in speech. In gesture, however, she points at all four numbers (the 7, the 6, the left 5, and the right 5), thus giving an add-all-numbers strategy in gesture (frames B1–B4 in Figure 6). In this case, the child produces two different strategies on the same problem, but both strategies are incorrect.

Children also produce gesture-speech mismatches in which one strategy is correct and the other is incorrect. For example, for the problem $4 + 5 + 6 = \_\_ + 6$, the child puts 15 in the blank and gives an add-to-equal-sign strategy in speech to justify this solution. At the same time, however, the child indicates an awareness of the two numbers that can be grouped and summed to get the right answer—she points with a "horns" handshape at the 4 and 5, thus producing a grouping strategy in gesture (frame C in Figure 6).

Finally, children produce gesture-speech mismatches containing two different correct strategies. For example, on the problem $7 + 5 + 8 = 7 + \_\_$, the child solves the problem using correct strategies (although she actually adds wrong—she thinks that $7 + 5 + 8$ equals 19, and she puts 12 in the blank to make the right side of the equation equal 19). She says "this equals 19 and this equals 19" and thus produces an equalizer strategy in speech. She also produces an equalizer strategy in gesture (see Figure 7B)—she sweeps her hand from the 8 to the 7 on the left side of the equation (frame B2) and then sweeps her hand from the 7 to the 12 on the right side of the equation (frame B3). So far, the response looks like a gesture-speech match—equalizer in both speech and gesture. However, just before doing her first sweep, the child points with a "horns" handshape at the 5 and the 8, thus also producing a grouping strategy in gesture (frame B1). This child knows how to solve the problem and even seems to know that there is more than one way to arrive at the correct solution. But she doesn't yet seem to have an explicit framework within which she can comfortably unify these various correct strategies.

After generating a lexicon of correct and incorrect gestural strategies and establishing that our coding system was reliable, the next important step was to use the gestural lexicon in a training study (Perry, Church, and Goldin-Meadow 1988). We gave children in the fourth and fifth grades a pretest of six addition problems and assessed their understanding of mathematical equivalence. We also used the pretest to determine whether the children were matchers or mismatchers. As before, we classified children as mismatchers if they produced three or more

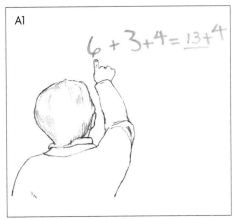

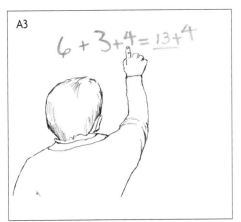

Figure 6 (above and on facing page). Children explaining their incorrect solutions to a mathematical equivalence problem. All of the children say that they added the numbers on the left side of the equation (that is, they describe an add-to-equal-sign strategy in speech). The child in frames A1–A4 conveys the same information in gesture (he points at the three numbers on the left side of the equal sign and the answer in the blank on the right)—he has produced a gesture-speech match. The children in frames B1–B4 and C convey different information in their gestures. In B1–B4, the child conveys a different yet still incorrect strategy in gesture (she points at the last number on the right side of the equation as well as the three on the left, that is, an add-all-numbers strategy). In C, the child conveys a correct strategy in gesture (she indicates the two numbers which, when summed, give the correct answer, that is, a grouping strategy). Both children have thus produced gesture-speech mismatches.

B1

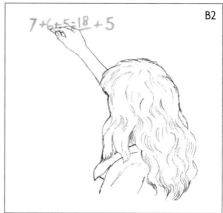

B2

B3

B4

C

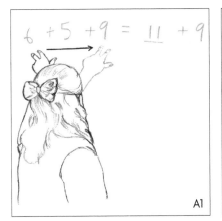

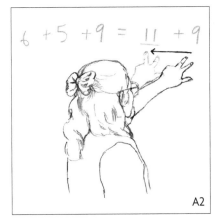

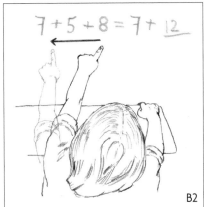

Figure 7. Children explaining their correct solutions to a mathematical equivalence problem. Both children say that they made the sums on the two sides of the equation be the same (that is, they describe an equalizer strategy in speech). The child in frames A1–A2 conveys the same information in gesture (she sweeps her hand under the left side of the equation and then sweeps her hand under the right)—she has produced a gesture-speech match. The child in frames B1–B3 also conveys an equalizer strategy in gesture (B2, B3), but, in addition, she produces a grouping strategy in gesture (she indicates the two numbers that can be summed to give the correct answer in B1). She has produced a gesture-speech mismatch, but one in which both strategies are correct.

mismatching explanations on the problems, and as matchers if they produced fewer than three. We then gave the children instruction in the principle underlying the addition problems—the children were told that the goal of the problem was to make both sides of the equation equal. After the instruction session, the children were again given six addition problems and a series of novel addition and multiplication problems that tested their ability to generalize what they had learned.

As in our conservation studies, many more mismatchers than matchers were successful on the post-test, including the generalization test (.62 versus .25, $p < .03$). The mismatchers had learned not only how to solve the equivalence problems, but also how to extend that knowledge to different problem types. Again, mismatch predicted who would learn and who would not.

Is mismatch an index of readiness-to-learn in older learners as well? We don't really know. Stone and his colleagues (1991) looked for a relation between mismatch and learning in adolescents performing a bending rods task, and didn't find one (although there might have been some problems in how they did the looking, see Perry, Church, and Goldin-Meadow 1992). However, Perry and Elder (1997) did find a relation between mismatch and learning in adults performing a gears task. The adults were asked to predict the direction in which a target gear would rotate when one of the gears in the configuration was moved, and to explain their predictions (see Figure 1 in Chapter 2). Not surprisingly, the adults often gestured during their explanations (it's hard to talk about gears without moving your hands), and some produced a large number of gesture-speech mismatches. The adults were then given instruction in how gears work, and some, but not all, profited from this instruction. The relevant result from our point of view is that those adults who learned produced more mismatches during their explanations than those who didn't (although the result only approached statistical significance). Here again, mismatch may signal that the learner is ready to take in, and profit from, new input.

Mismatchers Learn in the Real World

One advantage of a training study (as opposed to waiting for learners to change on their own) is time—the changes we want to observe occur over a short rather than a long time period (hours as opposed to weeks). However, another advantage is that we can control the instruction that the learner gets—which means that, if we find differential effects after instruction (as we do), those effects can be attributed not to differences in input but, rather, to differences in the learners themselves (their status as a matcher or mismatcher).

There are also benefits, however, to looking at learning as it occurs in more naturalistic circumstances, not the least of which is that it would be nice to know whether gesture-speech mismatch has anything to do with learning in the real world. We have conducted two studies which suggest that it does.

In the first, Melissa Singer and I asked math teachers to individually instruct nine- and ten-year-old children in mathematical equivalence (Goldin-Meadow and Singer 2003). The teacher watched while an experimenter gave the child a pretest consisting of six mathematical equivalence problems. Children who solved even one problem correctly were eliminated from the study. The teacher then instructed the child using any techniques that he or she thought appropriate. After the tutorial, we gave the child a post-test comparable to the pretest. We found that, on the basis of the explanations they produced during the pretest and training, the children could be divided into three groups: those who never produced mismatches at any point during the testing or instruction; those who produced mismatches only during instruction; and those who produced mismatches during the pretest and typically during instruction too.

The interesting result is that the children's post-test scores reflected these groupings: children who produced mismatches on the pretest solved 3.2 problems correctly on the post-test (out of 6), children who produced mismatches only during instruction solved 2.1 correctly, and children who never produced mismatches solved 0.5 correctly. Thus the children who produced mismatches were far more likely to profit from the teacher's instruction than the children who didn't. Of course, the teachers may have altered their instruction as a function of the children's gestures, treating matchers differently from mismatchers. If so, it may have been the child's gestures that let the teacher know the child was ready for a different kind of input, thus playing a pivotal role in the learning process. We return to this very real possibility in Chapter 9.

In our second naturalistic study, we observed very young children making the transition from one- to two-word utterances (Goldin-Meadow and Butcher 2003). These children encountered the naturalistic input that all young language learners experience. The question was who would be the first to profit from this input and make the transition to two-word speech. All six of the children we observed produced gestures along with their one-word utterances. Moreover, all six began producing utterances in which gesture and speech conveyed different information (that is, mismatches, such as "dada" + point at dad's hat) prior to their first two-word utterance ("dada hat"). The crucial point for us here is that the age at which the children first produced these mismatches correlated with the age at which they first produced two-word utterances ($r_s = .90$, $p < .05$, Spearman rank correlation coefficient, correcting for ties; see Figure 8, top graph). Even without Joseph, who was substantially older than the other children and thus ranked at the top on all measures (the point to the far right in the figure), the correlation was .82 (correcting for ties). Thus the children who were first to produce mismatches were also first to produce two-word utterances.

Importantly, the correlation between mismatches and two-word speech was specific to utterances in which gesture and speech conveyed different information—we didn't find the pattern for utterances in which gesture and speech conveyed the same information (that is, matches, such as "hat" + point at dad's hat). The correlation between the onset of matches and the onset of two-word utterances was low and unreliable ($r_s = .46$, n.s.) and, without Joseph, dropped to .03 (correcting for ties; see Figure 8, bottom graph). Thus it is the ability to use gesture and speech to convey different components of a proposition—and not just the ability to use gesture and speech in a single utterance—that predicts the onset of two-word utterances (see also Capirci, Montanari, and Volterra 1998; Goodwyn and Acredolo 1998). Mismatch tells us who is ready to take advantage of input, whether that input is administered by an experimenter or comes naturally through the child's interactions with the world.

A Step along the Way

The studies I have described thus far show that gesture-speech mismatch is associated with a propensity to learn, but they don't in any way shed light on the path of learning. To do so, Martha Alibali and I conducted a "microgenetic" study—that is, we assessed children repeatedly as they were exposed to instruction in mathematical equivalence (Alibali and Goldin-Meadow 1993b).

Gesture-speech mismatch appears to be a transitional step, but from where to where? We guessed that prior to a period of mismatch, children would produce gesture-speech matches in which both gesture and speech convey incorrect information (matching explanations that are

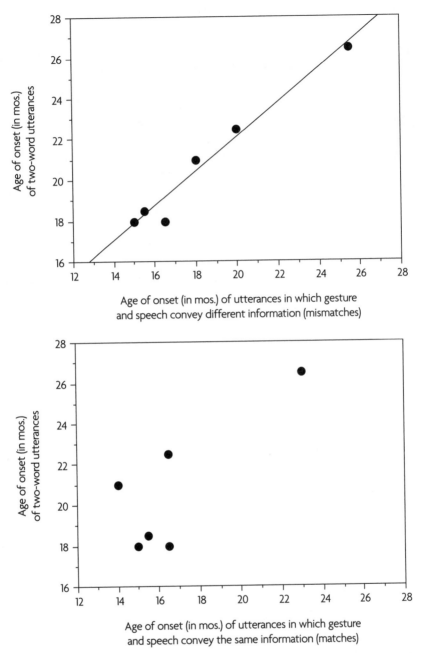

Figure 8. The age at which each child first produced two-word utterances as a function of the age at which that child began producing gesture-speech mismatches (top) and the age at which that child began producing gesture-speech matches (bottom). The onset of two-word utterances is reliably related to the onset of gesture-speech mismatches, but not matches.

incorrect; see, for example, Figure 6A). After a period of mismatch, children might again produce gesture-speech matches, but this time gesture and speech convey *correct* information (matching explanations that are correct; see Figure 7A). Thus we hypothesized that the typical developmental trajectory with respect to a particular task would take a child from a period of incorrect matching explanations, through a period of mismatch (either two different incorrect explanations, or one correct and one incorrect), and back to a period of matching correct explanations (see Table 2).

To test this hypothesis, we gave children instruction in problems of the $4 + 5 + 3 = \_\_ + 3$ variety, and assessed them three times over the course of the training period. The children began the study at different levels of understanding of mathematical equivalence (although none could solve the problems correctly), and made different gains as a result of instruction. Indeed, some made no progress at all, and a small number regressed. The interesting point, however, is that the vast majority of the thirty-five children who gestured and made progress on the task did so following the hypothesized path. Over the course of the study, eleven children traversed the first two steps of the path (incorrect match to mismatch), fifteen traversed the last two steps (mismatch to correct match), and three traversed all three steps (incorrect match to mismatch to correct match), accounting for 83 percent of the thirty-five children (a number significantly higher than that expected by chance, $p < .001$, binomial test). Only six of the children who gestured and progressed on the task did so by skipping the mismatching step. Thus, gesture-speech mismatch appears to be a stepping-stone on the way toward mastery of a task.

Long-Lasting Knowledge

What about the six children in our microgenetic study who arrived at a correct state without passing through mismatch? The question we ask is whether skipping mismatch makes any difference. Once having arrived at a correct state, it may not matter at all how you got there—only that you're there. To address this question, we tested the breadth and longevity of the children's understanding of mathematical equivalence after instruction.

To tap breadth of knowledge, we gave the children a post-test requiring them to generalize what they had learned on the addition problems to multiplication. This post-test was given immediately following the

Table 2. Sample explanations children use on the path to mastering mathematical equivalence

	Responses generated for the problem $6 + 4 + 7 = \_\_ + 7$		
Modality	Matching explanations (incorrect)	Mismatching explanations[a]	Matching explanations (correct)
Speech	"I added the 6, the 4, and the 7" (Add to equal sign)	"I added the 6, the 4, and the 7" (Add to equal sign)	"I added 6 and 4 and got 10" (Grouping)
Gesture	Points at the 6, the 4, and the 7 on the left side of the equation (Add to equal sign)	Makes "horns" shape with the hand under the 6 and 4 (Grouping)	Makes "horns" shape with the hand under the 6 and 4 (Grouping)

a. Children also produce mismatching explanations in which speech and gesture both convey incorrect procedures (for example, "add to equal sign" in speech, accompanied by a point at each of the four numbers in the problem—that is, "add all numbers" in gesture, see Figure 6, frames B1–B4) and, far less frequently, mismatching explanations in which speech conveys a correct problem-solving procedure and gesture conveys an incorrect procedure (for example, "grouping" in speech accompanied by "add to equal sign" in gesture).

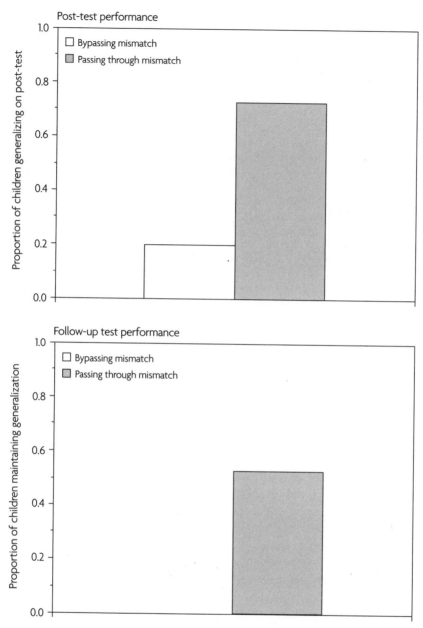

Figure 9. The proportion of children who successfully generalized their mathematical equivalence training to the post-test immediately following the instruction (top), and who maintained that progress two weeks later on a follow-up test (bottom). All of the children were correct matchers by the end of training. Children who arrived at that state by passing through mismatch (gray bars) were significantly more likely to generalize their training and maintain that progress than children who arrived at the state by skipping mismatch (white bars).

training period. To tap longevity, we gave the children the same test two weeks after training. We focused on two groups: children who gestured and progressed to a matching correct state by passing through a mismatching state, and those who gestured and progressed but did so by skipping the mismatching state. We found that children who skipped the mismatching state were significantly less likely to generalize their knowledge on the post-test, and significantly less likely to maintain their gains on the follow-up test two weeks later, than children who went through a mismatching state (Figure 9; Alibali and Goldin-Meadow 1993b).

These findings suggest that, when gesture-speech mismatch is a step on a child's path to mastery, learning is deep and robust. They provide the first hint that gesture, when taken in relation to speech, may not only reflect learning but also contribute to it.

5

Only the Hands Know for Sure

Speakers can reveal in gesture information that they may not know they have. Consider a child explaining how he solved the math problem 4 + 5 + 3 = __ + 3. The child says, "I added 4 plus 5 plus 3 plus 3 and got 15," demonstrating no awareness that this is an equation bifurcated by an equal sign. His gestures, however, offer a different picture: he sweeps his left palm under the left side of the equation—pauses—then sweeps his right palm under the right side. His gestures demonstrate that, at some level, he knows the equal sign breaks the string into two parts. But how widespread is his knowledge? Is the child able, on another problem of this type, to express this knowledge in speech? Or is the knowledge expressed by gesture in a mismatch accessible only to gesture—a thought that the child can express with his hands but not with his mouth?

Is Information in Gesture Accessible to Speech?

The information conveyed by gesture in a gesture-speech match is obviously accessible to speech. But what about the information conveyed by gesture in a gesture-speech mismatch? The child does not express the information in speech in that response—else we would not call it a mismatch. But the child might express this information in speech in some other response. The only way to address this question is to look at all of the responses that a child produces—that is, to describe the child's *repertoire*.

We did this for a group of fourth-grade children who gestured when solving and explaining six mathematical equivalence problems (Goldin-Meadow, Alibali, and Church 1993). We first listed all of the different types of problem-solving strategies that a particular child expressed. We then determined which modalities the child used to express each strategy. If the child expressed a particular strategy only in gesture across all six problems, the strategy was assigned to the *Gesture-Only* repertoire. If the child expressed the strategy only in speech, the strategy was assigned to the *Speech-Only* repertoire. Finally, if the child expressed the strategy in both gesture and speech, the strategy was assigned to the *Gesture + Speech* repertoire. Note that a child need not have expressed a strategy in gesture and speech on the same problem in order for that strategy to be counted as part of the Gesture + Speech repertoire.

We found two striking results. First, the children's Speech-Only repertoires were very small. On average, they produced only 0.3 different strategies uniquely in speech. What this means is that whatever information the children were able to express in speech, they were also able to express in gesture—not necessarily on the same problem, but at some point during the task.

Second, the children's Gesture-Only repertoires were relatively large. On average, they produced 1.6 different strategies uniquely in gesture— about the same number of strategies as they produced in Gesture + Speech (1.3). The children thus knew some strategies that they did not express in speech, not just on a single problem but across an entire set of problems.

Thus, at least on this task, when children can articulate a notion in speech, they are also able to articulate that notion in gesture. But the converse is not true—when children express a notion in gesture on the mathematical equivalence task, sometimes they are also able to express that notion in speech and sometimes they are not.

Even in judgments of others' explanations, there may be an asymmetric relation between gesture and speech—when children notice a speaker's words, they also notice that speaker's gesture, but not vice versa. Graham (1999) asked very young children to "help" a puppet learn to count. Half the time the puppet counted correctly, but the other half of the time the puppet added an extra number (for example, the puppet would say "one, two, three" while counting two objects). In addition, when the puppet made these counting errors, he either produced the same number of pointing gestures as number words (three in this example), a larger or smaller number of pointing gestures (four or two pointing gestures), or no pointing gestures at all. The child's job was to tell the puppet whether his counting was correct and, if incorrect, to explain why the puppet was wrong. The interesting result from the point of view of this discussion concerns whether children made reference to the puppet's number words (Speech-Only) or points (Gesture-Only) or both (Gesture + Speech) in their explanations: two-year-olds did not refer to either gesture or speech; three-year-olds referred to gesture but not to speech (Gesture-Only); and four-year-olds referred to both gesture and speech (Gesture + Speech). Very few children across all three ages referred to the puppet's speech without also referring to the puppet's gesture. In other words, when they noticed the puppet's speech, they also noticed his gesture, but not necessarily vice versa.

Thus having the ability to express a notion in gesture does not guarantee that the speaker can express the notion in speech. However, having the ability to express a notion in speech almost always does mean that the speaker is able to express that notion in gesture. This asymmetry makes sense if gesture is a learner's entry into a domain. The learner first acquires information about a task through gesture, and over time comes to express that information in speech as well as in gesture. The strong claim is that, in order to acquire information in speech, the learner must first process it in gesture. The strong claim is not likely to be true in all domains. It might, however, be an accurate picture of how we learn in domains that are particularly well suited to gestural representation, that is, in spatial and visual domains.

Is Information in Gesture Tied to the Hands?

We now know that speakers can express knowledge in gesture that they do not express in speech. But is there some other means by which speakers can tell us that they "have" this knowledge, or is this knowledge tied to the speakers' hands? Knowledge that is accessible to gesture but not to speech, by definition, cannot be articulated. But perhaps one can gain access to this knowledge in some other, less explicit way, for example, by a rating task (see Acredolo and O'Connor 1991; Horobin and Acredolo 1989; Siegler and Crowley 1991). In a rating task, all the raters need do is make a judgment about information provided by the experimenter. They do not need to express the information themselves. A rating task thus seems ideal for our purposes.

Our goal, then, is to figure out whether speakers display in a rating task the information that they express in gesture but not speech (Garber,

Alibali, and Goldin-Meadow 1998). The goal requires two steps. Our first step is to determine which information speakers express uniquely in gesture. We observed a group of fourth-grade children solving and explaining mathematical equivalence problems and, on the basis of the explanations they gave to six problems, we divided each child's problem-solving strategies into one of three categories: (1) strategies that the child expressed in speech (with or without gesture), (2) strategies that the child expressed only in gesture (and never in speech), and (3) strategies that the child did not express at all. We focus here on only those children who had some strategies in each category.

Our next step was to look at the child's responses to the rating task. We asked the child to rate possible solutions to a particular mathematical equivalence problem. For example, we presented the problem $4 + 5 + 3 = \_\_ + 3$ and asked the child if it would be okay to put 12 in the blank. Note that this particular answer can be gotten by adding up the numbers on the left side of the equal sign (an add-to-equal-sign strategy). We then asked, for the same problem, if it would it be okay to put 15 in the blank. Adding up all of the numbers in the problem gives 15 as an answer (an add-all-numbers strategy). Interestingly, the children were quite happy to accept more than one possible solution for the same problem (that is, they would say that both 12 and 15 were good answers for this problem)—a finding that, in itself, suggests the children were not too sure what mathematical equations are all about.

The crucial question is whether the children would be more likely to accept 12 as an answer if they had expressed an add-to-equal-sign strategy uniquely in gesture than if they had not expressed this strategy in either modality. They were. Children rated solutions significantly higher if they had expressed the strategy that generated the solution in gesture than if they had not expressed the strategy at all (see Figure 10). Thus knowledge expressed uniquely in gesture, though never spoken, can nevertheless be accessed and utilized in another context.

Not surprisingly, children also rated solutions significantly higher if they had expressed the strategy that generated the solution in speech than if they had expressed it uniquely in gesture. Thus solutions derived from strategies children conveyed uniquely in gesture were rated *higher* than solutions derived from strategies they did not convey at all, but *lower* than solutions derived from strategies they conveyed in speech (see Figure 10).

These findings underscore two points. The first is methodological. As we saw in Chapter 3, we tested to make sure that the system we use to code gesture is reliable, that is, when one experimenter attributes a par-

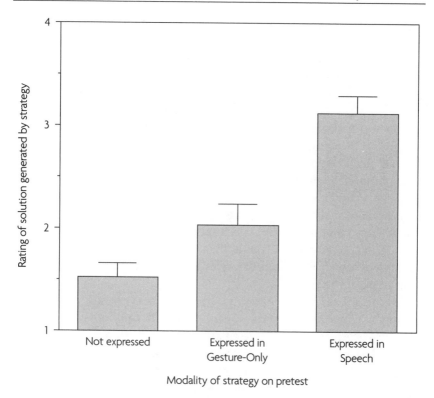

Figure 10. Mean ratings of solutions generated by strategies that, on the pretest, the children (1) never expressed, (2) expressed in gesture but not in speech, or (3) expressed in speech (with or without gesture). Solutions derived from strategies expressed uniquely in gesture were rated *higher* than solutions derived from strategies not expressed at all, but *lower* than solutions derived from strategies expressed in speech. The error bars indicate standard errors.

ticular meaning to a gesture, a second independent experimenter is very likely to attribute this same meaning to the gesture. Until now, however, we have not tested the validity of our coding system—is the meaning that we attribute to a particular gesture the meaning that the child intends?

The findings from this study suggest that the answer to this question is yes, and that our coding system is indeed valid. The gestures that the children produced on the explanation task were classified into strategies on the basis of our coding system. On a separate and independently administered rating task, the children were asked to judge the acceptability of solutions derived from these strategies. We found a systematic relation between a child's judgments on the rating task and our classifications of that child's gestures on the explanation task, and it is this systematic relation that validates our gesture-coding classifications.

This is a particularly satisfying result in the case of mathematical equivalence gestures. The typical gestural explanation on this task involves a series of points. Rather than interpret this series of points merely as a list of numbers (that is, 4, 5, 3), we have chosen to attribute procedural meaning to the gestures (that is, add the 4, the 5, and the 3). The fact that there was a systematic relation between the child's rating of a solution and the presence of the strategy that generated that solution in the child's explanations (a relation that held even for strategies expressed uniquely in gesture) suggests that our coding decision is justified—that is, that it is legitimate to attribute a procedural meaning to these strings of gestures. Overall, the study buttresses a research methodology designed to capture knowledge that would be missed using a purely verbal protocol.

The second point is theoretical. Knowledge expressed uniquely in gesture is neither fully explicit nor fully implicit. Children could not express in speech the knowledge that they conveyed only through their hands—indeed, they did not express this knowledge anywhere in their verbal repertoires. Moreover, on a rating task, they gave less credence to knowledge expressed uniquely in gesture than to knowledge expressed in speech. Thus knowledge expressed uniquely in gesture is not fully explicit. This knowledge, however, is not fully implicit either. Children did have access to the knowledge they expressed uniquely in gesture and could apply it in other contexts—the rating task. Thus knowledge expressed uniquely in gesture represents a middle point along a continuum of knowledge states, bounded at one end by the fully implicit and embedded in action, and at the other by the fully explicit and accessible to verbal report (compare Dienes and Perner 1999; Goldin-Meadow and Alibali 1994, 1999; Karmiloff-Smith 1986, 1992).

Mismatchers Know More and It's All in Gesture

We saw in Chapter 4 that children who produce many gesture-speech mismatches—mismatchers—are more likely to profit from instruction than children who produce few. Are mismatchers also more likely to have knowledge that they can express uniquely in gesture?

This question is easy to address. All we need do is describe the repertoires of mismatchers and compare them with the repertoires of matchers. We looked again at our fourth-grade children (Goldin-Meadow, Alibali, and Church 1993) and divided them into matchers and mismatchers on the basis of the explanations they produced before instruction (mismatchers produced three or more mismatches in six problems; matchers produced fewer than three). Looking across the entire set of six problems, we then classified each of the problem-solving strategies that a child produced as Gesture-Only (strategies that the child expressed in gesture and never in speech), Speech-Only (strategies that the child expressed in speech and never in gesture), or Gesture + Speech (strategies that the child expressed in both gesture and speech, but not necessarily on the same problem). The results of this analysis are presented in Figure 11.

The only significant differences between the matchers and the mis-

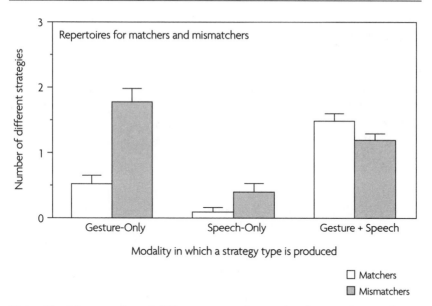

□ Matchers
■ Mismatchers

Figure 11. Mean number of different types of strategies that matchers and mismatchers produced (1) in Gesture-Only, (2) in Speech-Only, and (3) in Gesture + Speech. Matchers and mismatchers have approximately the same small number of different strategies in Speech-Only, and approximately the same larger number of different strategies in Gesture + Speech. The difference between the groups lies in Gesture-Only, where mismatchers have more different strategies than matchers. The error bars indicate standard errors.

matchers were in the Gesture-Only repertoire: mismatchers produced more types of strategies uniquely in gesture than matchers. Interestingly, matchers and mismatchers produced approximately the same number of different strategies in Gesture + Speech, and both produced very few strategies in Speech-Only. What this means, of course, is that mismatchers have more types of strategies at their disposal than matchers (3.4 versus 2.1), which perhaps accounts for the mismatchers' ability to profit from instruction.

It is worth noting, however, that all of the "extra" strategies that the mismatchers have in their repertoires are unique to gesture—that is, the children seem unable to express these extra strategies in speech. To have an accurate picture of what mismatchers know, we must look at their hands.

Repertoires in Transition

Up to this point, we have looked across children, showing that children who mismatch are in a different knowledge state from children who do not mismatch. But producing mismatches is not a personality trait—it reflects speakers' knowledge with respect to the particular task they're describing. Children move between states of match and mismatch as their understanding of mathematical equivalence changes (see Table 2 in Chapter 4). Thus we need to ask what happens to a child's knowledge state as that child moves in and out of mismatch. The data presented in Figure 11 lead to specific predictions:

- A child moving into a state of mismatch ought to *increase* the number of different types of strategies he or she produces in Gesture-Only.

- A child moving out of a state of mismatch ought to *decrease* the number of different types of strategies he or she produces in Gesture-Only.

- There should be no changes in the size of the child's Speech-Only repertoire as the child moves in and out of mismatch.

- There should be no changes in the size of the child's Gesture + Speech repertoire as the child moves in and out of mismatch.

To address these questions, we need to look at children whose knowledge of a task is changing—children who are making progress on a task, or children who are regressing.

CHILDREN WHO PROGRESS AND REGRESS

We return to the microgenetic study described in Chapter 4 in which we observed the steps gesturers took when provided with instruction in mathematical equivalence (Alibali and Goldin-Meadow 1993b). In that study, we found twenty-nine children who made progress when given instruction, but also eleven who regressed. Children who made progress either moved from a matching state into a mismatching state (that is, the children were incorrect matchers at first and became mismatchers), or they moved from a mismatching state into a matching state (that is, the children were mismatchers at first and then became correct matchers). Similarly, children who regressed either moved from a matching state into a mismatching state (that is, the children were correct matchers at first and fell back to become mismatchers), or they moved from a mismatching state into a matching state (that is, the children were mismatchers at first and then fell back to become incorrect matchers).

We found first that, as predicted, there were no significant changes in either the Speech-Only or the Gesture + Speech repertoires during any of these transitions. There were significant changes, however, in the Gesture-Only repertoires in each of the transitions, and those transitions are presented in Figure 12. The top two graphs display children who made progress on the task, those who moved into a state of mismatch on the left ($N = 12$) and those who moved out of a state of mismatch on the right ($N = 17$). The bottom graphs display the children who regressed on the task, again with those who moved into a state of mismatch on the left ($N = 6$) and those who moved out of a state of mismatch on the right ($N = 5$).

As predicted, when moving into a state of mismatch (either by making progress or by regressing), children increased the numbers of different strategies they produced uniquely in gesture. Conversely, and again as predicted, when moving out of a state of mismatch (either by making progress or by regressing), children decreased the numbers of different strategies they produced uniquely in gesture. The size of a child's "bag of tricks" waxes and wanes as the child moves in and out of transition.

CHILDREN WHO STAY PUT—APPARENTLY

Instruction jostles learners. It can catalyze a learner to move forward or, in some cases, to regress. But sometimes instruction seems to do nothing at all, at least on the surface.

In an attempt to observe the smallest steps children make when learning a task, Alibali (1994, 1999) gave a group of fourth-grade children

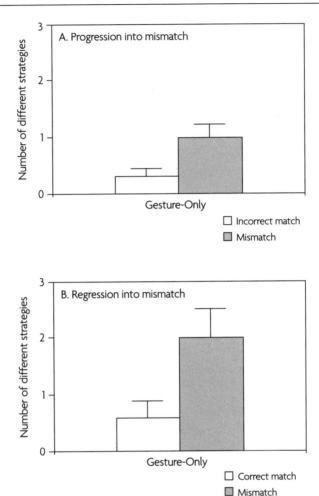

Figure 12 (above and on facing page). Mean number of different strategies children produce in Gesture-Only when they progress into or out of mismatch (graphs A and C)
and when they regress into or out of mismatch (graphs B and D). Children increase
the size of their Gesture-Only repertoires as they move from a matching state (white
bars) *into* a mismatching state (gray bars), whether by progression or regression
(graphs A and B). Moreover, they decrease the size of their repertoires as they move
out of a mismatching state (gray bars) into a matching state (white bars), whether by
progression or regression (graphs C and D). The error bars indicate standard errors.

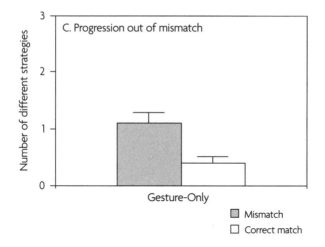

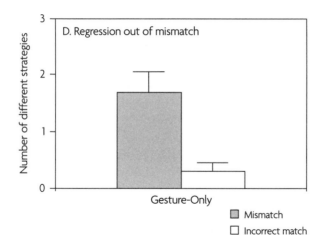

enough instruction in mathematical equivalence to alter their understanding of the task but not enough to get them to master it. And, indeed, as intended, the children in the study changed very little, some not changing at all. Predictably, given the findings in Figures 11 and 12, children who were incorrect matchers at first and progressed to being mismatchers increased the total number of different strategies in their repertoires. And children who were mismatchers at first and regressed to being incorrect matchers decreased their total number of strategies (Goldin-Meadow and Alibali 1995).

But there were also two groups of children who went nowhere—children who were incorrect matchers at the beginning of the study and stayed there, and children who were mismatchers at the beginning of the study and stayed there. Not surprisingly, the size of these children's repertoires didn't budge over the course of the study—the incorrect matchers' repertoires were relatively small (2 strategies) throughout the study, and the mismatchers' were relatively large (4 strategies).

Before concluding that these children behaved like unchanging lumps throughout the study, however, we need to look more carefully at *how* children alter the size of their repertoires. In fact, almost all of the children maintained at least one strategy over the course of the study, which suggests that change may be a more gradual than abrupt process (compare Alibali 1999; Kuhn and Pearsall, 1998; Siegler and Chen 1998). But what about abandoning old strategies or generating new ones? As we might expect, incorrect matchers who became mismatchers not only maintained old strategies but also generated new ones—thus enlarging

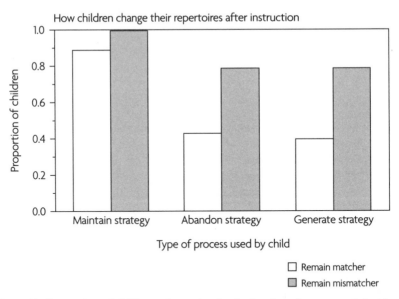

Figure 13. Proportion of children who maintained, abandoned, or generated at least one strategy after instruction. The matchers maintained the size of their repertoires by keeping their old strategies and not adding new ones. The mismatchers did it by constantly revamping their repertoires, maintaining and abandoning old strategies and generating new ones.

their repertoires. Conversely, mismatchers who regressed to being incorrect matchers abandoned old strategies but did not generate new ones—thus shrinking their repertoires (Goldin-Meadow and Alibali 1995).

The interesting contrast comes from the children who went nowhere. These two groups of "stayers" maintained the size of their repertoires but did so in different ways. Children who remained incorrect matchers, predictably, neither abandoned old strategies nor generated new ones—they maintained the same (small) number of strategies in their repertoires by not changing those repertoires at all (see Figure 13).

In contrast, children who remained mismatchers maintained the same number of strategies in their repertoires by continuously revamping those repertoires. The children not only maintained old strategies but, at the same time, generated new strategies and abandoned old ones (Figure 13). Thus the mismatchers' strategies were continuously changing—the children only appeared to be unchanging lumps. In fact, they were doing a great deal of short-lived experimentation. Moreover, all of that experimentation took place in gesture. Many of the new strategies that the mismatchers generated in gesture were incorrect and were quickly abandoned. Gesture may thus be an arena where children can air ideas that may not, in themselves, be all that sound but may be able to serve as stepping-stones for progress nonetheless. And the variability that this constant revamping provides may be just what the learner needs.

Mismatch, Variability, and Learning

Variability exists at every level in children's thinking (Siegler 1994). It's not just that children vary from one another, but the same child can vary from time to time, or from problem to problem. Siegler describes three types of within-child variability common to children.

First, a child may solve the same type of problem in different ways. For example, a child uses the "add-to-equal-sign" strategy to solve the problem $4 + 5 + 3 = \_ + 3$ but the "add-all-numbers" strategy to solve $7 + 5 + 4 = \_ + 4$. The second problem has the same structure as the first and differs from it only in its particular numbers. The child thus has more than one way of solving problems of this type at her disposal.

Second, a child may solve precisely the same problem in different ways. If the child were given the $4 + 5 + 3 = \_ + 3$ problem twice, such a child might solve it first using an "add-to-equal-sign" strategy and then an "add-all-numbers" strategy (compare Siegler and McGilly 1989; Siegler and Shrager 1984; Wilkinson 1982).

Finally, a child may use two different strategies when solving a single problem. The prototypical example of this type of within-child variability is mismatch—the child solves the problem using an "add-to-equal-sign" strategy that he expresses in speech while at the same time expressing an "add-all-numbers" strategy in gesture (see Figure 6B in Chapter 4). By definition, a mismatch is an utterance in which gesture conveys different information from speech—it is a response that, in a sense, contains two responses.

Children who produce a large number of gesture-speech mismatches have variability in their cognitive systems in at least two of these senses. They have variability within a single response and, as we have seen in this chapter, they have a relatively large repertoire of responses at their disposal and thus have variability across responses as well as within them.

Why should we care about variability? There are both theoretical and empirical reasons to believe that variability is important to change. Theories that posit internal conflict as a mechanism of change (for example, Piaget's equilibration theory [1975] 1985) assume that the impetus for transition comes from having more than one rule for solving a problem, and noting discrepancies among those rules. Detecting discrepancy leads to disequilibrium that then acts as an impetus for change (see, for example, Langer 1969, Snyder and Feldman 1977, Strauss 1972, Strauss and Rimalt 1974, within the Piagetian tradition; and Turiel 1969, 1974, within the domain of moral development). Even traditions that are distinctly non-Piagetian have proposed that multiple solutions to a problem may be characteristic of a changing state. Take, for example, Keil (1984), who lists resolution of internal inconsistencies as a possible mechanism of change, and Fischer (1980), who argues that change comes about when two or more skills with an old structure are transformed into skills with a new structure. From an information-processing perspective, Klahr (1984) lists conflict-resolution rules—rules that apply when two productions are eligible to be activated on a single problem—as an important mechanism of change in self-modifying systems. From a Vygotskian perspective, Griffin and Cole (1985) argue that the zone of proximal development embodies multiple levels, both next steps and previous steps. Finally, a number of contemporary descriptions of cognitive change argue that new understanding emerges when two different levels of knowledge are integrated (for example, Bidell and Fischer 1992; Thelen and Smith 1994; Zelazo, Frye, and Rapus 1996). The common thread running through all these theories is the notion that more than one approach is activated or considered in solving a problem, and that the simultaneous activation of a variety of approaches is good for learning.

Empirical work supports the link between variability and change. Across a range of tasks, individuals display variability just prior to making a cognitive change (Thelen and Smith 1994; Turiel 1969, 1974; Walker and Taylor 1991). Take, for example, children in the process of discovering a new way to solve a simple addition problem. The children exhibit variable behavior on trials immediately before the discovery and when the discovery itself is made (Siegler and Jenkins 1989). As another example, adults who profited from instruction in how gears work had a variety of approaches to the problem in their repertoires prior to instruction—many more than adults who did not profit from the instruction or who understood how gears work from the start (Perry and Elder 1997). And, of course, there is our own finding that children who produce many mismatches on a task (two responses on a single problem) are more likely to profit from instruction on that task than children who produce few (Church and Goldin-Meadow 1986; Perry, Church, and Goldin-Meadow 1988; Goldin-Meadow and Singer 2003). Variability is associated with learning.

Gesture-speech mismatch is one type of variability that is associated with learning, but is it special in some way? Mismatch does, in fact, have some unique features. First, the different approaches are activated on a single problem in a mismatch, which could encourage comparison across the approaches. Second, the different approaches are expressed in different modalities, one in speech and the other in gesture. Perhaps the variety of representational formats is itself important for learning.

Church (1999) addressed this question empirically, comparing the impact on learning of three different kinds of variability: (1) variability within a response and across modalities, that is, gesture-speech mismatch; (2) variability within a response in a single modality, speech (the number of different spoken explanations children produce within a single response), that is, within-speech variability; and (3) variability across responses within a single modality, again speech (the number of different spoken explanations children produce across the set of problems), that is, across-task variability. Church observed children's performance on a conservation task before and after instruction, and asked which pretest measure of variability best predicted learning.

All three measures reliably predicted who profited from instruction and who did not. For each measure, children who displayed variability were more likely to learn than children who didn't, telling us once again that variability is good for learning. However, of the three measures, gesture-speech mismatch was the strongest predictor. When all of the measures were entered into a logistical regression, only the mismatch measure emerged as a significant predictor of improvement. Perhaps not surprisingly, since they both involved speech on its own, the within-speech and across-task variability measures correlated with one an-other—and neither speech measure correlated with gesture-speech mis-match. The fact that mismatch involves within-problem variability across modalities may be what gives it its uniqueness. We will return to this hypothesis in later chapters.

Where to Next?

We have discovered that gesture is associated with learning. It can index moments of cognitive instability and reflect thoughts not yet found in speech. Gesture is therefore an ideal tool for researchers interested in identifying who is on the verge of learning, and figuring out what those learners know that they can't say. But might gesture do more than just reflect learning? Might it be involved in the learning process itself? In the next two parts of the book, I consider two non-mutually exclusive possibilities.

First, gesture could play a role in the learning process by displaying, for all to see, the learner's newest, and perhaps undigested, thoughts. Parents, teachers, and peers would then have the opportunity to react to those unspoken thoughts and provide the learner with the input neces-sary for future steps. Gesture, by influencing the input learners receive from others, would then be part of the process of change itself. I con-sider this possibility in Part II.

Second, gesture could play a role in the learning process more directly by influencing the learners themselves. Gesture and speech externalize ideas differently and therefore each may draw on different resources. Conveying an idea across modalities may, in the end, require less effort than conveying the idea within speech alone. In other words, gesture may serve as a "cognitive prop," freeing up cognitive effort that can be used on other tasks. If so, using gesture may actually ease the learner's processing burden and, in this way, function as part of the mechanism of change. I consider this possibility in Part III.

Gesture thus has the potential to contribute to cognitive change in at least two ways—directly by influencing the learner, and indirectly by in-fluencing the learning environment. Our task now is to see whether ges-ture lives up to its potential.

part two

Communicating

6

Everyone Reads Gesture

When someone looks at us with a wrinkled brow and frown, we assume that the person is not happy, even if she says "It's a pleasure to be here." We make inferences about people's attitudes and emotions all the time, and are aware enough of those inferences to be able to display them on "tests" asking us to read facial expressions (for example, Ekman, Friesen, and Ellsworth 1972). Can we do the same for gesture?

There is clearly information to be gotten out of gesture. If individuals are trained to code handshape and motion forms and to attribute meanings to those forms, they are able to reliably describe the information that gesture conveys—independent coders arrive at the same descriptions (see Chapter 3). Moreover, we have good evidence that those gesture descriptions are valid—they reflect the meanings that the gesturer intends (see Chapter 5). But just because trained individuals can get meaning from gesture doesn't mean that ordinary folk can.

Although there is little disagreement in the field about whether there is information displayed in gesture, there is great disagreement about whether ordinary listeners take advantage of that information. Can someone who has not taken a course in gesture coding understand gesture? Do gestures communicate? Some researches are completely convinced that the answer is yes (for example, Kendon 1994). Others are equally convinced that the answer is no (for example, Krauss, Morrel-Samuels, and Colasante 1991).

Before entering the fray ourselves, we need to spend a moment figuring out why we should care if gestures communicate. In Part I, we found that often the information conveyed in gesture is different from the information conveyed in speech. These "mismatches" are of great interest to researchers, who can use them to predict who will learn and who will not. But the same information that is useful to researchers could also be useful to ordinary listeners. How much of what people say with their hands is accessible to others? Do we treat people as if they know the information they express in their hands, or must they actually say it for us to react to it?

Gesture has the potential to change the course of a conversation or lesson—but only if listeners can get meaning from gesture. If they can, a host of questions opens up. When are listeners most likely to get information from gesture? Are some listeners (teachers, for example) better at getting information from gesture than others?

Over the course of this chapter, it will become clear that I come down on the yes side of the "Do listeners get information from gesture?" controversy. I have been convinced by the data that gestures do communicate. However, it is not always easy to see the impact of gesture—you have to know where to look. We can look at how individuals interpret *gesture* when it is produced with speech or without it. Or we can look at how individuals interpret *speech* when it is produced with gesture or without. But neither of these approaches is ideal for figuring out whether listeners glean substantive information from the gestures they see. The best approach is to look at listeners' reactions to mismatches.

Gesture with and without Speech

The most obvious way to see if people understand gesture is to present it to them without speech and ask them what they think it means. Note, however, that unless we are looking at emblems (wordlike gestures that often are produced without speech), we are taking gesture out of its normal habitat—it isn't meant to be interpreted away from the framework provided by speech. Nevertheless, recipients do seem to be able to get some sort of meaning from gesture when it's presented on its own.

To do such a study, we first need the gestures, and we need to know their meanings. Feyereisen, van de Wiele, and Dubois (1988) made video recordings of two lecturers addressing university students. From these lectures, they selected segments containing two types of gestures, iconic gestures that seemed to express some aspect of the content of what the speaker said, and beat gestures that did not but were linked to points of emphasis or some other prosodic aspect of the speech. They then presented these segments to a panel of adults who viewed them with speech and without speech. The panel's job was first to decide whether a gesture was an iconic or a beat and, if iconic, to give the meaning of the gesture. The panel did better at deciding whether a gesture was an iconic or a beat when the gesture was presented along with speech. Some gestures, however, were consistently classified as iconic with or without sound, and these were used in the next part of the study. The panel's meaning guesses served to generate plausible and implausible meanings for these iconic gestures.

All this was in preparation for the real test—presenting the gestures with and without speech to a group of adults, and asking them to select the meaning that came closest to what they thought the real meaning of the gesture was. The adults had three meanings to choose among: the correct interpretation (the words that the original lecturer used when producing this gesture), a plausible interpretation (the words most frequently guessed by the panel), or a relatively implausible interpretation (the words offered by only one person on the panel). When attributing meaning to the gestures consistently classified as iconic, the adults chose the correct or plausible meaning more often than they chose the implausible meaning. But they were no more likely to attribute the correct meaning to the gesture than the plausible meaning. The plausible meaning was, in fact, the consensus response of a wide group of people, so it's not a surprise that it was so frequently chosen. What Feyereisen and colleagues neglected to tell us was how much (or little) the plausible meaning overlapped the correct meaning in the first place. Thus we know there is consensus, but we're not sure whether the consensus reflects the meaning that the gesturer intended.

Note that by choosing gestures whose meanings reflect their accompanying words, the researchers have included only gesture-speech matches. This is also a feature of the only other study that has asked adults to interpret gesture on its own. Krauss, Morrel-Samuels, and Colasante (1991) extracted segments from video recordings of seventeen different speakers describing a set of pictures depicting a variety of subjects (landscapes, abstractions, buildings, machines, people, and so on). A panel of judges viewed the segments with sound. The tape was stopped at clause boundaries, and the judges were asked, first, if they had seen a gesture and, if so, which word or phrase in the accompanying speech was related to that gesture—what Krauss and colleagues call the gesture's "lexical affiliate." Gestures whose lexical affiliates were agreed on by eight of ten judges went into the pool that supplied the stimuli for the real study.

The gestures were shown to a group of adults who were asked to choose between two possible lexical affiliates—the actual affiliate of the gesture, and another affiliate chosen at random. The adults were somewhat more likely to choose the actual lexical affiliate than the one randomly selected (75 percent, where chance is 50 percent). When asked in the next study to generate the meaning of the gesture (rather than recognize it), adults were able to do so reliably for gestures representing actions and locations, but not for object names or descriptions.

Finally, adults were asked to assign a gesture to a semantic category (action, location, object name, description) when it was viewed with speech and without. The results were not the same—adults assigned gestures to categories differently when they saw them in the context of speech (gesture with speech) than when they saw them alone (gesture alone). These results are striking, because they suggest that even if adults are able to glean meaning from gesture on its own, this ability tells us absolutely nothing about how they glean meaning from gesture when it occurs with speech—which is how we always see gesture.

Krauss and his colleagues went on to make one further comparison, one which suggests (according to Krauss et al.) that gesture contributes very little to the entire enterprise. In addition to assigning a gesture to a semantic category when it was viewed in the context of speech, adults were also asked to listen to the speech on its own and assign it to semantic categories. Judgments of a gesture's semantic category made in the presence of speech (gesture with speech) were not reliably different from judgments made when only speech was available (speech alone). In other words, gesture added nothing to the decisions made on the basis of speech alone. When people can hear the words that accompany a gesture, their understanding of that gesture (or at least the gesture's semantic category) is largely a product of what they hear rather than what they see. This result may not be all that surprising, given that the only gestures included in the study to begin with were those that conveyed the same information as speech, that is, those with lexical affiliates—gesture-speech matches.

So where are we? We have learned that people can glean some information from gestures when those gestures are viewed without speech, but not much. The question is whether, realistically, we should have expected even this. The fact that there is variability in the meanings attributed to gestures when they are viewed without speech makes sense if we recognize that the gestures produced along with speech do not form a stable lexicon (see Chapter 3). As McNeill (1992) makes very clear, gestures are spontaneous accompaniments of talk, drawn not from a list of lexical items but constructed "on the fly" to capture nuances of meanings that are important at that moment. They are consequently idiosyncratic, varying from person to person and even from time to time within the same person. Thus in a very real sense we have been looking in the wrong place. We have been looking at gesture as though it were a system unto itself—but it isn't. It forms an integrated system with the speech it accompanies. Just because we cannot reliably interpret gestures when they appear on their own does not mean that we cannot reliably interpret them when they are viewed as they are meant to be viewed—in the context of speech.

Speech with and without Gesture

SPONTANEOUS CONVERSATION

Do we pay attention to gesture when it accompanies speech? There are hints that we do, from observations of how listeners behave in conversation. Heath (1992, cited in Kendon 1994), for example, describes several interchanges in which the recipient seems to grasp the meaning of an utterance before its completion, and to do so on the basis of gesture. A doctor is explaining that a particular medicine will "damp down" a symptom and makes several downward movements of his hand as he does so. The timing, however, is important. He says "they help sort of you know to dampen down the inflammation," and has already completed three downward strokes of his gesture by the time he says "you know"—he gestures before he actually produces the word "dampen." It is at this point, after the gesture but before the word "dampen," that the recipient looks at the doctor and begins to nod. The recipient appears to have gotten the gist of the sentence well before its end, and to have gotten that gist from gesture.

Examples of this sort are suggestive but not at all definitive. We have no idea what the recipient is actually understanding when he nods his head. The recipient may think he's gotten the point of the sentence, but he may be completely mistaken. He may even be pretending to understand. We need to know exactly what recipients are taking from gesture in order to be sure that they have truly grasped its meaning. To do that, we turn to a more experimental approach.

ASKING SPEAKERS NOT TO GESTURE

Graham and Argyle (1975) conducted one of the very first studies designed to explore the effect of gesture on the recipient. An encoder described a series of abstract line figures to decoders who could not see the figures and were asked to make drawings of the shapes described to them. Each encoder described half of the pictures using gesture freely, and half with his or her arms folded. A separate panel of judges analyzed the decoders' drawings for similarity to the original drawing and assigned each drawing an "accuracy" score. The accuracy score is the measure we're looking for—an assessment of how much information the decoder takes from the encoder's message. This measure can be compared for drawings done following messages with gesture versus messages without gesture.

The effect was large. Decoders created significantly more accurate drawings when listening to messages that were accompanied by gesture than when listening to messages that were gesture free. The effect was particularly large for line drawings that were difficult to describe in words (that is, low-codability pictures). Allowing gesture to accompany speech improves the accuracy with which shapes can be communicated.

There is, however, one difficulty with the Graham and Argyle study that the authors themselves point out. When speakers are forced not to use their hands, they may change the way they speak. In other words, the speech in the two conditions (messages with gesture versus without it) may differ, and this difference could be responsible for the accuracy effect. In a separate study, Graham and Heywood (1975) analyzed the speech in these two conditions and did find some differences. The messages produced without gesture had more words describing spatial relations, fewer demonstratives, and more pauses than the messages produced with gesture. The first two changes in speech make perfect sense. Gesture can do the job of conveying spatial information, but when gesture is eliminated, speech must take over. Demonstratives such as "this" or "that" often rely on gesture for their interpretation, and when gesture is eliminated, these terms must be replaced with more complete descriptions. Note, however, that gesture seems to be better at the task of conveying two-dimensional objects than speech—accuracy was higher with gesture than without it.

The last difference—an increase in pauses—is more worrisome. It may be that asking encoders to keep their hands folded while talking added to their cognitive burden, which then increased their need to pause. And it is possible that decoder accuracy was adversely affected by all that pausing in the no-gesture condition. The difference in decoder accuracy across conditions might then be attributable to the awkwardness and artificiality of the no-gesture condition, rather than to the absence of gesture per se. All in all, although the Graham and Argyle (1975) results are very suggestive, it might be more convincing to keep speech constant when exploring the beneficial effects of gesture. We can easily do this with videotape.

WATCHING AND LISTENING VERSUS LISTENING ALONE

If we want to get some sense of what gesture adds to communication, we can determine what people understand when they watch and listen to a videotape of a speaker who is gesturing versus when they only listen to the soundtrack of the videotape. Krauss, Dushay, Chen, and Rauscher (1995) did just that. In three separate studies, they asked speakers to describe abstract graphic designs, novel synthesized sounds, or samples of tea. Decoders either saw and heard the videotape of the speakers or heard only the soundtrack, and were asked to select the object being described from a set of similar objects. Accuracy was straightforwardly measured by the number of times they selected the correct object. In none of the experiments was accuracy enhanced by allowing the decoder to see the speaker's gestures.

We now know that, in certain situations, gesture can add nothing to the information conveyed by speech (at least from the listener's point of view). Unfortunately, however, Krauss and his colleagues give us no information, other than rate, about the gestures that the speakers produced. Speakers produced more gestures per minute when describing the graphic designs than the sounds, and very few gestures at all when describing the teas—and rate of gesture made no difference (there was no beneficial effect of gesture for any of the three types of descriptions). But what about the types of gestures the speakers produced? Did they produce emblems? Deictic gestures? Iconic gestures? Does it matter? Other researchers have asked the same question as Krauss and colleagues but have focused their attention on particular types of gestures—and have found effects of gesture.

SPEECH WITH AND WITHOUT EMBLEMS

Berger and Popelka (1971) asked groups of decoders to write down exactly what they heard when simple sentences were spoken to them in a "soft" voice by a speaker standing more than five feet away. Half of the sentences they heard were accompanied by gestures—emblems—and half were not. For example, the speaker in the gesture condition said, "I see him on the horizon," while raising a flat palm to the forehead, with the fingers together, parallel to the floor, and the thumb resting on the eyebrows (the "looking in distance" gesture).

Accuracy scores were twice as high for sentences presented with gestures as for sentences presented without gestures. But emblems, of course, truly do form a stable lexicon—they ought to be easily interpreted by listeners. Moreover, Berger and Popelka introduced another factor that could be important—how easy or hard it is to understand the speech (all of the sentences they presented were produced in a soft voice and thus were relatively hard to hear). Gesture may be important to the listener when speech is difficult to hear, but may contribute very little when speech is easily accessible (see Rogers 1978).

SPEECH WITH AND WITHOUT DEICTIC GESTURES

Thompson and Massaro (1986) explored how pointing gestures affect listeners' perception of ambiguous speech sounds. Decoders saw two objects, a ball and a doll, and heard synthesized speech sounds that corresponded either to /ba/ or /da/ or to sounds intermediate between these two syllables. The decoder's job was to indicate whether the ball or the doll had been referred to in speech. Decoders either heard the sounds on their own or heard them in conjunction with a gesture (a person was seated behind the objects and pointed to one of the two objects). Sometimes the object that was pointed to was the same as the object referred to in speech (point at ball + /ba/) and sometimes it wasn't (point at doll + /ba/).

Perhaps not surprisingly, the decoders' decision about which object had been referred to was strongly influenced by the pointing gesture—they were more likely to choose the ball when they saw a point at the *ball* while hearing /ba/ than when they saw a point at the *doll* while hearing /ba/. Moreover, reminiscent of Berger and Popelka's (1971) results with soft speech, the pointing gesture influenced the decoders' judgments to a greater extent when the speech information was ambiguous (that is, when points were used in conjunction with the intermediate sounds between /ba/ and /da/).

Pointing gestures can convey important information to listeners, but speakers often draw attention to their pointing gestures with their talk (for example, "I'd like this one"). In contrast, speakers are frequently not even aware that they have produced an iconic gesture, and listeners seem not to overtly notice either. Can gestures that are, in this sense, "invisible" have an impact on the listener?

SPEECH WITH AND WITHOUT ICONIC GESTURES

Riseborough (1981) showed decoders extracts from videotapes of a speaker describing an object (for example, a fishing rod) to another person. The extracts were presented with both picture and sound, or with sound alone. The decoder's job was to guess the object being described. Decoders guessed the correct object more rapidly when they could see the iconic gestures that accompanied the description than when they could not. In a subsequent experiment, Riseborough made sure that it wasn't just the hand waving that mattered. She compared responses (this time accuracy scores) to speech accompanied by vague movements versus well-defined iconic gestures, and found that accuracy was much better with the real gestures. Finally, Riseborough examined the effect of noise on comprehension of stories presented with and without gesture, and found that gesture improved comprehension even at low noise levels.

It is, of course, possible that listeners aren't really gleaning specific information from gesture in these situations. Gesture could be doing nothing more than heightening the listener's attention to speech which, in turn, results in more accurate and faster responses—although the fact that vague hand waving doesn't do the job as well as real gesture makes this hypothesis less viable. Beattie and Shovelton (1999b) avoid this concern by examining in detail the types of information that listeners take from a message when they hear it with and without gesture.

Beattie and Shovelton (1999b) asked speakers to narrate three cartoon stories. Using McNeill's (1992) gesture definitions and criteria (see Chapter 1), they isolated eighteen different iconic gestures (from five different speakers), all of which depicted different events from the cartoons. The gesture was presented along with the clausal unit in speech in its immediate vicinity. Each decoder saw six clips in the audio + video condition (soundtrack and picture), heard six in the audio condition (just the soundtrack), and watched six in the video condition (just the picture). After each clip, the decoder answered a series of planned questions about the objects and actions in the clip (for example, "what object(s) are identified here?" "what are the object(s) doing?" "what shapes are the object(s)?").

The results were quite clear. When the decoders could see the iconic gestures as well as hear the speech, they answered the questions more accurately than when they just heard the speech. And all ten decoders showed the effect. Interestingly, however, some decoders seemed to be better gesture readers than others. One decoder increased the amount of information he got out of a clip by as much as 27.6 percent when he saw and heard the clip versus just hearing it—another increased information intake by only 0.9 percent. Thus there appear to be large individual differences in how much information a listener can glean from gesture. We have no idea, however, how stable these differences are. That is, will someone who gleans a great deal of information from gesture when watching and listening to a video clip also glean a great deal of information from gesture when participating in a conversation, listening to a story, and so on? Very little work has been done on this question—it's a wide-open issue.

It also turned out that in the Beattie and Shovelton (1999b) study, gesture was more beneficial with respect to certain semantic categories than to others—for example, the relative position and the size of objects. Take as an instance one video clip in which the speaker said "by squeezing his nose" while opening and closing his left hand. All of the decoders in both the audio + video and the audio condition accurately reported the squeezing action. However, decoders in the audio + video condition were much more likely than those in the audio condition to accurately report the size and shape of the nose, its position with respect to the squeezing hand, and whether it was moving. It's not surprising that the decoders in the audio condition didn't report these pieces of information—they didn't hear them anywhere in the soundtrack they were given. But it is surprising (depending upon your point of view) that the decoders in the audio + video condition not only noticed the extra information conveyed in gesture, but were able to integrate that information into the mental image they were developing on the basis of speech. Listeners can glean specific information from gesture.

Mismatches Are Key

To summarize thus far, it looks like emblems and pointing gestures convey information that listeners can take advantage of. This is a noncontroversial claim that even Krauss and his colleagues are comfortable making (Krauss et al. 1995, 549). The argument centers on iconic gestures, and here it gets harder to tell what role gesture plays. When gesture conveys precisely the same information as speech, we can never be sure that the listener has gotten specific information from gesture. Even if a listener responds more accurately to speech accompanied by gesture than to speech alone, it could be because gesture is heightening the listener's attention to the speech—gesture could be serving as an energizer or focuser, rather than as a supplier of information.

Note that the data from the Beattie and Shovelton (1999b) study are not plagued by this problem. We are convinced that the listeners in this study are gleaning specific information from gesture simply because that information does not appear anywhere in speech. It must be coming from gesture—it has no place else to come from. In general, I suggest that the very best place to look for the effects of gesture on listeners is in gesture-speech mismatches—instances where gesture conveys information that is not found in speech.

UNNATURAL MISMATCHES

McNeill, Cassell, and McCullough (1994) asked decoders to watch and listen to a videotape of someone recounting a Tweety Bird cartoon. The decoder never sees the cartoon, only the narration. Unbeknownst to the decoder, the narrator is performing a carefully choreographed program of mismatching gestures along with a number of normally matching gestures. The decoder's task is to retell the story to yet another person, and that narration is videotaped. The question is whether we will see traces in the decoder's own narration of the mismatched gesture-speech combinations planted in the video narrative. A control group heard the soundtrack of the video but didn't see the picture.

Several types of mismatches were included in the narrative, some that never occur in natural communication and some that are quite common. The narrative also included naturally occurring matches. As an example of a match, the narrator might wiggle the fingers of a downward pointing V-handshape as he moves his hand forward while saying, "And he's running along ahead of it"—gesture and speech both convey running across. To create a mismatch, a relatively uncommon one in natural discourse, the narrator would produce precisely the same gesture while saying, "And he's climbing up the inside of it"—gesture again conveys running across, but speech conveys climbing up. Do decoders notice discrepancies of this sort and, if so, how do they resolve them?

McNeill and his colleagues have coded hundreds of narrations of this particular Tweety Bird cartoon—they know exactly what types of things people say and how they gesture when retelling this tale. The approach they took to analyzing the decoders' narrations was to examine them for unusual gestures, unusual linguistic phenomena, invented scenes, and omissions of scenes—anything that violated expectations. They found many violations and, most important, they found that almost all of these violations occurred when the decoders had watched gesture-speech mismatches. Very few violations occurred when the decoders had watched and listened to gesture-speech matches, and very few occurred when the control group had listened to the soundtrack. The decoders did indeed notice the mismatches.

What did the decoders do in the face of a mismatch? Let's look at an example. The narrator on the videotape says, "he comes out the bottom of the pipe," while bouncing his hand up and down—a verbal statement that contains no mention of how the act was done (that is, no verbal mention of manner), accompanied by a gesture that does convey manner. The decoder resolves the mismatch by inventing a staircase. In her retelling, the decoder turns the sentence into "and then goes down stairs across—back across into," while producing a manner-less gesture, a dropping-straight-down motion. Notice that the decoder not only has picked up the information conveyed uniquely in gesture (the bouncing manner), but has incorporated it into her speech. The decoder must have stored the bouncing manner in some form general enough to serve as the basis for her linguistic invention ("stairs").

Thus the information conveyed in gesture *is* noticed by listeners, but it is not necessarily tagged as having come from gesture. Bavelas (1994) notes a similar phenomenon. She describes a study done by Coughlan, who selected videotaped excerpts from a stand-up comedy routine and showed them to viewers. Key parts of the story were conveyed gesturally, with no verbal counterpart. When asked to retell or recall what they had seen, the viewers put the bits conveyed only in gesture into words. They sometimes made the gesture as well, but they never made the gesture without the words.

Some of the mismatches that McNeill and his colleagues (1994) included in their study are found in the gestures speakers spontaneously create (manner conveyed in gesture and not in speech is an example), but many of the examples they used are not found in natural discourse. Moreover, the mismatches that the listeners saw and heard were performed by an adult experimenter. We turn now to a series of studies done in my lab designed to examine how listeners react to gesture-speech mismatches that are spontaneously produced by children.

NATURAL MISMATCHES ON VIDEO

We have, over the years, asked a great many children to explain their solutions to conservation or math tasks. As a result, we have in our videotape library numerous examples of gesture-speech matches and mismatches. Our first step in figuring out whether untrained observers can glean information from gesture was to select examples from our store and present them to ordinary listeners. We conducted one study using examples from conservation (Goldin-Meadow, Wein, and Chang 1992) and another using examples from mathematical equivalence (Alibali, Flevares, and Goldin-Meadow 1997).

We selected the videotaped examples carefully: half were gesture-speech matches, and half were gesture-speech mismatches. Each example was shown twice to an adult, and the adult was simply asked to give us a sense of the child's reasoning on this particular problem. The adults had the conservation materials (for example, the containers, sticks, or checkers) or the addition problems in front of them while assessing the child's skills, and were permitted to refer to the props at any time.

In an example of a match on the conservation task, the child on the videotape explained that the two sticks were a different length by focusing in both speech ("you moved them") and gesture (the child moved his hand along the table as though to push one of the sticks over) on the transformation that the experimenter had performed. In an example of a mismatch, the child focused on the difference in the heights of the dish and the glass in speech ("because this one's lower than that one") but focused on the difference in the widths in gesture (she used two wide "C" hands to indicate the width of the dish and a narrower "C" to indicate the width of the glass, see Figure 3B in Chapter 3).

In an example of a match on the math task, the child on the videotape indicated that he solved the problem $3 + 4 + 5 = 3 + \_\_$ by adding up all of the numbers in the problem in both speech ("I added 3 plus 4 plus 5 plus 3 and got 15") and gesture (point at the left 3, the 4, the 5, the right 3, and the blank). In an example of a mismatch, the child indicated that she solved the problem $7 + 6 + 4 = 7 + \_\_$ by adding up the numbers on the left side of the equation in speech ("I added 7 plus 6 plus 4 and got 17") but by adding up all of the numbers in the problem in gesture (point at the left 7, the 6, the 4, the right 7, and the blank; the example shown in Figure 6B in Chapter 4 is another instance of this type of mismatch).

We thought that adults who interact with children on a daily basis and are constantly called upon to assess their skills might be particularly good gesture readers. We therefore arranged for half of the adults in each study to be teachers, and half to be undergraduate students. The entire session was videotaped so that we could not only hear what the adults had to say but also look at their gestures.

How might we expect adults to react to a child's gesture-speech mismatch? If adults are responding only to the fact that the children are moving their hands, they should react to mismatches in the same way that they react to matches. However, if adults are responding to the content of the children's gestures, they ought to react differently to mismatches than to matches.

A mismatch contains two messages, one in speech and one in gesture. If adults are gleaning information from gesture, we might expect them to say more when they assess a child who produces a mismatch than when they assess a child who produces a match. And they did. In both studies, the adults produced many more "additions"—that is, they mentioned information that could not be found anywhere in the speech of the child they were assessing—when evaluating children who produced mismatches than when evaluating children who produced matches.

In addition to producing many more "additions," the adults also produced more of their own gesture-speech mismatches when evaluating children who produced mismatches than when evaluating children who produced matches. Thus the adults responded to the variability in the children's explanations with variability of their own—variability within their own responses (that is, gesture-speech mismatches) and variability across responses (more different kinds of responses per evaluation).

Up to this point, we know that adults react with uncertainty to children who produce mismatches—they attribute knowledge to the child that they did not hear that child express, and they produce their own mismatches which reflect their uncertainty about what the child really knows. But is there evidence that the adults are gleaning specific information from the children's gestures? In fact, it turns out that over half of the "additions" that the adults in both studies produced could be "traced back" to the gestures that the children produced in their mismatches.

Consider this example. In the conservation task one child said that the rows contained different numbers of checkers after the top row had been spread out "because you moved 'em." However, in his accompanying gesture, the same child indicated that the checkers in one row could be matched in a one-to-one fashion with the checkers in the other row (he pointed to a checker in one row and then to the corresponding checker in the other row, and repeated this gesture with another pair of checkers; see Figure 4B in Chapter 3). The adult described the child as saying "you moved 'em" but then, the adult continued, "he pointed . . . he was matching them even though he wasn't verbalizing it," while producing a one-to-one correspondence gesture of her own. Thus the adult had attributed to the child reasoning that was explicitly mentioned in the child's speech (that is, reasoning based on the fact that the checkers had been moved), along with reasoning that appeared only in the child's gesture (that is, reasoning based on one-to-one correspondence). In this example, the adult explicitly refers to the child's gestures, but that doesn't happen in all cases, as the next example illustrates.

A child in one of the math video clips produced an "add-all-numbers" strategy in speech, and an "equalizer" strategy in gesture. One adult described this child as follows: "He doesn't understand the equal sign—that the two sides have to—that what's on the left and what's on the right have to be equal." The adult described in words the very strategy that the child had expressed uniquely in gesture (equalizer). Note that, in this example, the adult denies that the child understands a strategy that the child had actually produced in gesture. The interesting point is that the adult chose to mention this particular strategy for this particular child. We looked at how often adults mentioned the "equalizer" strategy when the child did not express it in gesture, and found that they did so far less frequently than when the child did express it in gesture. It wasn't just that this strategy happened to be on the adult's mind—this strategy was brought into focus in the adult's mind by the child's gestures.

Contrary to our expectations, teachers were no better at gleaning information from the children's gestures than were the undergraduates. At first glance, this finding seems surprising, given that teachers have both more experience with children and more knowledge about learning processes than undergraduates. From another perspective, however, the lack of difference suggests that integrating knowledge from both modalities is, in fact, a basic feature of the human communication system, as McNeill (1992) would predict.

As we have stressed many times, gesture and speech together form a single unified system and, within this system, are coexpressive. Both modalities contribute to a speaker's intended meaning, and the overall meaning is a synthesis of the information presented in the codified, linear, segmented speech mode and the information presented in the idiosyncratic, holistic, relational gestural mode. The findings from our mismatch studies suggest that listeners carry out this same synthesis—in the process of speech comprehension, listeners synthesize the information presented in speech and in gesture to form a single unified representation. Under this view, the ability to combine information presented in the verbal and gestural modalities is an integral and natural part of the process of communication, and thus requires no particular cultural or professionalizing experiences to cultivate it (compare Geary 1995). It then is not all that surprising that teachers of varied experience levels, as well as undergraduates with no formal teaching experience, are able to carry out this integration.

One final point deserves mention. Some of the adults in our study were very aware of the children's gestures and remarked on them in their assessments of the children's knowledge. In fact, in several cases, the adults mentioned the same aspects of the gestures that trained gesture coders used in assessing children's gestured strategies. For example, in describing a boy who expressed the "add-all-numbers" strategy in speech and the "equalizer" strategy in gesture, one undergraduate said, "He seemed to notice that there was an equal sign because he used both arms." In describing a girl who expressed the "add-to-equal-sign" strategy in speech and the "add-all-numbers" strategy in gesture for the problem $7 + 6 + 4 = 7 + \_\_$, the same undergraduate said, "Her finger sort of scanned over the [right] 7, and she ignored it. So I think that she notices that there are two 7's, but instead of canceling it out on both sides, she only canceled it out on the right side."

My first reaction was to try to hire these particular adults as gesture coders in my lab. However, it turned out, surprisingly, that they were no better at gleaning substantive information from the children's gestures than were the adults who failed to mention gesture. Being explicitly aware of gesture (at least enough to talk about it) is thus not a prerequisite for decoding gesture. Everyone does it, with or without training.

NATURAL MISMATCHES "LIVE"

When we pull out our very best examples of gesture-speech mismatches and show them to adults twice on a videotape so they can't help but notice the gesture, untrained adults are able to glean substantive meaning from gesture. But the gesture-reading situation we set up seems a bit removed from the real world. At the least, it would be nice to have adults looking at real-live children producing whatever gestures they please. We conducted such a study (Goldin-Meadow and Sandhofer 1999).

We asked adults to watch a series of children responding to Piagetian conservation tasks. Each adult watched from four to seven children chosen at random from a classroom. We could not, of course, stop the child after each task and ask the adult to assess the child's understanding of the task as we had done in our videotape studies. We needed a technique that allowed the adults to make assessments of the children while they were watching them. To solve this problem, we presented each adult with a checklist, one for each task that the child would perform. Each list contained the typical explanations that children produce on this task (both correct and incorrect). The adult's job was to check off all of the explanations that the child expressed on each task as the child was performing it. The checklist technique thus allowed adults to assess the child's performance on a task as it was being administered. At the same time we videotaped the sessions for later analysis.

Our first step after all of the data had been collected was to code and analyze the explanations that the children produced. Luckily for us, it turned out that a third of the children's explanations were gesture-speech mismatches, a third were gesture-speech matches, and a third were speech alone, containing no gesture. Thus the adults had watched just the right distribution of explanations for us to figure out whether they could read gestures on the fly.

Our next step was to determine whether the adults checked off the explanations that children produced uniquely in gesture (that is, explanations that children expressed in the gesture half of a gesture-speech mismatch). They did—37 percent of the time. We were concerned, however, that the adults might have checked off these explanations even if the child had not expressed them in gesture. To deal with this potential problem, we compared how often an adult checked a given explanation when it was produced by a child uniquely in gesture versus when that same explanation was not produced at all. Thus, for example, we compared how often an adult checked the one-to-one correspondence explanation on her list when the children she saw produced it in gesture in a mismatch versus when the children she saw did not produce it at all on that same task. As we predicted, the adults were significantly more likely to check an explanation when it had appeared uniquely in gesture (in mismatches) than when it had not appeared at all (37 percent versus 7 percent).

The adults were thus able to glean substantive information from a child's gestures, information that did not appear anywhere in that child's speech, and could do so in a relatively naturalistic context. Listeners can get meaning from gesture even when it is unedited and fleeting.

NATURAL MISMATCHES IN CONVERSATION

The study just described is naturalistic in the sense that listeners viewed gestures live, as they occurred. However, it hardly approaches conditions in the real world. First of all, the listeners were given a list which may have encouraged them to consider explanations that would not have otherwise come to mind (although, in fact, the explanations on the list were taken from those that adults spontaneously did produce when asked to assess children's knowledge on these same tasks; see Goldin-Meadow, Wein, and Chang 1992). Second, the listeners were not really listeners at all—they were "over-hearers." They were observing gesturers, but not participating in a conversation with them. Our next study looked at adults and children in a spontaneous communication situation, a teaching situation (Goldin-Meadow, Kim, and Singer 1999).

We asked eight teachers to individually instruct a series of children in mathematical equivalence. It turned out that all eight teachers gestured a great deal with each of the children they taught. However, as appears to be typical for math lessons (compare Pimm 1987), the teachers did most of the initiating, and the children did most of the responding. Thus the children talked and gestured very little, and as a result, we looked only at how the children responded to the teacher's gestures.

Did the children glean substantive information from their teacher's gestures? To answer this question, we examined the children's responses to the teachers' problem-solving strategies. Interestingly, the teachers produced a number of mismatches (in 19 percent of their instructions), and we focused on how the children responded to these mismatches (we consider what it might mean for a teacher to produce a mismatch in Chapter 9—for now, we exploit the fact that they do produce them). We used a very conservative measure of child comprehension—we required that the child paraphrase or reiterate the teacher's gestured strategy (in speech, gesture, or both modalities). If children don't pay attention to the gestures that their teachers produce, they will behave as though those gestures aren't really there (that is, as though the strategies conveyed uniquely in gesture have not been expressed). If, however, they do notice and pay attention to their teachers' gestures, they may well reiterate the strategies that their teachers convey uniquely in gesture.

The children reiterated strategies that the teacher produced in the gesture half of a gesture-speech mismatch 20 percent of the time. Although this may seem like a small percentage, the children reiterated strategies that the teachers produced in the speech half of a gesture-speech mismatch only 25 percent of the time. And, of course, asking for reiteration may be asking too much—a child may understand what the teacher says or gestures and not reiterate it. Although undoubtedly an underestimate of how often children interpret a teacher's gestures, the reiteration measure does make it clear that children can glean substantive information from teachers' gestures. Moreover, 78 percent of the children reiterated the teacher's gestures in a mismatch at least once. The children were indeed able to garner substantive information from their teachers' gestures.

Not only were children able to glean problem-solving strategies from the teacher's gestures, but they were able to recast them into their own speech. For example, on the problem $3 + 7 + 5 = \_\_ + 5$, the teacher conveyed a "grouping" strategy in speech ("You want to add the 3 and 7 to make both sides equal"), but an add-to-equal-sign strategy in gesture (point at the 3, the 7, the left 5, and the blank). In response, the child asked, "I add the 3 plus 7 plus 5 to get 15?" thus picking up on the teacher's (incorrect) gestured strategy and ignoring her (correct) spoken strategy. The children translated the information the teacher conveyed uniquely in gesture into speech almost all of the time. They were thus not merely miming teacher hand movements—for better or worse, they understood them.

We have since replicated this study with another group of teachers and another group of children (Goldin-Meadow and Singer 2003). This time we encouraged the teachers to get explanations from their pupils, so we had much more child participation. We were therefore able to look at how the teachers responded to the children's gestures, as well as vice versa. Both groups reiterated the gesture half of a gesture-speech mismatch. Moreover, both groups often recast the strategy that had appeared uniquely in gesture into their own words. They too were able to read their partner's gestures.

Children Can Do It Too

As these math studies suggest, the ability to interpret the gestures that accompany speech is not limited to adults—children can do it too. In fact, very early on, a gesture-plus-word combination may offer an easier route to the speaker's message than a word-plus-word combination.

ONE- TO TWO-YEAR-OLDS

Even before young children produce pointing gestures to orient another's attention toward an object, they respond to others' pointing gestures by directing their attention to the object indicated by the point (Lempers, Flavell, and Flavell 1976; Leung and Rheingold 1981; Murphy and Messer 1977)—unlike our dog, Kugel, who insists on looking at the end of my finger when I point out a toy to her. But do young children integrate the information they get from the pointing gesture with the message they're getting from speech?

Allen and Shatz (1983) asked one-and-a-half-year-olds a series of questions with and without gesture; for example, "what says meow," uttered while holding up a toy cat or cow. The children were more likely to provide some sort of response when the question was accompanied by a gesture. However, they were no more likely to give the right response, even when the gesture provided the correct hint (that is, holding up the cat versus the cow). From these observations, we might guess that gesture serves merely as an attention getter for young children, not as a source of information.

Macnamara (1977) presented children of roughly the same age with two gestures—the pointing gesture or the hold-out gesture (extending an object out to a child as though offering it)—and varied the speech that went with each gesture. In this study, the children did respond to the gesture—they looked at the objects that were pointed at and reached for the objects that were held out. Moreover, when there was a conflict between the information conveyed in gesture and speech, the children went with gesture. For example, if the pointed-at object was not the object named in the speech, the child looked at the object indicated by the gesture.

From these studies, we know that very young children notice gesture and can even respond to it appropriately. However, we don't know whether very young children can integrate information across gesture and speech. To find out, we need to present them with information that has the possibility of being integrated. We did just that in a study of children ranging in age from one to two and a half years (M. Morford and Goldin-Meadow 1992). We presented children, all of whom were in the one-word stage, "sentences" composed of a word and a gesture. For example, we said "push" while pointing at a ball, or we said "clock" while producing a give gesture (flat hand, palm facing up, held at chest level). We reasoned that if the children could integrate information across gesture and speech, they would respond to the first sentence by pushing the ball, and to the second by giving us the clock. If not, they might throw the ball or push some other object in response to the first sentence, and shake the clock or give us a different object in response to the second sentence.

As you might guess by now, the children responded by pushing the ball and giving the clock—that is, their responses indicated that they were indeed able to integrate information across gesture and speech. Moreover, they responded more accurately to the "push" + point-at-ball sentence than to the same information presented entirely in speech—"push ball." For these one-word children, gesture + word combinations were easier to interpret than word + word combinations conveying the same information.

One more point deserves mention—the gesture + word combinations were more than the sum of their parts. We summed the number of times the children pushed the ball when presented with the word "push" alone (0.7) with the number of times the children pushed the ball when presented with the point-at-ball gesture on its own (1.0). That sum was significantly smaller than the number of times the children pushed the ball when presented with the "push" + point-at-ball combination (4.9). In other words, the children needed to experience both parts of the gesture + word combination in order to produce the correct response. Gesture and speech together evoked a different response from the child than either gesture alone or speech alone.

THREE- TO FIVE-YEAR-OLDS

Kelly (2001) found the same effect in slightly older children responding to more sophisticated messages. The situation was as natural as possible. A child was brought into a room and the door was left ajar. In the speech-only condition, the adult said, "it's going to get loud in here" and did nothing else. In the gesture-only condition, the adult said nothing and pointed at the open door. In the gesture + speech condition, the adult said, "it's going to get loud in here" while pointing at the door. Each child participated in two speech-only conditions, two gesture-only conditions, and two gesture + speech conditions.

The adult wanted the child to get up and close the door, but he didn't indicate his wishes directly in either gesture or speech. The child had to make a pragmatic inference in order to respond to the adult's intended message. The children, even the three-year-olds, were able to make this inference, and were much more likely to do so when presented with gesture + speech than with either part alone. And again, the gesture + speech combinations were more than the sum of their parts. Kelly summed the proportion of times the three-year-olds responded correctly (that is, they closed the door) when presented with speech alone (.12) and when presented with gesture alone (.22). That sum (.34) was significantly smaller than the proportion of times the children responded correctly when presented with gesture + speech (.73).

Interestingly, the four-year-olds did not show this emergent effect—they were equally able to infer the correct response from the individual parts presented alone: .21 (speech alone) + .33 (gesture alone) = .54 versus .61 (gesture + speech). They already knew how to make pragmatic inferences from either speech or gesture on its own—in contrast to the younger children, who needed the gesture + speech combination to help them infer the adult's intended meaning.

Thus for very young children, neither gesture alone nor speech alone is sufficient to convey the speaker's intended meaning in sentences of this type. Rather, gesture and speech must work together to co-determine meaning. Gesture on its own is ambiguous in this context, and needs speech to constrain its meaning. However, speech on its own is also ambiguous, and needs gesture to constrain its meaning. It's a two-way street.

SEVEN AND BEYOND

Older children seem to look just like adults in terms of their ability to get meaning from gesture (Kelly and Church 1997, 1998). Kelly and Church (1997) asked seven- and eight-year-old children to watch videotapes of other children participating in conservation tasks. In half of the examples, the children on the videotape produced gesture-speech mismatches; in the other half, they produced gesture-speech matches. The children in the study watched the videotape twice. On one pass through, they described to the experimenter how they thought the child in the videotape explained his or her answer. On the other pass through, they filled out a checklist after watching each child on the videotape.

No matter which technique the children used, they were able to get substantive information from other children's gestures. They produced more "additions" when responding to the mismatches, and much of the added information could be traced back to the gestures on the videotape. They checked off explanations on the checklist that had appeared only in the gestures on the videotape. Thus children, like adults, are able to glean specific meaning from gestures when those gestures are produced along with speech and convey different meaning from that speech.

In Sum

We have discovered that the best way to decide whether listeners get substantive information from gesture is to observe responses to gestures that convey different information from the speech they accompany—gesture-speech mismatches. The alternatives just don't do the job. Looking at gesture on its own defeats the purpose, since our goal is to understand how gesture works in conversation; gesture rarely appears on its own in the real world. Looking at gesture when it conveys the same information as speech gives results that are hard to interpret. If listeners do respond appropriately, we can never truly tell whether they are getting specific meaning from gesture (it's the same meaning that they would get from the speech), or are merely energized by gesture.

When we look at people's responses to gesture-speech mismatches—mismatches created for the purpose as well as mismatches that occur naturally—we find that everyone can read gesture, even one-year-olds. Moreover, people don't have to be shown the very best examples of gesture-speech mismatches on a videotape with repeated presentations in order to be able to interpret gesture. They can do it on the fly, even when interacting with the gesturer. Gestures not only display information but communicate that information to listeners. The answer to the question "do gestures communicate?" is "yes, they do."

7

Understanding Speech

We now know that all listeners can read information off of the gestures that accompany speech. We also know that gesture and speech form an integrated system for speakers and listeners alike. From here, it's an easy step to our next hypothesis—that our ability to process speech depends on the gestures that accompany that speech.

How could gesture affect the message that listeners take from speech? When gesture conveys a message that is different from the message conveyed in speech, it might hinder the listener's ability to interpret that spoken message. In this instance, there are two messages that the speaker is conveying—one in speech and another in gesture—and two messages ought to be harder to understand than one. Put another way, the message conveyed in gesture may compete with the message conveyed in speech (the result may not be less information garnered overall, but less information garnered only from speech). On the other hand, when gesture conveys a message that matches the message conveyed in speech, it might facilitate the listener's ability to interpret the spoken message. In this case, the message conveyed in gesture is redundant with the message conveyed in speech and, on the grounds that more is better, ought to make the message more comprehensible.

In the Company of Gesture

To explore the effect of gesture on the speech it accompanies, we need a reasonable measure of comprehension and a good sense of what's being comprehended. We presented adults with a videotape displaying a series of children making a judgment in a conservation task and then explaining that judgment—and, of course, gesturing while doing so (Goldin-Meadow and Sandhofer 1999). We selected the videotapes carefully so that in half of the tapes the child's gesture conveyed the same explanation as the speech it accompanied, and in half the child's gesture conveyed a different explanation. To measure comprehension, we showed the adults the children on the video one by one and asked them to check off on a list the explanations they thought each child had considered when solving the task.

Not surprisingly, the adults were very good at checking off the explanations that the children expressed in speech, but they were better on some spoken explanations than others. Moreover, the differences looked like they could be attributed to the children's gestures—the adults correctly identified the child's spoken explanations in 5.8 of the 6 explanations accompanied by a matching gesture, but in only 5.1 of the 6 explanations accompanied by a mismatching gesture. This difference, though small, was statistically reliable.

But perhaps this difference is not about gesture at all. Perhaps children subtly change their words when they produce matching gestures versus mismatching gestures. If so, adults might be better at identifying the message children convey in speech when it is accompanied by a matching gesture simply because the speech is clearer (more straightforward, and so on) than it is when it's accompanied by a mismatching gesture. The best way to test this hypothesis is to get rid of gesture—which we can do by merely turning off the picture on the video. We asked a second group of adults to do the same task as the first group, but this time they heard only the soundtrack of the video and didn't see the picture. And the differences disappeared—the adults were just as likely to identify the message in speech when that message had originally been produced with a matching gesture (5.6 out of 6) as they were when the message had originally been produced with a mismatching gesture (5.6 out of 6). Thus the differences we find when the adults *can* look at the picture cannot be attributed to differences in speech—gesture is the likely culprit.

An adult's ability to receive a message conveyed in speech seems to be affected by the gestures that accompany that speech. However, we don't yet know whether a matching gesture improves the adult's ability to recognize an accompanying spoken explanation, or whether a mismatching gesture decreases the adult's ability to recognize an accompanying spoken explanation. To address this question, we need to look also at comprehension of speech when it is accompanied by no gesture at all.

When Gesture Hinders Our Understanding

Recall from Chapter 6 that when we asked adults to observe children participating in conservation tasks "live" (Goldin-Meadow and Sand-hofer 1999), the children not only produced gesture-speech matches and mismatches but also produced some speech-alone utterances with no gesture at all. We compared how often the adults were able to identify the explanation that the child produced in speech when that speech was accompanied by a mismatching gesture versus when the speech was accompanied by no gesture at all. The effect was relatively large and consistent. Adults were significantly worse at repeating a child's speech when that speech was accompanied by gesture conveying a different message (70 percent) than when the speech was gesture free (82 percent). Gesture can clearly hurt comprehension of speech.

This pattern seems to be robust. Kelly and Church (1998) found the same effect when adults were asked to look at conservation videotapes and describe what they thought the children understood—the adults were less likely to mention the explanation the child gave in speech when it was accompanied by a mismatching gesture than when it was accompanied by no gesture at all. We also found the effect in unscripted one-on-one math tutorials (Goldin-Meadow, Kim, and Singer 1999)—children were less likely to reiterate their teacher's speech when it was accompanied by a mismatching gesture than when it was accompanied by no gesture at all. Thus, for example, on the problem $5 + 4 + 3 = \_ + 3$, a child would be less likely to repeat the teacher's spoken grouping strategy ("all you have to do is add the 5 and the 4 and put the sum in the blank") when the teacher gestures an add-to-equal-sign strategy along with it (point at the 5, the 4, the left 3, and then the blank) than when she doesn't gesture at all.

In fact, in a replication of the math study with a new group of teachers and students (Goldin-Meadow and Singer 2003), we found that mismatching gestures work in precisely the same ways for children and for teachers. As in our first study (Goldin-Meadow, Kim, and Singer 1999), the children were less likely to reiterate a problem-solving strategy in their teacher's speech when it was accompanied by a mismatching gesture than when it was accompanied by no gesture at all. But we also found that the teachers were less likely to reiterate a problem-solving strategy in their student's speech when it was accompanied by a student's mismatching gesture than when it was accompanied by no gesture at all. Figure 14 displays the data for both children and teachers. In both graphs, the gray bar in the left panel (responses to gesture-speech mismatches) is lower than the white (responses to speech without gesture).

Looking at the left panels in the graphs in Figure 14, we might reasonably assume that listeners get less total information from a message when that message contains a gesture-speech mismatch than when it contains no gesture at all. But that assumption would be wrong, simply because we're forgetting about the information listeners glean from gesture. Recall from Chapter 6 that listeners glean substantive information from the gesture half of a gesture-speech mismatch (see the right panels in both graphs, which present reiterations of the information conveyed in the gestural component of a mismatch). That information, when added to the information gleaned from speech, increases the total amount of information the listener gets from the speaker. Indeed, for children, the amount of information gleaned from both gesture and speech in a mismatch (the two gray bars in the top graph in Figure 14) equals the amount of information gleaned from speech when it's not accompanied by gesture. Children get the same amount of information from a gesture-speech mismatch as from speech alone, but that information comes from both modalities. So although mismatching gesture reduces the amount of information listeners get from speech, it makes up for the loss by providing information of its own.

When Gesture Eases Our Understanding

Does gesture *always* hurt the comprehension of speech? No. When it conveys the same information as speech, gesture does not make it any harder for the listener to understand that speech. Somewhat to my surprise, however, it doesn't always make it easier. In our study of adults watching children perform a conservation task "live" (Goldin-Meadow and Sandhofer 1999), the adults were more likely to repeat the child's speech when it was accompanied by a matching gesture (88 percent) than when it was accompanied by no gesture at all (82 percent), but the difference wasn't reliable. And Kelly and Church (1998), in their study of adults watching children perform a conservation task on videotape, found that the adults were no more likely to repeat the child's speech

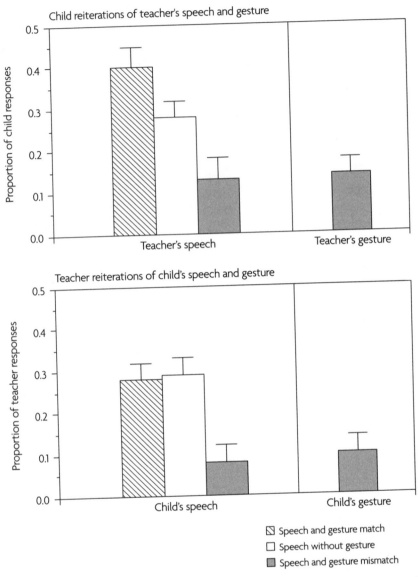

Figure 14. Proportion of responses in which the child reiterated the teacher's speech and gesture (top) and the teacher reiterated the child's speech and gesture (bottom). Both children and teachers were significantly *less* likely to reiterate the message in speech when that speech was accompanied by gesture conveying different information (gray bars on left) than by no gesture at all (white bars). Only the children were significantly *more* likely to reiterate the message in speech when that speech was accompanied by gesture conveying the same information (striped bar, top) than by no gesture at all (white bar, top). In addition, both children and teachers reiterated the strategy conveyed in the gestural component of a mismatch as often as they reiterated the strategy conveyed in the speech component of a mismatch (compare the two gray bars in each graph). The error bars indicate standard errors.

when it was accompanied by a matching gesture than when it was accompanied by no gesture at all. However, the adults were already repeating the child's speech almost 100 percent of the time without gesture—gesture didn't have much room to improve adult performance.

Our math tutorial studies offer a better test of the hypothesis simply because response rates are not even close to 100 percent. Note that in the top graph in Figure 14, the striped bar (responses to gesture-speech matches) is higher than the white bar (responses to speech without gesture). When children respond to a teacher, they are more likely to reiterate the teacher's speech if that speech is accompanied by a matching gesture than if it is accompanied by no gesture at all (this difference is reliable and replicates the effect found in Goldin-Meadow, Kim, and Singer 1999). In this case, gesture helps. For example, on the problem 5 + 4 + 3 = __ + 3, the child would be more likely to repeat the teacher's grouping strategy ("all you have to do is add the 5 and the 4 and put the sum in the blank") when the teacher gestures a grouping strategy along with it (point at the 5 and the 4 and then the blank) than when he doesn't gesture at all.

When teachers respond to a student, however, they are no more likely to reiterate the child's speech when that speech is accompanied by a matching gesture than when it is accompanied by no gesture at all. In the bottom graph in Figure 14, the striped bar is no higher than the white bar. Here, gesture does not help (although it doesn't hurt either). Matching gesture seems to boost children's attention to their teacher's speech, but it doesn't have the same effect on teachers—at least in this situation.

Sometimes Gesture Helps, Sometimes It Doesn't

What do we now know about gesture's effect on the comprehension of speech? We know that gesture can help listeners secure a message conveyed in speech when it too conveys that message, but that it doesn't always help. Sometimes gesture will augment the listener's apprehension of the information conveyed in speech, and sometimes it won't.

At the moment, we don't have any idea why gesture that is redundant with speech makes it easier to grasp the speaker's message in some cases but not in others. Before conducting the studies, I had guessed that redundant gesture would help in all situations. We know that when visual images are presented simultaneously with a spoken message, listeners do better at remembering the message (Baggett 1984) or solving problems with information contained in the message (Mayer and Anderson 1991). Why shouldn't it work the same for gesture? And it does sometimes, just not all of the time.

The key may be in how much overlap there is between the visual and spoken information. As we saw in Chapter 3, it's not quite fair to call gesture "redundant" with speech. Gesture never conveys precisely the same information as speech—it's grounded in a different modality with very different representational resources. Perhaps it's the way in which gesture complements speech that is crucial in determining whether listeners use it to help secure the spoken message. Gesture's effectiveness could well depend on how much overlap there is between the information conveyed in gesture and the information conveyed in speech—and on whether the listener can appreciate that overlap, a topic to which we return in the next chapter.

Note, however, that even though matching gesture may not always facilitate a listener's comprehension of speech, it clearly does not hurt the listener's comprehension. This is an important result for the following reason—when gesture does hurt comprehension (that is, when gesture conveys different information from speech), those negative effects can't be blamed on the distraction of hand waving. Speakers wave their hands when they produce gesture-speech matches too, but matching gestures don't adversely affect comprehension of the speech they accompany. Only mismatching gestures do that. I suggest that it is precisely because listeners grasp the meaning conveyed in a mismatching gesture and recognize (at some level) that it is not the same meaning as is conveyed in speech, that mismatching gesture reduces comprehension of its accompanying speech. Here again, we see that gesture does have an impact on communication.

If, as we have seen in this chapter, gesture can affect the way listeners hear speech, it is likely to play a role in the classroom. Gesture could have a big impact on how children interpret their teacher's words and, conversely, on how teachers interpret their students' words. Gesture could affect learning just by changing the nature of the conversation. We explore these possibilities in the next chapter.

8

In the Classroom

We have seen that an undercurrent of conversation takes place in gesture alongside the acknowledged conversation in speech. The underground information conveyed in gesture is integrated with the information conveyed in speech by both speaker and listener. In Part I, we saw that speakers integrate the gestures they produce with the speech they utter. In Part II, we are learning that listeners integrate the gestures they see with the speech they hear. This integration need not be done consciously. Indeed, speakers are often not aware that they are moving their hands when they speak, and listeners rarely know whether the information they glean from a conversation comes from the speaker's hand or mouth (see Alibali, Flevares, and Goldin-Meadow 1997; Goldin-Meadow and Sandhofer 1999).

This state of affairs makes it very likely that there is more happening in a conversation than meets the ear—in all conversations, even those that take place in the classroom. In order to more completely understand the dynamics of teaching and learning, we need to know about the parts of classroom conversations that are seen but not heard. And we need to know whether these parts have an impact on the teaching and learning process.

Gesture's impact on teaching and learning might be felt in at least two ways. First, the gestures that children produce might signal to their teachers what they know and don't know about a task. Teachers might then be able to use those gestures to help them "diagnose" each child's current state of understanding. Second, the gestures that teachers produce might affect what children learn. We have already seen that children pay attention to the gestures that their teachers produce (Goldin-Meadow, Kim, and Singer 1999). The question is whether those gestures have an impact on learning.

Diagnosing What a Child Knows

WHAT THE CHILD KNOWS BUT CANNOT SAY

How can teachers benefit from a student's gestures? If gesture conveys information that overlaps with speech, it can serve to emphasize, highlight, or draw attention to that information. Gesture could then make it easier to grasp the child's message. As we saw in Chapter 7, sometimes gesture is effective in just this way, and sometimes it isn't.

But gesture can benefit teachers in other ways. When a student's gestures convey information that is different from the information found in speech, those gestures can inform the teacher of thoughts that the student has but cannot (or at least does not) express in speech. Gesture may be one of the best ways that teachers have of discovering thoughts that are on the edge of a student's competence—what L. S. Vygotsky (1978) called the child's "zone of proximal development" (the set of skills a child is actively engaged in developing).

In fact, teachers do notice, and rely on, the gestures children produce in a classroom situation. Crowder and her colleagues (1996; Crowder and Newman 1993), focusing not only on speech but also on gesture, have elegantly described the give-and-take between teacher and student in science lessons (see also Roth and Welzel 2001). There are times when the students express views through their hands that are not evident in their speech, and the teacher notices. For example, students were asked whether the shadows cast by a streetlight (actually a light bulb hung from a ladder) on a line of 20-centimeter sticks would get longer, shorter, or stay the same as the sticks got farther away from the ladder. In response, Malik said, "I think that the longer one's gonna have a longer shadow and the shorter one's shadow gonna be . . . ," while pointing to sticks *farthest* from the ladder. The teacher restated his ideas for the classroom as follows: "so the ones up here closer to the light bulb are gonna have shorter ones and the ones further away are gonna have longer ones" (Crowder 1996, 196). The teacher focused on the objects that Malik had referred to in gesture rather than in speech. It is not clear, in this instance, whether the teacher knew she was making inferences about her student's thoughts on the basis of his gestures. At times, however, teachers can be quite aware of their students' gestures and even ask the students directly to make their gestures more explicit (Crowder and Newman 1993).

Not surprisingly, teachers do not always notice the comments that their students make uniquely in gesture. When students produce gesture-rich but lexically limited expressions, teachers often overlook those gestured contributions even if they are key to the discussion (Crowder and Newman 1993)—the student's gestured comments receive no reaction or are misrepresented in subsequent summaries. Not being ratified by the teacher, the comments that appear uniquely in gesture—which often are at the forefront of the student's knowledge—may then be lost to the group and to subsequent discussion.

Why might a teacher ignore the comments that a student contributes in gesture? The most obvious answer is that the teacher just doesn't notice the student's gestures. The other possibility, however, is that the teacher sees and understands the gestures but finds it difficult to integrate the information they convey with the information conveyed in speech. Recall that in our studies of teachers instructing children individually in mathematical equivalence (Goldin-Meadow, Kim, and Singer 1999; Goldin-Meadow and Singer 2003), gesture reading came at a cost—teachers were less likely to reiterate the message in a child's speech when it was accompanied by a mismatching gesture than when it was accompanied by no gesture at all (see Figure 14 in Chapter 7). If they got information from gesture, they didn't get it from speech—and vice versa.

DOES MISMATCHING GESTURE ALWAYS COMPETE WITH SPEECH?

The nagging question for me is whether mismatching gesture must always hurt the speech it accompanies. I can certainly imagine situations where the information conveyed in gesture, though different from the information conveyed in speech, ought to be relatively easy to integrate with the information in speech. For example, consider a child participating in a liquid conservation task. The child says that the amount of water is different "because this one [the glass] is taller than this one [the flat dish]" while at the same time indicating, in gesture, first the skinny diameter of the glass and then the wide diameter of the dish. In situations of this sort, the pieces of the argument are relatively easy for an adult listener to fit together into a coherent whole, even if the child himself hasn't fitted them into the whole. The wide diameter of the dish compensates for the short height of the water—an observation that is central to the notion of conservation (that is, the belief that the amount of water doesn't change when it's poured from the glass to the dish). A teacher responsive to both gesture and speech might be able to attribute to this child an understanding of both dimensions, height and width.

In other situations, in contrast, the information conveyed in gesture appears—at least at first blush—to be difficult to integrate with the information conveyed in speech. Consider, for example, a child explaining how she solved the problem $6 + 3 + 7 = \_\_ + 7$. She says, "I added the 6, the 3, and the 7 and put 16 in the blank" (an add-to-equal-sign strategy), while pointing at all four numbers in the problem, the 6, the 3, the left 7, and the right 7 (an add-all-numbers strategy). Is it possible for a listener to integrate these two very different problem-solving strategies, strategies so different that they result in different solutions (16 versus 23)?

In fact, there is a framework within which these strategies are not only compatible but essential for solving the problem correctly. In order to arrive at the correct answer, the child must recognize that the equation has two parts, an insight that she reveals in speech by referring only to the numbers on the left side of the equation (the add-to-equal-sign strategy). However, the child must also take into account the addend on the right side of the equation, an insight that she reveals in gesture by pointing at all four numbers in the problem (the add-all-numbers strategy). Although the answers that these strategies give are contradictory, the mathematical insights upon which the strategies are based are not at all contradictory—indeed they are both essential to understanding mathematical equivalence.

I argue that there is always a framework that can unite the message in a mismatching gesture with the message in its accompanying speech. The speaker need not—and, indeed, probably does not—have control of that framework. The listener, however, might well have the framework in mind. If so, he or she might profitably use that framework when interpreting the speaker's gesture and speech.

For example, the child solving the math problem in the instance above has signaled the pieces relevant to a correct solution, but hasn't yet mastered the framework within which these pieces fit. However, the teachers who instruct this child do have in their repertoires an overarching framework that could integrate the child's pieces. Perhaps if teachers were to read the child's gestures and speech in relation to that framework, they could glean information from both modalities. In other words, it might be possible to avoid the competition that seems to arise naturally between the gesture and speech components of a mismatch by searching for a framework that can integrate the two modalities.

Indeed, we know that even very young children are able to combine the information conveyed in gesture and speech into a single message when they have at their disposal a framework that can integrate that information. As described in Chapter 6, when an adult says "push" and points at a ball, children as young as one and a half can get a single message from the two modalities—they push the ball (M. Morford and Goldin-Meadow 1992). These are children who are on the cusp of two-word speech themselves. In fact, the children who are the first to produce gesture-speech combinations of this sort will be the first to produce two-word utterances conveying propositions (Goldin-Meadow and Butcher 2003). They appear to have at their disposal a framework that can integrate the information coming to them across modalities and, importantly, they make use of that framework when interpreting the information conveyed in gesture and speech.

The situation for teachers is much more complex. It may be very difficult, particularly in the heat of an interaction, to figure out a framework that can integrate the information a child is conveying in gesture and speech. But perhaps teachers could be taught to look for such frameworks in their students' communications. The first step, of course, is to make sure that the teacher can reliably read the child's gestures. Although we found in Chapter 6 that adults can glean information from a speaker's gestures, we also found that they don't do it all the time. Can we get teachers to improve their rates of gesture reading, which, in turn, might then help them get as much as they can out of their students' hands and mouths?

APPRECIATING STUDENTS' HANDS

To find out whether teachers can be taught to appreciate their students' hands, we gave adults instruction in how to read gesture (Kelly et al. 2002). We conducted a number of studies, teaching adults to read the gestures that children produce on either conservation or mathematical equivalence tasks. In some studies, we tested the adults' ability to read gesture by giving them a checklist on which they were to indicate the information the child in the videotape had expressed; in others, we asked them to tell us what they thought the children knew about the task. We gave the adults a pretest, then gave them instruction, and finally tested them once again on a post-test. We varied our instruction from just giving a hint ("pay close attention not only to what the children on the videotape say with their words, but also to what they express with their hands"), to giving general instruction in the parameters that experts use when describing gesture (handshape, motion, placement), to giving specific instruction in the kinds of gestures children produce on that particular task.

The adults did improve with instruction, even with just a hint. After getting a hint to attend to gesture, they picked up 30 percent more explanations that the child had expressed uniquely in gesture than before, and after getting specific instruction in the gestures in the task, they picked up 50 percent more than before. In fact, after the adults were given specific training, they were able to accurately decode the children's gestures 90 percent of the time on the conservation task and 60 percent on the math task (improvement was the same on the two tasks—before instruction, the adults were at a 40 percent level on conservation but at a 10 percent level on math). Moreover, on both tasks, the adults were able to generalize the instruction they received to new gestures they had not seen during training.

Importantly for our discussion here, improvement in reading gesture did not affect the adults' ability to glean information from the children's speech on the conservation task—they identified the child's spoken explanations perfectly before and after instruction in gesture reading. There was, however, a slight decrement in the number of spoken explanations the adults reported after instruction on the math task (as in the naturalistic situations we've studied, this decrement was offset by an increase in the number of gestured explanations the adults reported after instruction).

The challenge for us in future studies is to figure out ways to encourage teachers to glean information from their students' gestures while at the same time not losing their words. The technique that seems fruitful to me is to instruct teachers to look for a framework that can unite the information the student conveys in both gesture and speech. Having such a framework in mind should make it easier for the teacher to process the information coming in from the two modalities. The added benefit is that the teacher can also make the framework explicit to the student—and the framework may be just what the student needs at this particular moment. The student already has the pieces. It's the whole that could unify those pieces that the student doesn't have—but seems (if the student's gesture and speech are any indication) very ready to accept.

Changing What a Child Knows

We have seen that teachers can use their students' gestures to discover the thoughts those students are unable to express in words. But students are not the only ones who gesture—teachers gesture too. Do those gestures play a role in teaching and in learning?

The first question is "do teachers use gesture in their classrooms?" Gesture crops up in talk about topics that are frequently taught in schools—for example, counting (Graham 1999), addition (Alibali and Goldin-Meadow 1993b; Perry, Church, and Goldin-Meadow 1988), control of variables (Stone, Webb, and Mahootian 1991), gears (Perry and Elder 1997), rate of change (Alibali et al. 1999). It should come as no surprise, then, that gesture also crops up in classrooms (Crowder and Newman 1993; Flevares and Perry 2001; Neill 1991; Roth and Welzel 2001; Zukow-Goldring, Romo, and Duncan 1994), particularly in classrooms of experienced teachers (Neill and Caswell 1993). But does gesture occur often enough to make a difference?

We know that in a one-on-one math tutorial situation, teachers express 40 percent of the problem-solving strategies they convey to their students in gesture (Goldin-Meadow, Kim, and Singer 1999)—that's quite a lot. And gesture is equally frequent in the classroom. Flevares and Perry (2001) found that math teachers used from five to seven nonspoken representations of mathematical ideas per minute (almost one every 10 seconds) in their classrooms, and gesture was by far the most frequent nonspoken form for all of the teachers (the other nonspoken forms were pictures, objects, and writing). Moreover, when the teachers combined the various forms of nonspoken representations, they always included mathematically relevant gestures—gesture was the glue that linked the different forms of information to one another and to speech. It grounded speech in the world of objects and actions (see Glenberg and Robertson 1999). Interestingly, the teachers used their nonspoken representations strategically, often responding with a nonspoken representation to a student's confusion. The teachers would repeat their own speech while clarifying the meaning of their utterance with gesture. And it worked—the children would frequently then come up with the correct answer.

Thus teachers use gesture in the classroom (at least in science and math classrooms and probably in all classrooms), and they seem to use it to good effect to clarify and correct misconceptions. We don't yet know, however, whether gesture promotes learning. To address this question, we need to move to more experimental circumstances. The few studies that have been done are suggestive, though by no means definitive. Perry, Berch, and Singleton (1995) presented grade-school children with scripted instruction in mathematical equivalence. One group received instruction in speech with no gestures; the other group received precisely the same verbal instruction accompanied by natural-like but scripted gestures. More children in the verbal + gestural condition than in the verbal-only condition were successful after instruction. Along the same lines, Valenzeno, Alibali, and Klatzky (2003) presented preschool children with one of two videotaped lessons on symmetry. The audio track was the same in both videos, but only one included pointing and tracing gestures. Children who saw the verbal + gestural lesson scored higher on the post-test than children who saw the verbal-only lesson.

Finally, Church, Ayman-Nolley, and Estrada (n.d.) presented grade-school children with one of two videotaped lessons on conservation. As in the Valenzeno, Alibali, and Klatzky study, the audio track was the same in both videos, but only one video included gesture, this time iconic gestures typically found in conservation tasks. The one unique aspect of this study was that two groups of children participated—children who were native Spanish speakers and were just learning English, and children who were native monolingual English speakers. The native English speakers performed better on the conservation task, both before and after instruction, than the children who were learning English as a second language (the study was conducted in English). The important point, however, is that gesture helped both groups of children and in equal measure. Both groups were twice as likely to improve after instruction when that instruction included gesture than when it didn't. Thus gesture helped these children learn, whether they were proficient speakers or just learning the language. Taken together, these findings begin to suggest that gesture can play an important role in teaching.

One obvious question is whether gesture always promotes learning. For example, we might guess that gesture would get in the way of learning when it conveys information that is different from the information conveyed in speech. Take the following interchange that occurred in one of our studies in which we asked teachers to instruct children individually in mathematical equivalence. The teacher had asked the child to solve the problem $7 + 6 + 5 = \_\_ + 5$ and the child put 18 in the blank, using an add-to-equal-sign strategy to solve the problem. In her speech, the teacher made it clear to the child that he was using this strategy: she said, "So you get this answer by adding these three numbers." In her gestures, however, she produced an add-all-numbers strategy: she pointed at the 7, the 6, the 5 on the left side of the equation *and* the 5 on the right side of the equation (see Figure 15). In fact, the string of gestures that the teacher produced is identical to the string children produce when giving an add-all-numbers explanation in gesture (see Figure 6B in Chapter 4). After these gestures, the teacher went on to try to explain how to solve the problem correctly but, before she could finish, the child offered a new solution—23, precisely the number you get if you add up all of the numbers in this problem. The teacher was genuinely surprised at her student's answer, and was completely unaware of

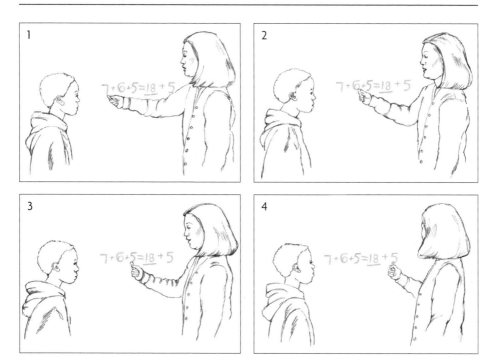

Figure 15. In her speech, the teacher points out to the child that he added the first three numbers to get his incorrect answer of 18. In her gesture, however, she points at all of the numbers in the problem, including the last number on the right side of the equation (frames 1–4). The child's response was to add up all of the numbers in the problem and give 23 as his answer. He had paid attention to his teacher's gestures.

the fact that she herself might have given him the idea to add up all of the numbers in the problem.

A teacher's gestures can lead a child astray. The larger point, however, is that the gestures teachers produce have an impact on what children take from their lessons. The example in Figure 15 illustrates just how potent a teacher's gestures can be—in this case, for the worse. But gesture can also be used to good effect. As we will see in Chapter 9, there are times when a teacher's mismatching gesture might be just what the child needs.

Indeed, when gesture conveys information that complements the information conveyed in speech, a two-modality communication can be highly effective. The information conveyed in gesture may be particularly suited to the manual modality and may work with the information conveyed in speech to convey a richer message. For example, consider a teacher who describes in speech where a set of trenches were dug during World War I, but indicates in gesture the zigzagging course the trenches took (Neill and Caswell 1993, 113). Gesture can provide students with a second representation, and multiple representations can enhance learning.

Current recommendations for math curricula, in fact, encourage teachers to present ideas through a variety of representations—diagrams, physical models, written text (National Council of Teachers of Mathematics 1989). For example, Shavelson, Webb, Stasz, and McArthur (1988) recommend that teachers translate among alternative symbolic representations of a problem (for instance, math symbols and number line) rather than working within a single symbolic form. Gesture can serve as one of these representational formats, one which has a strong visual component.

Gesture is unique, however, in that unlike a map or a diagram, it is transitory—disappearing in the air just as quickly as speech. But gesture also has an advantage—it can be, indeed must be, integrated temporally with the speech it accompanies. And we know that it is important for visual information to be timed appropriately with spoken information in order for it to be effective (Baggett 1984; Mayer and Anderson 1991). Thus gesture used in conjunction with speech may present a more naturally unified picture to the student than a diagram used in conjunction with speech. If gesture were to become recognized as an integral—and inevitable—part of conversation in a teaching situation, it could perhaps be harnessed, offering teachers an excellent vehicle for presenting to their students a second perspective on the task at hand.

Legal and Clinical Worlds

The gestural undercurrent I have been describing may be particularly significant in situations where speakers are not aware of the messages they convey. In classrooms, students convey unintended messages through their gestures, and teachers use those gestures to assess their skills. Conversely, teachers convey unintended messages through their gestures, and their students react to those gestures. There are at least two other situations in which unintended messages may be particularly important—legal interviews and clinical therapy sessions.

Legal interactions are, in Philips's (1985, 206) terms, "structured through talk." What this means is that the interaction can, for the most part, be understood without reference to the nonverbal environment. Philips acknowledges that facial expressions, gaze direction, and gestural patterns provide relevant information, but when nonverbal cues are missing (as in an audio recording or a transcript of the session), the conversation remains more or less comprehensible. The question, however, is whether participants in a legal interview reveal through gesture knowledge that they do not reveal in speech. If so, this information will go undetected in a transcript, but may not go undetected by the participants in the interview.

For example, given the prevalence of gesture, it is not hard to imagine that children will gesture when responding to questions in a forensic interview—and that those gestures will, at times, convey information that is not found in their speech. If so, the interesting question—both theoretically and practically—is whether adult interviewers are able to pick up on the information that children convey uniquely in gesture, and whether the interviewers are aware of doing so. The flip side of the question is also of great importance—do adult interviewers convey information in their gestures, information that they do not consciously intend to convey, and if so, does that information influence how children respond to their queries? In other words, is there a sub-rosa conversation taking place in gesture that does not make it onto the transcripts that become the legal documents for forensic interviews? Given that the details children recall of an event can often be influenced by the way in which the interviewer poses the question (for example, Ceci 1995), this issue becomes a timely and important one.

Let's take a hypothetical case. Imagine an interviewer who suspects that a child has been mistreated by someone wearing a beard. Although the interviewer may be careful not to mention her suspicions in her words (she is aware of the swaying effects that leading questions can have on young children), she might inadvertently produce a "beard" gesture on her face while questioning the child. The child may then describe a person with a beard, not because the person really had a beard, but in response to the interviewer's (unintended) suggestion through gesture. The idea here is that suggestions can be introduced into an interview through gesture as well as through talk. But interviewers typically are much less aware of their gestures and therefore don't monitor them as well as they monitor their talk to children.

Conversely, consider a child who produces a gesture for a beard when describing the person who hurt her. The interviewer picks up on the gesture and asks in her next question, "Did he have a beard?" To someone reading the transcript of the exchange (and not watching the video), the interviewer has produced a leading question—when in reality, the "lead" came from the child. In this case, information that has spontaneously come from the child is wrongly interpreted as having been introduced by the adult interviewer—all because gesture is not considered part of the legal world.

In her dissertation at the University of Chicago, Sara Broaders is currently investigating one side of this question—the impact of an interviewer's gestures on how a child recalls an event. She is building on a paradigm that has successfully been used to demonstrate that the words an interviewer produces to probe an event can shape the way children remember that event (for example, Ceci 1995). A musician comes to the children's classroom to demonstrate a variety of different instruments. During the performance, which is carefully scripted (and videotaped so that we really do know what happened in the classroom), the musician knocks over a glass of water, shakes the teacher's hand, and plays some but not all of his instruments. In other words, he does a number of things that might be memorable to young children. Sara then conducts a series of interviews with each child in the class over a period of time, asking them about the performance. So far the study is no different from previous studies. However, Sara deliberately introduces gestural details into her questions, details that could mislead the children if, in fact, they are paying attention to gesture. For example, she asks, "what was he wearing?" while producing a "put-on-hat" gesture. A child who notices Sara's gesture and is swayed by that gesture might say that the musician was wearing a hat when, in reality, he was not. Sara's first wave of results is quite clear—the way the children remember the performance is influenced by the gestures she produces when asking them about the performance (Broaders and Goldin-Meadow, n.d.). Although far from a forensic interview, studies of this sort establish that children can be swayed by an interviewer's gestures—a potentially important fact that the legal world might want to take note of.

In clinical therapy sessions, patients may also reveal through gesture ideas that they do not necessarily have conscious control over. For example, Lee and Beattie (1998) did a detailed analysis of an adult talking to a researcher about an event that evoked a powerful negative emotion. They found that the adult's nonverbal behaviors during the interview were just as important as her verbal behavior in revealing her sense of self. The implication is that the interviewer would have come away with a different sense of this person if he or she had just read a transcript of the interview.

If patients in therapy sessions reveal through gesture information that is not found in their speech, the therapist then has yet another window into the patient's current state—and yet another yardstick by which to measure the patient's progress (for example, characteristics of the patient's gestures may change as a function of progress in therapy). It might indeed help therapists to be aware of the fact that they are gathering information about their patient from the patient's hands. Again, the flip side of the issue is also important—do therapists convey information in their gestures, information that they may or may not consciously intend to convey? If so, does that information influence the course and outcome of the therapeutic sessions? As in the case of legal interactions, we do not yet know what role, if any, gesture plays in clinical therapy sessions—it remains an open and important question.

In all of these situations and many others, the knowledge conveyed in gesture is there for the taking. As listeners, we often do take it, although we rarely acknowledge its source. Particularly in domains where it is important to keep track of what is said and by whom, we may want to begin tracking gesture as well as speech.

9

Learning by Gesturing to Others

Children can express thoughts in gesture that they don't even know they have. And those thoughts tend to be on the cutting edge of their knowledge. Gesture, then, is an ideal tool for researchers who can use it to make inferences about a child's up-to-the-minute knowledge of a task. But gesture may have a wider reach.

One of gesture's most salient features is that it is "out there," a concrete manifestation of ideas for all the world to see, not just researchers. Gesture could be a signal to parents and teachers that a particular notion is already in a child's repertoire, though not quite accessible. These listeners could then alter their behavior accordingly, perhaps offering instruction in these specific areas. If so, children would be able to shape their own learning environments just by moving their hands. In this way, gesture would not only reflect a child's understanding, but play a role in shaping it as well. Gesture would be part of the mechanism that brings about cognitive change.

Several facts need to be established in order for this hypothesis to be credible.

1. Ordinary listeners must be able to process the gestures children produce and glean substantive information from them, not just in laboratory situations but in real live interactions with children.

2. Those listeners must change their behavior in response to the children's gestures, treating children differently simply because of the gestures they produce.

3. Those changed behaviors must have an effect on the child, prefer-
ably a beneficial effect.

Chapters 6 and 7 established the first point—ordinary adult listeners
can interpret a child's gestures even if they have had no instruction in
how to read gesture, and even if they are participants in the conversation with the child. The goal of this chapter is to explore the second and
third points. In fact, we will find that listeners—teachers, in particular—
do change their behavior in response to the gestures their pupils produce, and that the changes in their behavior may promote learning. The
teachers seem to be exquisitely sensitive to the child's knowledge state,
and seem to know just what to do to teach to that state—although I'd be
willing to bet that they have no conscious awareness of the feat they are
accomplishing. Gesture looks like it may indeed be part of the mechanism of cognitive change. Here its impact is through the listener and
thus indirect. In Part III we will explore the direct effect that gesture can
have on cognitive change.

Teachers' Responses to Students' Gestures

The question here is whether adults adjust the way they interact with
children in response to the gestures those children produce. To address
this question, we need to observe adults conversing with children in
spontaneous, unscripted interactions. Teachers are reasonable adults to
observe, on the grounds that they routinely attempt to adjust their input
to their pupils' skills, and indeed I have already described pieces of a
study that addresses this question in Chapters 4, 6, and 7.

Recall that we asked eight math teachers to individually instruct nine-
and ten-year-old children in mathematical equivalence (Goldin-
Meadow and Singer 2003). The experimenter gave the child a pretest
consisting of six mathematical equivalence problems and the teacher
watched. In this way, the teacher had some idea of his or her pupil's
abilities before picking up the chalk. The teacher then instructed the
child at the blackboard, using any techniques that he or she thought
appropriate. After the instruction, the experimenter gave the child a
post-test comparable to the pretest. The entire session was videotaped
for later analysis.

On the basis of the explanations the children produced during the
pretest and during instruction, they could be divided into three groups:
those who never produced gesture-speech mismatches at any point during the testing or instruction (No Mismatch); those who produced mis-

matches only during instruction (Mismatch in Instruction); and those who produced mismatches during the pretest and typically during instruction as well (Mismatch in Pretest and Instruction).

In Chapter 4, I reported that the children's post-test scores reflected these groupings. Children who produced mismatches in the pretest and instruction solved more problems correctly on the post-test than children who produced mismatches only in instruction, and these children, in turn, solved more problems correctly than children who produced no mismatches at all. Our assumption was that the first group of children were more ready to learn mathematical equivalence than the second group who, in turn, were more ready than the third. But, of course, we don't yet know what the teachers were doing during instruction. Did they provide different instruction to each of the three groups of children? Did they teach children who (from our point of view) were particularly ready to learn mathematical equivalence differently from children who were not yet ready?

To determine how sensitive the teachers were to the presence or absence of gesture-speech mismatch in a child's explanations, we calculated how many different types of correct and incorrect strategies each teacher produced when instructing children in the three groups. The number of different types of strategies gives us some idea of how diversified the teacher's lesson was. The top two graphs in Figure 16 present the data. Teachers used significantly more different types of correct and incorrect strategies when teaching children who produced mismatches during pretest and instruction (gray bars) and only during instruction (striped bars) than when teaching children who produced no mismatches at all (white bars). In all cases, the teachers used their incorrect strategies to instruct children in what *not* to do (for example, "You don't add up all of the numbers in the problem") or to comment on what a child had just done ("You just added up all of the numbers in the problem"). Expressing incorrect strategies in this context seemed to be part of the teacher's instructional plan.

Another index of variability, this time within an utterance rather than across utterances, is gesture-speech mismatch. At times, the teachers produced mismatches of their own, conveying one strategy in speech and a different strategy in gesture (often both strategies were correct, yet different). The bottom graph in Figure 16 displays the mismatch data. The teachers produced significantly more of their own mismatches when teaching children who produced mismatches during pretest and instruction (gray bars) and only during instruction (striped bars) than

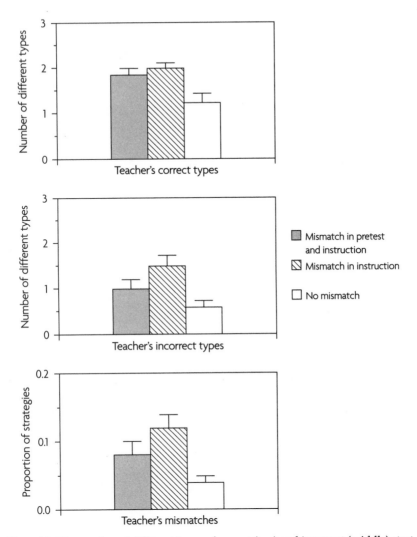

Figure 16. The number of different types of correct (top) and incorrect (middle) strategies, and the proportion of mismatches (bottom), that teachers used when instructing children in mathematical equivalence. Teachers produced more different types of correct and incorrect strategies, and more mismatches of their own, when teaching children who produced mismatches during the pretest and instruction (gray bars) and only during instruction (striped bars) than when teaching children who produced no mismatches (white bars). The error bars indicate standard errors.

when teaching children who produced no mismatches at all (white bars).

Several points are important to make at this juncture. First, all eight of the teachers taught children who produced mismatches on the pretest and during instruction; all but one taught children who produced mismatches during instruction only; and all but two taught children who never produced mismatches. In other words, the phenomenon seen in Figure 16 is not tied to individual teachers or children. Most of the teachers had the opportunity to teach all three types of children.

Second, the adjustments that the teachers made in the *types* of correct and incorrect strategies they produced during instruction did not extend to the tokens, or instances, of correct and incorrect strategies they produced. We looked at the proportion of correct and incorrect strategies that the teachers produced, counting each token (instance) of a strategy rather than each type. Not surprisingly, the teachers produced many more correct than incorrect strategies when teaching the children. The important point, however, is that they used the same distribution of strategies when teaching children in all three groups—the proportion of correct strategies the teachers produced did not differ across the three child groups, nor did the proportion of incorrect strategies. Thus the teachers made adjustments in the *variety* of correct and incorrect strategies in their lessons, not the *number* of correct and incorrect strategies.

Third, the adjustments that the teachers made in their mismatches did not extend to other types of utterances—they produced the same proportion of gesture-speech matches and speech-alone utterances with all three groups of children. Thus the adults adjusted their utterances containing more than one strategy, one in speech and one in gesture (that is, mismatches). But they did not adjust their utterances containing a single strategy, either the same strategy presented in speech and gesture (that is, matches) or a single strategy presented in speech in an utterance containing no gesture (that is, speech-alone utterances). The adults made adjustments in utterances containing a variety of strategies within a single response, not in all utterances.

Finally, and importantly, the teachers did seem to be responding to the children's gesture-speech mismatches, and not to the correctness or incorrectness of the children's responses. We calculated the number of types of correct and incorrect strategies the children produced during instruction, and also the proportion of correct and incorrect tokens they produced. There were no reliable differences across the three child groups in either types or tokens of correct and incorrect strategies.

The *only* difference that we could find across these three groups was their production of gesture-speech mismatches.

More convincing still, the variables that the teachers altered during instruction (the number of types of strategies they produced, and their own mismatches; see Figure 16) correlated with child mismatch during instruction. The more *mismatches* a child produced during instruction, the more types of strategies ($r_s = .39, p = .01$) and more mismatches ($r_s = .58, p < .001$) a teacher was likely to produce during instruction. However, the number of *types of strategies* the children produced was not significantly correlated with either teacher types ($r_s = .18$, n.s.) or teacher mismatch ($r_s = .13$, n.s.).[1] Adjustments in teacher instruction thus correlated only with child mismatch.

Did the children's mismatches offer the teachers useful information about a child's knowledge state? Knowing what we know about mismatches, it should come as no surprise that the children's mismatches were quite informative. The children produced more different types of strategies in their mismatching utterances (2.4) than in their matching (1.5) or speech-alone (1.8) utterances. Thus they conveyed more information in mismatches than in other types of utterances. In addition, the information that the children conveyed in their mismatches was often unique and not found anywhere else in their repertoires. Overall, the children produced 33 strategies in their mismatches (out of a total of 110) that appeared in neither their speech-alone utterances nor their gesture-speech matches. It was essential to pay attention to mismatches in order to discover the complete set of strategies that the children had in their repertoires. And the teachers seemed to do just that.

Take the following example. Working on the problem 7 + 6 + 5 = ___ + 5, one child added up all of the numbers in the problem and put 23 in the blank. The teacher asked the child to explain his incorrect solution and he produced this mismatch:

Child Speech: "I added 13 plus 10 equals 23" [add-all-numbers, an incorrect strategy]

Child Gesture: Hold hand under 7 and 6, point at blank, point at 7 and 6 [grouping, a correct strategy]

---

1. Although teacher mismatch was correlated with child mismatch during instruction, the teachers' mismatches were not immediate responses to the children's mismatches. Only 10 of the 221 (.05) mismatches that the teachers produced during instruction were preceded by a child mismatch. Indeed, in only 39 mismatches (.18 of 221) could the

In response to the child's mismatch, the teacher said, "I am going to cover this up [while covering up the 7 and 6 with her hand]. Now what do you see on both sides? Five and five, right?" The teacher ignored the child's incorrect solution and spoken explanation, and used the child's gestures as the basis for her next instructional step. She covered the two numbers that the child had indicated in gesture (the two numbers which, if added together, give the correct answer), thereby forcing the child to notice that there was a 5 on each side of the problem (equal addends). The gestures that the child produced in his mismatch gave the teacher insight into what this child was thinking—the teacher noticed and responded accordingly.

To summarize thus far, the fact that the teachers respond differently to children who produce mismatches is the first bit of evidence that teachers not only notice the gestures their students produce but also use those gestures to decide how to teach the students. We are thus one step closer to making the case that gesture can play an indirect role in cognitive change. We have secured step 2 in the hypothesis with which we began this chapter—listeners change their behavior in response to children's gestures, treating children differently simply because of the gestures they produce. We turn now to step 3—where our evidence is, at this point, more tentative.

Teachers' Changes Promote Learning

We have learned that teachers spontaneously provide a more diversified and variable input when teaching children who produce gesture-speech mismatches than when teaching children who don't produce mismatches. Is there any reason to believe that this type of variability is good for learning? We know that the teachers' instruction does matter. If provided with no instruction whatsoever, children do not make progress on this mathematical equivalence task, whether they produce gesture-speech mismatches or not (Alibali 1999; Goldin-Meadow and Alibali 2002). The question is whether the variable instruction that the teachers in our study gave the mismatching children was particularly effective in promoting learning.

Unfortunately, the phenomenon that we have discovered—that teachers tailor their input to the child's initial state—makes it difficult to assess whether teacher instruction had an impact on learning above and

---

teacher's strategies be traced back to a strategy in the child's preceding utterance. The teachers' mismatches were therefore not driven in a response-by-response fashion by child utterances.

beyond the effect of the child's initial knowledge state. Since the teachers tailored their input to the children, teacher instruction and child initial state are to a great extent confounded.

Nevertheless, there are suggestions in the data that the particular adjustments the teachers made were good for learning. We divided children into those who received more different types of strategies than the average (4 and above) or fewer than the average (below 4) and calculated their scores on the post-test. Children receiving many types performed better on the post-test than children who received few (2.75 versus 1.17). We did the same analysis for mismatches and found that children who received a larger proportion of mismatches (.08 and above) performed better on the post-test than children who received a smaller proportion (2.54 versus 1.72). Moreover, children who received many types and many mismatches did better on the post-test (3.00) than children who received many types *or* many mismatches (2.00), who, in turn, did better than children who received few types and few mismatches (1.31).

Variability seems to be good for learning, at least in these mathematical equivalence problems. We now have preliminary evidence for step 3—the changes in the listener's behavior that came about in response to the child's gestures (an increase in variability) seemed to have a beneficial effect on the child (improved performance on the post-test).

But we can't ignore the child's state. I've been arguing that the teachers were, in fact, teaching to that state. We need to look at how variability affects children who do and don't produce mismatches. And here again, the data are suggestive. We divided each of the three groups of children into those who received instruction that was above average in terms of both teacher types and teacher mismatches (high variability), and those who did not (low variability). We then examined how well children in each group did on the post-test.

We first confirmed the phenomenon described in the last section—not one of the twelve children in the "No Mismatch" group received high-variability instruction. And, of course, these children did not do well on the post-test (0.50). The findings from Perry, Church, and Goldin-Meadow (1988) make it clear that, even if these non-mismatchers had received extensive instruction, they would not have made progress on the task. The teachers seemed instinctively to know that the children in this group were not ready to learn mathematical equivalence and didn't waste time giving them diversified instruction. They gave the children a narrow and very consistent input and the children made no visible progress after instruction.

In contrast, children in both of the other two groups did receive high-variability instruction. Moreover, it looked like this instruction had some beneficial effect. Six of the twelve children in the "Mismatch in Instruction" group received high-variability instruction, and these children performed better on the post-test than the six children who received low-variability instruction (2.50 versus 1.67). Five of the fourteen children in the "Mismatch in Pretest and Instruction" group received high-variability instruction. All of the fourteen children in this group did relatively well on the post-test (they were indeed ready to learn mathematical equivalence), but these five performed slightly better on the post-test than the nine who received low-variability instruction (3.60 versus 3.00).

These numbers are small, but suggestive. We will, of course, need to conduct an experimental study in which we manipulate how much variability each child receives in order to be certain that variability in instruction is good for child learning. We are currently conducting just this type of study (Singer and Goldin-Meadow n.d.). The teachers in our previous studies instinctively increased the variability in the instruction they gave to children who were ready to learn, and it clearly did not hurt to do so. The next step is to do the kind of study that can establish conclusively that it actually helps.

The Pedagogical Value of Teacher Mismatch

It is not difficult to imagine why an adult (particularly one who is a trained educator) might instinctively increase the range of approaches taken to a problem when instructing a child who is on the cusp of grasping that problem. Offering many different types of solution strategies to a learner seems intuitively to be good for learning. Indeed, the literature suggests that having a variety of approaches to a problem in one's repertoire is associated with cognitive change (Siegler 1994, 1996). Siegler and Stern (1998) have also shown that high-variability instruction can lead to sharper understanding of a concept (in particular, to less unwarranted overgeneralization) than low-variability instruction, although it can also bring with it slower initial learning. More globally, studies of teaching across nations have shown that Japanese students are exposed to more alternative solution methods to math problems than American students and they learn more (Stigler and Hiebert 1999)—although there is as yet no evidence of a causal link between variable instruction and child outcome.

It is less easy to imagine why an adult would produce a large proportion of mismatches. To get a handle on this question, we looked at the teachers' mismatches and compared them with the children's mismatches. And we made an interesting discovery. The mismatches that the teachers produced during instruction were different from the mismatches that the children produced. The children produced more types of strategies in their mismatching utterances than in their matching or speech-alone utterances. The teachers did not—they produced the same number of types of strategies in all of their utterances. In addition, the children often produced strategies that could be found only in their mismatches and not in their other utterances. The teachers did not—in fact, they never produced a strategy in the gesture half of a mismatch that they did not also produce in speech in some other utterance. Unlike the children's mismatches, there was nothing unique about the teachers' mismatches, at least in terms of content.

Not surprisingly given that their goal was to instruct, the teachers produced correct strategies in the majority of their mismatches and incorrect strategies in very few (.72 versus .17 of mismatches). As a result, many of the teachers' mismatches contained correct strategies in both gesture and speech. Despite the lack of overlap between the correct strategy in speech and the different but also correct strategy in gesture (or maybe because of it, see below), the children were able, at times, to pick up one of the strategies in a teacher's mismatch. For example, a teacher was using the problem $3 + 7 + 9 = \_\_ + 9$ to teach the child the equalizer strategy and produced the following mismatch:

Teacher Speech: "We're going to do it like before. We're going to make this side equal to this side" [equalizer, a correct strategy]

Teacher Gesture: Hold hand under 3 and 7 [grouping, a correct strategy]

In response to this mismatch, the child exclaimed "Oh!" and solved the problem correctly. When asked to explain her solution, the child produced the following match:

Child Speech: "We have the 9's so we need the same [equal addends] and we can't put two numbers so I just added these two and put it here and it equaled 10" [grouping]

Child Gesture: Point at left 9, point at right 9 [equal addends], point between 3 and 7 twice, point at blank, point at 3, point at 7 [grouping]

The child had picked up the correct grouping strategy that the teacher displayed uniquely in gesture, thus making it clear that children can glean information from teacher mismatch.

But are mismatches particularly effective in teaching children a strategy? Mismatches do expose children to strategies in the gestural modality, and the gestural modality might be particularly accessible to a child who has not yet mastered the task. But why then doesn't the teacher present the gestured strategy in a gesture-speech match? A match would give the child an opportunity to see the strategy in both the spoken and gestural modalities (and indeed, as we saw in Chapter 7, children pay attention to teacher matches, reiterating spoken strategies more often when they are accompanied by matching gesture than by no gesture at all). Perhaps teachers ought to consider increasing the number of gesture-speech matches they produce when instructing children who are on the cusp of learning.

Gesture-speech mismatch does, however, have one unique feature—it makes the contrast between strategies salient by placing two different strategies side by side within a single utterance. This contrast may highlight the fact that different approaches to the problem are possible—an important concept for children who are grappling with mathematical equivalence. As described in Chapter 3 and again in Chapter 8, the two pieces of information conveyed in a mismatch can always be integrated within a larger framework. In other words, they are not two conflicting approaches to the problem, but rather two complementary approaches that need to be integrated. With respect to mathematical equivalence, children need to appreciate all of the strategies that lead to a correct solution—and the relations among them—in order to fully understand the concept. It is in the spirit of fostering integration across strategies that teacher mismatch may have a special pedagogical role to play in child learning. If so, our teachers' instinctive reaction to offer more mismatches to those who are ready to learn may have been just right.

Does Change Depend on Awareness of Gesture?

What is remarkable about the phenomenon we have been describing is the teachers—they notice a child's gestures, make inferences about the child's knowledge as a function of those gestures, and then provide the child with instruction that may be just right for that child. Do the teachers know what they're doing? Would it help if they did?

We have no idea whether the teachers knew they were responding to the children's gestures, or knew that variability might be a good type of instruction for some of the children. We didn't ask them, though in future studies, we certainly will. I can easily imagine that the teachers responded to the children's gestures without being aware of what they were doing. Consider an actual example from one of our studies.

On the problem $5 + 3 + 4 = \_\_ + 4$, the child pointed simultaneously at the left 4 with her left hand and the right 4 with her right hand while expressing an incorrect strategy in her speech. The teacher did not reiterate the notion conveyed in the child's gestures—that there are "equal addends" on each side of the equation. Indeed, the teacher may not have been consciously aware of the fact that the child had conveyed an equal-addends strategy. Nevertheless, the teacher behaved as though she had processed the child's gestures. She expressed the grouping strategy in both speech and gesture—"you can solve the problem by adding the 5 and the 3 and putting the sum in the blank," accompanied by a V-shaped point at the 5 and 3. Note that the grouping strategy works in this problem because there are equal addends, one on each side of the equation, that can be canceled. The fact that the child demonstrated some awareness of equal addends in gesture seemed to give the teacher license to introduce grouping, a strategy that the child then picked up in her next attempt at solving the problem and continued to use throughout the interaction. This was the right moment to introduce grouping to the child and, whether or not she was aware of it, the teacher seemed to have learned that this was the right moment from the child's gestures.

Thus adults need not be aware of the fact that they have been influenced by a child's gestures in order to act on the information they get from those gestures. Indeed, the adult may get it just wrong and still be able to provide useful input to the child. Consider, for example, the following case described by Alibali, Flevares, and Goldin-Meadow (1997). The child said he solved the problem $5 + 6 + 7 = \_\_ + 7$ by adding the 5, 6, and 7 (an add-to-equal-sign strategy), while pointing only at the 5 and 6 (a grouping strategy). After observing this child, the teacher said that the child did *not* understand the grouping strategy:

> What I'm picking up now is [the child's] inability to realize that these [indicates 5 and 6] are meant to represent the same number . . . there isn't a connection being made by the fact that the 7 on this side of the equal sign [indicates left side] is supposed to also be the same as this 7 on this side of the equal side [indicates right side], which would, you know, once you made that connection it should be fairly clear that the 5 and 6 belong in the box.

Note that at some level the teacher was incorrect—the child *did* indeed have an understanding, however implicit, of the grouping strategy, an understanding that the child expressed only in gesture. I think it's very likely that the teacher chose the grouping strategy to highlight as the one the child didn't know because she detected the strategy in the child's gestures. The fact that the teacher did not explicitly recognize the child's grasp of this strategy may not matter if, in instructing the child, the teacher focuses on what she thinks the child needs most—input about the grouping strategy. Instruction about grouping might be especially effective at this moment for this particular child because it might help him to transform or "redescribe" his emerging knowledge into a problem-solving strategy that he could apply and articulate in speech (see Karmiloff-Smith 1992).

As a final example, consider an adult in the study in which we taught teachers how to read gesture (Kelly et al., 2002). The adult paraphrased the child's spoken add-to-equal-sign strategy in speech, while at the same time reiterating the child's gestured add-all-numbers strategy in gesture—and only in gesture. It is likely that this adult was aware of repeating the child's speech, but not aware of repeating the child's gestures. Nonetheless, adult actions of this sort could have an impact on the child simply because children do pay attention to the gestures their teachers produce (Goldin-Meadow, Kim, and Singer 1999; Goldin-Meadow and Singer 2003). When an adult "seconds" a child's gestures, it may serve to reinforce the meaning of those gestures for the child—whether that meaning is correct or, as in this case, incorrect.

Thus adults can respond to the gesture component of a child's mismatch by "seconding" it in their own gestures, translating it into their own speech, or acting on it without articulating the information at all. In all three cases, the adults might—but they also might not—be aware of the fact that they are responding to gesture.

Given that gesture is an unavoidable part of classroom activity, teachers might do well to increase their awareness of the way gesture is used in the classroom. There have been some successful attempts to train teachers to pay attention to their students' nonverbal cues in general (Jecker, Maccoby, and Breitrose 1965; Machida 1986) and gestures in particular (Kelly et al. 2002). However, aside from an occasional training manual (for example, Neill and Caswell 1993), no systematic efforts have been made to increase teacher awareness of how they themselves use their hands. Making teachers more aware of what they and their students do with their hands may create new avenues for teachers to exploit in instructing their students about math and probably other areas as well.

On the other hand, there is always a danger in tampering with a process that is working. If we raise gesture to conscious awareness, do we run the risk of altering the privileged access it has to unspoken knowledge? Do we run the risk of disrupting the elegant synchrony that exists between gesture and the speech it accompanies? We consider these issues in the final chapter of the book, after we have completed our exploration of the role gesture plays in thinking in Part III.

Why Do Teachers Produce Mismatches?

Why might a teacher present one strategy in one modality and a different strategy in the other modality? In other words, why might a *teacher* produce a gesture-speech mismatch? I argued in Chapter 4 that children produce a large number of gesture-speech mismatches on a task when they are in transition with respect to that task—that is, when they are "ready" to profit from instruction and improve their performance on the task. Children who produce many mismatches are in a state of cognitive uncertainty, possessing knowledge about the task that they cannot quite organize into a coherent whole.

Unlike their students, the teachers conducting the math tutorials were not at all uncertain about the principle of mathematical equivalence underlying the problems they taught. This difference in cognitive state between teacher and child was apparent in the types of mismatches the two produced. Children frequently conveyed information in their mismatches that was not found anywhere else in their repertoires— teachers rarely did. Children produced more types of strategies in their mismatching utterances than in their matching and speech-alone utterances—teachers produced the same number of types of strategies in all of their utterances. Children's mismatches contained an equal number of correct and incorrect strategies—teachers' mismatches primarily contained correct strategies.[2]

What then does teacher mismatch in this situation reflect? Although

2. Note that the mismatches produced by an adult who is teaching a confused learner may be quite different from the mismatches produced by an adult who is herself the learner. I suspect that when adults are on the cusp of learning a task, they will produce the same types of mismatches that our child learners produce—that is, they will produce more information and unique information in their mismatches.

the teachers were not uncertain about the principle underlying mathe-matical equivalence, they may have been uncertain about how best to teach this principle, particularly in light of all of the inconsistent strate-gies that their mismatching pupils were producing. It is this uncertainty that may then have been reflected in the teachers' mismatches. In gen-eral, a mismatch reflects the fact that the speaker is holding two ideas in mind (see Chapter 12; Garber and Goldin-Meadow 2002; Goldin-Meadow et al. 1993)—two ideas that the speaker has not yet integrated into a single unit—in this case, a single instructional unit. This way of describing mismatch is, at least plausibly, as applicable to adults when teaching as it is to children when explaining.

Teacher mismatch may even be a reaction to child mismatch (though not a direct mimicry of the child's utterances, see note 1). A teacher who is attempting to be responsive to her pupil may recognize, at least im-plicitly, the child's confusion about how the problem ought to be solved. She may respond to that confusion by incorporating one of the strate-gies the child has for solving the problem in her speech and another in her gestures. The within-response variability that the teacher displays may be a general reaction to the within-response variability the child displays. This line of reasoning leads to the prediction that teachers will produce their own mismatches most often when interacting with chil-dren who produce mismatches. And they did.

Whatever the cause of teacher mismatch, it looks as though it may be good for learning. One important question that Melissa Singer is cur-rently pursuing in her dissertation is whether the across-modality vari-ability found in mismatch is what's crucial for learning. After all, it could be variability of any sort (for example, different strategies, all ex-pressed in speech, but presented to the child within the same teaching session) that matters for learning, as opposed to variability that involves two modalities (different strategies expressed in speech and gesture pro-duced in the very same response). We have constructed four different lessons to explore this question:

- one incorporating variability within a modality and across re-sponses (that is, different strategies presented in speech);
- one incorporating variability across modalities and within a re-sponse (that is, different strategies presented in mismatch);
- one incorporating both types of variability;
- a control condition with no variability at all.

The question is whether one type of variability is more effective than others in bringing about child learning, particularly for children at different points in the learning process. Our results to date are clear and surprising—the only variability that appears to lead to learning is variability across modalities and within a single response, that is, gesture-speech mismatch (Singer and Goldin-Meadow n.d.).

If teacher mismatch is effective in promoting learning, it could be because it encourages children to continue producing mismatches of their own. A child producing a mismatch may be forced to confront, and perhaps to resolve, the multiple ideas that he or she is expressing within a single response. In other words, the very act of producing a mismatch could change the child's course and rate of growth. If so, a child's gesture could be playing a role in cognitive change, not only indirectly through listeners (as we have shown in this chapter), but also more directly through its effect on speakers themselves. This is the question to which the next part of the book is devoted—does gesture have an impact on how we think?

part three

Thinking

10

Gesturing in the Dark

We now know that gesture has an impact on listeners. But gesture crops up even when there are no listeners in the room. How often have you found yourself gesturing while on the telephone unseen by your listener? Or, even more embarrassing if caught, gesturing while talking to yourself? Even though gesture's purpose—its function—is likely to involve communication, the process by which gesture is produced—its mechanism—may not. Gesture production could be the result of processes within the speaker alone, independent of the listener.

Here is an example of the distinction between function and mechanism, taken from a distant domain. Consider the Mississippi alligator. In the evening, the Mississippi alligator goes down into the river. Because the alligator is cold-blooded and because the night air becomes quite cold, often much colder than the water, the evening trip into the river has an important function for the alligator—it serves to regulate its temperature. Given this function, one might assume that the trigger for the evening river trips—that is, the mechanism that leads to the trips—would also involve the alligator's temperature regulation system in some way. But, in fact, the mechanism underlying the evening river trips involves sensitivity to light—the dimming light is the stimulus that triggers the alligator's entrance into the water. The independence of mechanism and function is particularly apparent if the light and temperature stimuli are artificially separated. If the temperature is dropped but the lights do not dim, the alligator will remain on land and risk freezing to death. If, however, the light dims but the temperature remains constant, the alligator will enter the water even though the trip is not needed to keep warm (Lang 1976).

Gesture appears to serve an important function for human listeners (communication), just as evening river trips do for alligators (temperature regulation). The mechanism by which we produce gestures, however, need not involve communication and the listener. An alternative possibility is that we produce gestures as part of the process of thinking, and that (reminiscent of the Mississippi alligator) we would continue to gesture whether or not a listener was around. Do we, so to speak, gesture in the dark and, if so, does gesturing when no one is around tell us anything about how (and why) we gesture?

Driven by the Need to Communicate?

Our goal in this chapter is not to figure out whether listeners get meaning from gesture (we've already ascertained that they do), but to figure out whether the need to communicate information to others is the force that drives us to gesture. The easiest way to explore this question is to ask people to talk when they can see their listener and when they can't. If the need to convey information to others is what motivates us to gesture, we ought to gesture more when others are around and can see those gestures.

A number of studies have manipulated the presence of a listener and observed the effect on gesture. In most studies, the speaker has a face-to-face conversation with a listener in one condition, and a conversation in which a barrier prevents the speaker and listener from seeing each other in the second condition. In some studies, the second condition is conducted over an intercom, and in some the first condition is conducted over a videophone. In some studies, the camera is hidden so that the speakers have no sense that they are being watched. It doesn't really seem to matter. In most studies (though not all), people gesture more when they can see their listener than when they can't.

Cohen and Harrison (1973) used a face-to-face versus intercom comparison and hid the camera. They asked speakers to role play as an executive who has to give directions to different locations to a new secretary. Sometimes the secretary asked for directions through the intercom, and sometimes she came into the room. The speakers produced almost nine gestures per minute when they could see the secretary, but only about five when they could not see her.

Krauss, Dushay, Chen, and Rauscher (1995) conducted a similar study without the executive ruse and without the hidden camera. They asked speakers to describe graphic designs, novel synthesized sounds, or samples of tea to a listener who then tried to select the described object from a set of similar objects. Speakers produced approximately fifteen gestures per minute when describing the graphic designs to a visible listener versus twelve to a nonvisible listener. They produced almost thirteen gestures per minute when describing sounds to a visible listener versus eleven to a nonvisible listener. Although small, the differences were statistically reliable for both the designs and the sounds. The speakers produced almost no gestures at all when describing the teas, whether or not someone was watching (the tea stimuli elicited very terse and inarticulate descriptions in general—it looks like it's not easy to either talk or gesture about tea).

Emmorey and Casey (2001) asked speakers to solve a series of spatial puzzles. They had to decide where to place a group of blocks so that the blocks completely filled a puzzle grid—the catch was that they could not manipulate the blocks themselves. Instead the speakers told an experimenter where to place the blocks, and the experimenter was either visible or not. Emmorey and Casey did not look at gesture rate per minute, but they did calculate the percentage of orientation instructions that were accompanied by gesture—58 percent when the speakers could see the experimenter versus 28 percent when they could not.

Finally, Bavelas, Chovil, Lawrie, and Wade (1992) and Alibali, Heath, and Myers (2001) have both found listener visibility to have an effect on some gestures but not on all. Bavelas and her colleagues asked speakers to talk about a "close-call" incident (an incident in which the speaker almost got hurt or something bad almost happened but, in the end, everything was okay) to a visible versus a nonvisible listener. Speakers produced more interactive gestures (gestures that refer to the listener) when they could see their listener than when they couldn't, but not more topic gestures (gestures that refer to the topic of conversation). Alibali and her colleagues asked speakers to watch an animated cartoon and narrate the story to a visible versus a nonvisible listener. Speakers produced more representational gestures (gestures that depict semantic content) when they could see their listener than when they couldn't, but not more beat gestures (simple, rhythmic gestures that do not convey semantic content). It's not exactly clear how Bavelas's interactive-topic gesture split corresponds to Alibali's representational-beat gesture split, but it is clear that speakers do increase their production of at least some gestures when someone is watching.

Now we come to the two exceptions. Rimé (1982) asked speakers to describe how they felt about movies (their opinions on movies and what they liked to find in the cinema) to a face-to-face listener and to a listener sitting behind a screen. The camera was hidden. Speakers were not reliably more likely to gesture when they could see their listener than when they couldn't. One reason may be the topic (see Alibali, Heath, and Myers 2001). Movies (like tea) don't seem to elicit much gesture—the speakers produced thirteen gestures in a seven-minute period, which comes to a little less than two gestures per minute. Gesture may not play much of a role in conversations about the cinema between unacquainted people.

Lickiss and Wellens (1978) asked speakers to describe photographic portraits to a listener who would then select duplicate copies of the target photos from a larger set of similar pictures. In one condition, the speaker communicated with the listener via a two-way videophone; in the other, via a voice intercom. The speakers did gesture and at rates comparable to many other studies (eight to ten gestures per minute). However, they didn't reliably produce more gestures when they could see their listener than when they could not. One unusual feature of the design deserves mention. The speakers were asked to continuously depress two floor-mounted foot switches while they were talking (this constraint was included to contrast with yet another condition in which the speakers were asked to depress two desk-mounted hand switches). It may be that the speakers were thinking more about their feet than about their listeners.

Another creative way to approach this problem is to vary some aspect of the listener, rather than merely varying the listener's presence or absence. Özyürek (2000, 2002) did just that—she asked speakers to retell a cartoon story to different numbers of listeners sitting in different locations. She found that speakers changed their gestures as a function of the positioning of their listeners—in particular, as a function of how the speaker's and listeners' gesture spaces intersected and constituted their shared space. For example, when describing how granny threw Sylvester the cat onto the street, speakers would change the direction of their gesture so that it moved out of the shared gesture space, wherever that space was. If the speaker shared the space with two listeners sitting at her right and left sides, that space was larger than it would be if the speaker shared the space with one listener sitting at one side—and the outward motion of the speaker's gesture varied accordingly. Perhaps not surprisingly, "out of" looked different depending on what was considered "in." What's important for our discussion here is that the speakers took their listeners into account when fashioning their gestures, suggesting that they were, at least in part, making those gestures for the listeners.

Do Increased Gestures Arise from Changes in Speech?

But do speakers really intend to produce gestures for their listeners? There is no doubt that speakers change their talk in response to listeners. Perhaps the changes in gesture come about as a by-product of these changes in speech. Speakers could alter the form and content of their talk and those changes could "automatically" bring with them changes in gesture. To address this possibility, we need to examine not only changes that occur in gesture as a function of who the listener is, but also changes that occur in the accompanying speech. Only two studies have taken this step.

Speakers might use more words when speaking to listeners they can see than when speaking to listeners they cannot see. Those extra words could then bring with them extra gestures. Alibali, Heath, and Myers (2001) examined the amount of speech in their face-to-face and screen conditions, but found no evidence to support this hypothesis—speakers used essentially the same number of words whether or not a listener was present.

Formulating speech might be effortful in the absence of a face-to-face listener. If so, speakers might be more hesitant and more errorful when speaking to listeners they cannot see than when speaking to listeners they can see. Those errors might then affect gesture production. Alibali and her colleagues (2001) found no convincing evidence to support this hypothesis either—speakers made the same number of speech errors whether or not a listener was present.

Finally, and most important, speakers might change the content of their speech when addressing listeners they cannot see. If so, that changed content could bring with it changes in gesture. Alibali and her colleagues (2001) selected the aspects of talk that they thought might be most likely to vary according to the listener and bring along changes in gesture. They examined the speakers' choice of verbs of motion, their use of narrative as opposed to non-narrative talk, and their use of spatial prepositions. They found no differences anywhere—speakers said essentially the same things whether or not a listener was present. Thus when the speakers in this study produced more gestures with visible than with nonvisible listeners, it wasn't because they had changed their talk—it looks like they meant to change their gestures.

Along the same lines, the changes in gestures that Özyürek (2000, 2002) found were also not derived from changes in speech. The speakers did not change the content of their speech when their listeners sat in different locations; that is, unlike their gestures, their speech did not vary as a function of shared space. The speakers seemed to be designing their gestures (but not their talk) for their listeners. Moreover, they used common space rather than their own space or the listener's space in designing those gestures. In this sense, gesture use parallels a more general focus on common ground (see Clark 1996)—speakers fashion their gestures in the context of the common space they share with their listeners, just as they fashion their words in the context of the common ground they share with their listeners.

It is worth noting that the adjustments Özyürek (2000, 2002) found in gesture production may be particular to speakers who convey direction using a relative frame of reference. English speakers tend to set up a stage and gesture within that stage. In contrast, speakers of the language Guugu Yimithirr in Queensland, Australia, use an absolute rather than a relative frame of reference to represent direction, both in their spatial language and in their gestures (Haviland 1993, 2000). For example, when describing how a boat overturned many years ago, a speaker produced a rolling motion away from his body when facing west since the boat had actually rolled from east to west. However, when telling the story on another occasion, he happened to be facing north rather than west. In this retelling, he produced the same rolling-over gesture but this time his hands rolled from right to left rather than away from his body. The gesture was accurate with respect to the actual event (an east-to-west roll) and was not affected at all by the listener, only by the speaker's orientation with respect to the original event.

I can't imagine an English speaker (me, in particular) exhibiting such directional authenticity in a gesture. For me, it would be odd (and very stressful for my inadequate sense of direction) to do anything but produce the overturning motion away from my body. For these speakers, however, gesture is not free to vary with frame of reference but must be oriented according to the compass. It is possible, indeed probable, that in such communities, listener location and shared space might not have the same effects on gesture that they have in English speakers. Gesture use is quite likely to vary with linguistic and cultural community. However, if the studies reviewed in this chapter are correct in suggesting that the communicative needs of the listener inspire us to gesture, speakers across the globe might still be expected to adjust their gestures to their listeners, but in culturally and linguistically appropriate ways.

The issue of intention still remains—do we really intend to gesture? My intuition is that we intend to communicate, and gesture comes for free with that intention (see also Kita and Özyürek 2003). But we do seem to know at some level that communication involves gesture—we increase gesture production when our listeners can see us, and we design our gesture movements to take advantage of the space we share with those listeners. Perhaps we pay attention to gesture at the same level that we pay attention to speech. I don't explicitly think about whether I should refer to you as "you" or "me," or whether my next verb ought to be singular or plural. The correct form comes out automatically. Whatever speech production mechanism we devise to describe this process has to be able to account for the regularities in my speech, but I need not be granted explicit awareness of the steps in this process. In the same way, I may not be aware of moving my hand in a particular direction (in fact, I may not be aware of moving my hand at all). However, whatever gesture production mechanism we devise will have to be able to account for the fact that I gesture more when there is a listener in front of me, and that I adjust the direction of my movements to the spot that the listener occupies. The mechanism underlying gesture production will have to involve at least these components of communication.

The Ultimate Test: Congenitally Blind Individuals

Up to this point, I have been stressing the fact that speakers gesture more when they address visible listeners than nonvisible listeners. There does appear to be a communicative aspect to gesturing. In another sense, however, the more striking finding in each of these studies is that speakers continue to gesture even when there is no listener there at all. Although statistically less likely, gesture was produced in all the experimental conditions in which there was no possibility of a communicative motive. Why? If the need to communicate to the listener is the only force behind gesturing, why do we continue to move our hands when listeners can no longer see us?

One possibility is that we gesture out of habit. We are used to moving our hands around when we speak to others, and old habits die hard. This hypothesis predicts that if someone were to spend a great deal of time talking only to unseen people, eventually that person's gestures would fade away. It's possible, but I wouldn't bet on it. Another more likely possibility is that, even when no one is around, we imagine a listener and we gesture for that listener.

The only way to test these hypotheses is to observe speakers who have never spoken to a visible listener. Individuals who are blind from birth offer an excellent test case. Congenitally blind individuals have never seen their listeners and thus cannot be in the habit of gesturing for them. Moreover, congenitally blind individuals never see speakers moving their hands as they talk and thus have no model for gesturing. Do they gesture despite their lack of a visual model? And even more to the point, do they gesture when speaking to a blind listener?

Jana Iverson asked twelve children and teens blind from birth to participate in a series of conservation tasks, and compared their speech and gesture on these tasks with that of age- and gender-matched sighted individuals (Iverson and Goldin-Meadow 1998, 2001). We found that all twelve blind speakers gestured as they spoke, despite the fact that they had never seen gesture or their listeners. The blind group gestured at the same rate as the sighted group, and conveyed the same information using the same range of gesture forms. For example, the speaker shown in Figure 17 is congenitally blind. She understood conservation of liquid quantity—that is, she thought that the water had not changed in quantity after it was poured from a big container into two smaller containers—and justified this belief in both speech and gesture. She said that the amount was the same "because you poured the big container that had the same amount as in the other big container into those two glasses," while also focusing on the pouring motion in gesture: she traced a pouring trajectory in the air with her index finger (Figure 17). Her gesture is comparable to gestures sighted children produce on this task. Blind speakers apparently do not require experience receiving gestures before spontaneously producing gestures of their own.

We next asked whether blind speakers continue to produce spontaneous gestures along with their speech even when they know that their listener is blind and therefore unable to profit from whatever information gesture offers. We asked four additional children, each blind from birth, to participate in the conservation tasks. However, these children were tested by a blind listener and were explicitly informed of this fact. We found that all of the blind speakers gestured when addressing the blind listener. Moreover, they gestured at the same rate as the sighted-with-sighted dyads and the blind-with-sighted dyads. Speakers apparently do not gesture solely to convey information to a listener.

Figure 17. A child blind from birth arcs a pointing hand in the air, tracing the trajectory that the water followed when it was poured from one container to another. This gesture is comparable to the gestures that sighted children produce on this task, suggesting that we don't ever need to see gesture in order to be able to produce gestures of our own.

Conservation tasks involve objects (glasses, dishes, sticks, and so forth), and, indeed, all of the speakers in our studies—blind and sighted alike—often produced their gestures in relation to those objects. It is possible that blind individuals produce gestures only for concrete objects and actions—they may, for example, be unable to produce abstract metaphoric gestures. However, there is evidence that blind children gesture in a variety of situations (for example, describing small-scale spatial layouts, Iverson 1999; talking spontaneously in play sessions, Iverson et al. 2000), though not all situations (for example, giving route directions, Iverson and Goldin-Meadow 1997). More work is needed to determine the breadth of the blind individual's gestural repertoire. Nevertheless, the bottom line for us is that congenitally blind individuals do gesture. And when they gesture, they produce gestures at the same rate, and in the same manner, as sighted individuals. This phenomenon underscores the robustness of the gestures that accompany speech—and it makes us begin to think that we produce gestures not only for the sake of others, but also for ourselves.

Why Do We Gesture?

Gesture frequently accompanies speech in reasoning tasks where the speaker must think through a problem. In conservation tasks, for example, participants must consider and manipulate relationships between several different spatial dimensions of the task objects simultaneously (for example, in the liquid quantity task, the relationship between container height and width and water level). It may be easier to express aspects of these dimensions and their relationships in the imagistic medium offered by gesture than in the linear, segmented medium provided by speech (see McNeill 1992). Gesture may thus provide speakers with a channel for expressing thoughts that are difficult to articulate in speech. As a result, speakers—even blind speakers—may produce gestures when explaining their reasoning in a conservation task because some of their thoughts about the task lend themselves more readily to gesture than to speech. Gesture, in other words, might simply reflect a speaker's thoughts in a medium that happens to be relatively transparent to most listeners. This medium is such a natural accompaniment to speech that it is exploited by speakers even when its use has not been explicitly modeled for them, and when its communicative function is not immediately apparent.

I am, in effect, suggesting that gesture is an inevitable part of speaking. We don't need to have others around in order to gesture (although having others around does increase our gesture rate). Indeed, we don't need to have ever seen anyone gesture in order to produce gestures of our own. Gesture thus appears to be integral to the speaking process itself, and the mechanism by which gesture is produced must be tied in some way to this process.

But what about gesture's function? We saw in Part II that gesture serves to convey information to others (whether or not the speaker intends for it to convey this information is a separate issue). But gesture could, in principle, serve more than one function. The question we address in the next chapter is whether gesture serves a function for speakers as well as for listeners. The fact that we persist in gesturing even when there are no obvious communicative gains is what propels us to seek a within-speaker function. And there is indeed some evidence that gesturing is a boon to the gesturer.

11

Gesturing Helps

Is it good for speakers to gesture? We know that gesturing can benefit the listener, but does it also benefit the speaker? I argued earlier that
gesture reflects a speaker's thoughts, often offering a novel view of
what's on a speaker's mind. But perhaps gesturing does more than reflect thoughts; perhaps it also plays a role in shaping them. We know, for
example, that writing a problem down often makes it easier to solve the
problem, either by reducing demands on memory or by providing a
new perspective. Might gesturing work in the same or analogous ways?
If so, we may be altering the way we think just by moving our hands.

As the Task Changes, So Does Gesture

If the act of gesturing is itself beneficial, we might expect that gesturing
will increase as problems become more difficult. And for the most part it
does.

WHEN SPEAKING ITSELF IS HARD

When we talk, we hear ourselves, and this feedback is an important part
of the speaking process. If the feedback we get from our own voice is delayed, speaking becomes much more difficult. McNeill (1992) carried
out a series of experiments observing what happens to gesture under
delayed auditory feedback—the experience of hearing your own voice
continuously echoed back. As is typical of McNeill's studies, speakers
watched a Tweety Bird cartoon and then recounted the story to a lis-

tener. But this time, the speakers wore earphones during the narration. For the first half of the narration, speakers heard their own voices through the earphones as they normally would; for the second half, they heard their voices delayed about 0.2 seconds.

Delayed auditory feedback had a dramatic effect on speech. It slowed down, and stuttering and stammering became frequent. The question, however, is what happened to gesture? In fact, gesturing increased in all speakers but, interestingly, did not lose its synchrony with speech (as we might expect given that gesture and speech form a unified system). The most striking case was a speaker who produced absolutely no gestures at all under conditions of normal feedback, and began gesturing only during the second half of the narration when feedback was delayed. When the act of speaking becomes difficult, speakers seem to respond by increasing their gestures.

We see a similar increase in gesturing in individuals suffering from aphasia. These individuals, typically as a result of stroke, trauma, or tumor, have greatly impaired language abilities relative to individuals without brain injury—speaking is difficult for aphasic individuals. Interestingly, when Feyereisen (1983) asked twelve aphasic individuals to describe how they passed an ordinary day, they produced many more gestures than six nonaphasic speakers.[1] Again, increased gesturing seems to be associated with difficulty in speaking.

Finally, bilinguals who are not equally fluent in their two languages have more difficulty speaking their nondominant language than their dominant language. Marcos (1979) asked sixteen bilinguals to talk about either love or friendship in their nondominant language. All were Spanish-English bilinguals, but some were dominant in English and others were dominant in Spanish. Marcos found that the less proficient a speaker was in his or her nondominant language, the more gestures that

1. Although many studies have explored the production and comprehension of what might be called "gesture" in individuals who suffer from aphasia, most of these studies examine gesture in experimental contexts that do not probe for spontaneous communication. For example, to tap comprehension, the experimenter mimes the act of strumming a guitar and the aphasic individual's task is to select a picture of a guitar out of a set of distractor pictures; to tap production, the experimenter asks the individual to "show me how you salute" or shows a picture of a guitar and asks the individual to indicate what the object is by pretending to use it. Some studies find correlations between performance on these tests and severity of aphasia (Duffy and Duffy 1981; Duffy, Duffy, and Pearson 1975); others do not (Goodglass and Kaplan 1963; see Wang and Goodglass 1992, for a recent review of this literature and compromise results). No one, however, has yet examined the relation between an aphasic individual's performance on tests of this sort and the spontaneous production of gestures as we define them here.

speaker produced when speaking that language (see also Gulberg 1998, who found that French-Swedish bilinguals produced more gestures in their nondominant second language than in their dominant native language). The assumption is that speaking the nondominant language is more difficult for these individuals, and they respond by increasing their rate of gesturing.

WHEN THE NUMBER OF ITEMS IN A TASK GOES UP

Gesturing also increases when the focal task is itself made more difficult. For example, Graham (1999) asked two-, three-, and four-year-old children to count sets of two-, four-, and six-object arrays. Children learn to count small numbers before learning to count large numbers (Gelman and Gallistel 1978; Wynn 1990). If children gesture only when the counting problem is hard, we might expect them to gesture more on arrays with four and six objects than on arrays with only two objects. The four-year-olds did just that (apparently, the two- and three-year-olds were challenged by all three arrays and gestured equally often on all of them). When the counting task is hard, children rely on gesture (see also Saxe and Kaplan 1981).

Gesturing has also been found to increase when speakers have options to choose among. Melinger and Kita (n.d.) asked native speakers of Dutch to describe maplike pictures, each depicting a path with several destinations (marked by colored dots). The speaker's task was to describe from memory the path that leads past all of the destinations. Importantly, some of the maps had routes that branched in two directions, which meant that the speaker had a choice of paths (more than one item to choose among). The question is whether speakers produced more gestures when describing the branching points on the maps than when describing points where there were no choices to be made. They did. Controlling for the amount of directional talk the speakers produced, Melinger and Kita calculated the percentage of directional terms that were accompanied by gesture at branching points versus non-branching points and found that the speakers gestured more at branching points. The presumption is that the branching points elicited more gesture because they offered the speaker more than one item to choose among and, in this sense, were conceptually challenging.

WHEN DESCRIBING FROM MEMORY

Describing a scene from memory seems as though it ought to be more difficult than describing a scene within view. We might therefore expect speakers to produce more gestures when asked to retrieve information from memory. De Ruiter (1998) asked Dutch speakers to describe pictures on a computer screen so that the listener could draw them. The pictures were simple line drawings, consisting of an ellipse, a circle, a triangle, and two straight lines. The pictures differed in where the elements were positioned in relation to one another. Half of the pictures were described while they were visible on the computer screen, and half were described from memory. The speakers produced more gestures when describing the pictures from memory than when describing them in full view.

Wesp, Hesse, Keutmann, and Wheaton (2001) found the same effect in English speakers. They asked speakers to describe still-life watercolor paintings so that the listener could later pick the painting out of a set of paintings. Half of the speakers were asked to look at the painting, form an image of it, and then describe it from memory. The other half were asked to describe the painting as it sat in front of them. Speakers who described the paintings from memory produced more gestures than those who described the paintings in full view. When the description task becomes difficult, speakers react by increasing their gesture rates.

WHEN REASONING RATHER THAN DESCRIBING

Let's up the ante even further. What would happen if we asked speakers to reason about a set of objects rather than merely describe those same objects? If the argument I've been making is correct, reasoning about a problem ought to elicit more gesture than simply describing the problem, because reasoning is more difficult than describing. Alibali, Kita, and Young (2000) asked a group of kindergartners to participate in both reasoning about and describing a set of objects. In the reasoning task, the children were given six Piagetian conservation problems that tapped their understanding of continuous quantity and mass (whether sand changes in amount when it is poured from one container to another, or clay changes in amount when it is reshaped into another form). In the description task, the children were presented with precisely the same objects, but this time they were asked to describe how the objects looked rather than to reason about their quantities. The children produced more iconic gestures (but not more deictic gestures) when reasoning about the objects than when describing the objects. In other words, they produced more gestures that conveyed substantive information when doing the harder task.

I must note, however, that an increase in task difficulty does not always bring with it an increase in gesture. For example, in the role-playing study described in the previous chapter, speakers were asked to pretend to be an executive giving a new secretary directions to various locations (Cohen and Harrison 1973). Half of the places were easy to get to (fewer turns and less distance), and half were difficult. The speakers produced the same number of gestures when describing the easy and hard destinations. Of course, the hard destinations may not have been particularly hard for the speakers to describe.

De Ruiter (1998) also found no differences in rate of gesturing for easy versus hard problems, but he made sure that the problems really were hard. As described above, speakers were asked to describe pictures of five geometrical shapes in different arrangements. Half were easy to describe—the relations between the shapes could be described using simple terms such as "above," "next to," "to the left of," and "below." The other half were hard—the relations between the objects could not be described using the simple terms and required more complex constructions. The speakers did indeed find the hard pictures hard. Speech rate was significantly lower than it was for the easy pictures. But the speakers did not produce more gestures when describing the hard pictures than when describing the easy pictures.

Null effects are difficult to interpret. Perhaps the task just wasn't hard enough to inspire gesture.[2] But then, of course, we have to ask "what's hard enough?" Even more problematic, just because gesturing increases on difficult tasks doesn't mean that gesturing plays a causal role in thinking. Gesture may be reflecting the speaker's thought processes, rather than causing them. If so, an increase in gesture would reflect the increased effort that the speaker is expending. It would play no role at all in how the task itself is processed.

Note, however, that while the studies we have just reviewed are not conclusive with respect to the *functions* gesture serves, they do provide rather convincing evidence with respect to the *mechanisms* that cause gesture. When we manipulate a cognitive task and make it more difficult, gesture increases, suggesting that one factor that causes gesturing is cognitive effort. Indeed, I have often felt that I gesture most when I'm thinking hardest, and the data seem to support this impression.

---

2. If gesture and speech are interlinked in a specific way, then we might expect only certain types of tasks and verbal difficulties to lead to an increase in gesture. Ideally, theories of how gesture and speech relate to each other ought to be sufficiently specified to predict the kinds of difficulties that will lead to more gesture—but we haven't achieved the ideal yet. None of the current theories can explain these null results. I thank Sotaro Kita for drawing my attention to this need for more theoretical specificity.

Saving the Speaker Cognitive Effort

We return now to exploring gesture's function and ask whether gesture plays a causal role in thinking. Unlike the previously reviewed studies which manipulated *thinking* and observed the effects on *gesture*, the study presented in this section manipulates *gesture* and observes the effects on *thinking*. The hypothesis is that speakers gesture in order to lighten their cognitive load. They produce more gestures on difficult tasks in order to make the task easier. Of course, to make an argument of this sort, we can't just observe gesture in relation to task difficulty. We have to manipulate gesture itself. We can take gesture away and see if the task itself becomes more effortful.

If gesturing merely reflects effort expended and doesn't contribute in any way to making the task easier, a change in gesture ought not affect the amount of effort expended. Under this view, we would expect no change in effort when speakers are prevented from gesturing (or, for that matter, when they are encouraged to gesture). If, however, gesturing actually makes the task easier, a change in gesture ought to have a demonstrable effect on the amount of effort expended. Under this alternative view, we would expect that if speakers are prevented from gesturing, they would have to increase the amount of effort they expend on the task in order to make up for the lost benefits of gesture.

How can we possibly measure the amount of effort an individual expends on a task? One technique often used by cognitive psychologists is to give individuals a second task to perform at the same time as they are performing the original task. If the first task is very costly (from a cognitive effort point of view), they will perform less well on the second task than they would have if the first task were less effortful (Baddeley 1986). In other words, we can use performance on the second task to gauge how much effort an individual is expending on the simultaneously performed first task.

My hypothesis is that gesturing reduces demands on a speaker's cognitive resources, thereby freeing cognitive capacity to perform other tasks—it lightens the speaker's cognitive load. There is, however, another possibility. Instead of lightening the load, gesturing while speaking (as opposed to speaking without gesture) might require motor planning, execution, and coordination of two separate cognitive and motor systems (Andersen 1995; Petersen et al. 1988). If so, gesturing ought to increase a speaker's cognitive load (Norman and Bobrow 1975; O'Reilly, Braver, and Cohen 1999; Wickens 1984). And, of course, as mentioned above, gesturing might simply reflect the cognitive resources a speaker expends but play no causal role in allocating those resources. If so, gesturing ought to have no effect on a speaker's cognitive load.

In order to distinguish among these three possibilities and to determine the impact of gesturing on a speaker's cognitive load, we explored how gesturing on one task (explaining a math problem) affected performance on a second task (remembering a list of words or letters) carried out at the same time (Goldin-Meadow et al. 2001). If gesturing reduces cognitive load, gesturing while explaining the math problems should free up resources available for remembering. Memory should then be better when speakers gesture than when they do not. If, however, gesturing increases cognitive load, gesturing while explaining the math problems should take away from the resources available for remembering. Memory should then be worse when speakers gesture than when they do not gesture. Finally, if gesturing merely reflects cognitive load but has no role in causing it, gesturing while explaining the math problems should have no effect on the resources available for remembering. Memory should then be the same when speakers gesture and when they do not gesture.

We individually tested children on addition problems of the form, $4 + 5 + 3 = \_\_ + 3$. But we also wanted to test our hypothesis on adults. As a result, we needed a math problem that would be challenging enough for adults and that would elicit gesture. We chose factoring problems, for example, $x^2 - 3x - 10 = (\ \ )(\ \ )$. The adults' job was to solve the problem and then explain how they got their solution. Figure 18 gives an example of the kinds of spoken and gestural responses the adults gave. The adult put "$x - 5$" in the first set of parentheses and "$x + 2$" in the second set of parentheses and then said, "negative 5 and positive 2 make negative 3 added together, multiplied together they make negative 10." At the same time, he produced the following string of gestures:

He pointed at the 5 and then at the 2 with his palm facing the board [frames 1 and 2];

He pointed at the 3 with his palm facing away from the board (that is, he changed the orientation of his palm) [frame 3];

He produced an "add-together" gesture (he wiggled his palm back and forth) [frame 4];

He produced a "multiply-together" gesture (he held a "C" hand near the 5 and 2 and brought the ends of the "C" together) [frame 5];

He pointed at the 10 [frame 6].

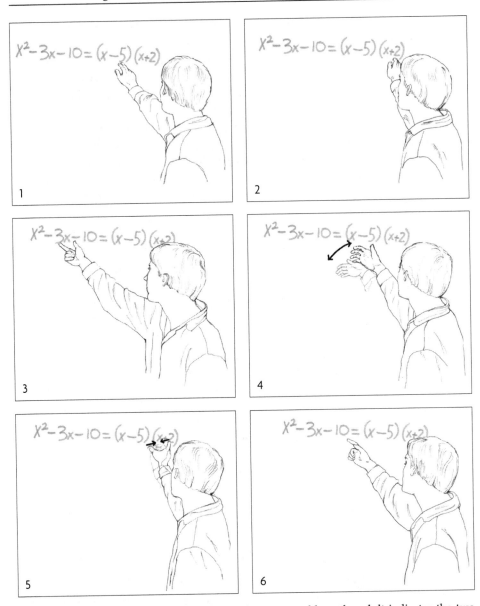

Figure 18. When explaining his solution to a factoring problem, the adult indicates the two numbers (−5, 2; frames 1–2) that need to be added to give −3 (frame 3) and multiplied to give −10 (frame 6). In addition to pointing out each of the numbers, he produces an "add" gesture (frame 4) and a "multiply" gesture (frame 5).

The adult not only used gesture to indicate the factors in the problem, but also managed to use his hands to convey that the two numbers are added together to give one number and multiplied together to give another. The factoring problem seemed perfect for our purposes. We therefore tested adults individually on a series of these problems.

We asked the children and the adults to solve a math problem at the blackboard. After doing so, they were given a list of items to remember (words for children, letters for adults—random letters are harder to remember than words). They were then asked to explain how they arrived at their solutions to the math problem. After completing the explanation, the children and adults were asked to recall the list. The crucial part of the design is that both children and adults had to keep the to-be-remembered list in mind while explaining how they solved the math problem—the two tasks were performed simultaneously. The memory task could then serve as a gauge of how much effort each child and adult expended on the explanation task (Logan 1979; Shiffrin and Schneider 1984).

Children and adults gave explanations under two conditions: (1) gesture permitted, in which their hands were unconstrained; (2) gesture not permitted, in which they were instructed to keep their hands still on the tabletop. Within each condition, lists were of two difficulty levels (three-versus one-word lists for children; six- versus two-letter lists for adults), a manipulation that allowed us to examine the effect of gesturing on memory when it is more versus less taxed.

Does gesturing on the math explanations affect memory? Both children and adults remembered a significantly larger proportion of items when gesturing than when not gesturing, particularly on the long lists that taxed their memories (Figure 19). Thus gesturing does not merely reflect cognitive load, but appears to have an impact on the load itself. Moreover, that impact is beneficial—gesturing reduces rather than increases cognitive load.

All of the adults in our study knew how to solve and explain the factoring problems correctly (they were University of Chicago students). Not all of the children, however, knew how to solve their math problems. Perhaps expertise affects the role that gesture plays in lessening cognitive load. If so, word recall ought to have been affected by how well the children understood the math problems. But it wasn't. Gesturing benefited memory independent of math knowledge. Not only did children who solved the math problems correctly remember the same proportion of words as children who solved them incorrectly but,

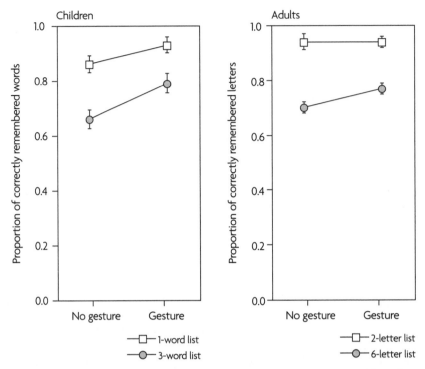

Figure 19. The proportion of correctly remembered items on the short and long lists. Children (left) and adults (right) both remembered more when gesturing while explaining their math solutions than when not gesturing. The effect was reliable for long lists but not for short lists, suggesting that gesturing benefits memory particularly when it is taxed. The error bars indicate standard errors.

more important for our purposes, gesturing improved memory to the same extent in the two groups. Thus the speakers' superior performance on the memory task was not a consequence of the *solutions* they gave on the math task—what mattered was whether they gestured while explaining those solutions. It's also worth noting that both the adults and the children produced the same types of explanations on the math task when they gestured and when they didn't gesture. Thus the speakers' superior performance on the memory task when they gestured versus when they didn't was not a consequence of the *explanations* they gave on the math task.

In this study we manipulated gesture directly—we instructed individuals not to move their hands on some problems, and found a consequent detrimental effect on memory. Manipulating gesture experimentally is, of course, essential if we are to determine whether gesture plays a causal role in cognition. By manipulating gesture, however, we run the risk of raising gesture to a conscious level and possibly altering the phenomenon we wish to study. For example, being forced not to gesture could itself hurt memory. If so, the effect seen in Figure 19 might be due, not to the beneficial effects of gesture, but to the deleterious effects of the constraining instructions. Asking speakers not to gesture is, in effect, asking them to do yet another task, which could add to their cognitive load.

The children and adults in our study saved us from this pitfall. A subset of the children and adults spontaneously (and presumably, unconsciously) gestured on only some of the problems where gesturing was permitted. In other words, there were problems on which these individuals could have gestured but chose not to. We were therefore able to compare the effects on memory of removing gesture by experimental design versus by the individual's spontaneous inclination. We reanalyzed the data from these children and adults, separating memory when they did not gesture by choice from memory when they did not gesture by instruction. As before, we found that memory was affected by gesturing, but only on the taxing long lists and not on the short lists. The crucial point is that both children and adults remembered more on the long lists when gesturing than when not gesturing *either* by choice *or* by instruction (see Figure 20). Memory was, if anything, worse under no-gesture-by-choice than under no-gesture-by-instruction for children (though the difference was not reliable), and equal for adults, suggesting that instructing individuals to remain still did not systematically add to their cognitive load.

We were worried by one other potential confound. It's possible that the math problems on which the children and adults in Figure 20 chose not to gesture were particularly difficult and that's why they remembered so little (that is, their relatively poor performance on these problems had nothing to do with the absence of gesture). We needn't have worried, however. We calculated the percentage of problems that these children and adults solved correctly when they gestured or did not gesture by choice or by instruction, and found no differences. Thus the patterns seen in Figure 20 cannot be attributed to difficulty in solving the math problem.

Another possible confound that we worried about was the time it took to explain the math problem. What if gesturing allows speakers

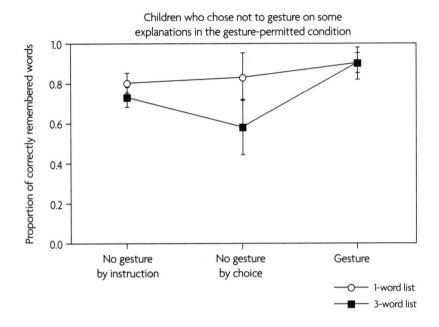

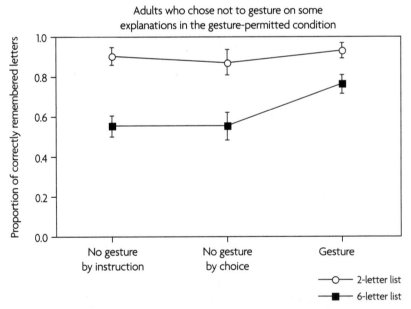

Figure 20. The proportion of correctly remembered items on the short and long lists for a subset of the children (top) and adults (bottom)—those who chose not to gesture on some (but not all) of their explanations of the math problem when gesture was permitted. Both children and adults remembered significantly more long lists when gesturing on the math task than when not gesturing, either by choice or by instruction. The error bars indicate standard errors.

to present more information in less time? If so, the speakers might have produced shorter explanations when they gestured than when they didn't. Since short-term memory deteriorates with time, a shortened explanation ought to lead to better recall. The shortened interval prior to recall (rather than the act of gesturing) might then be responsible for the better recall on problems accompanied by gesture. Again we needn't have worried—both children and adults spent slightly more time (not less) in explanation when gesturing than when not gesturing.

Finally, we were concerned about the effects that the number of words in an explanation might have on recall. If the speakers produced fewer words when gesturing than when not gesturing, the decrease in words (rather than the act of gesturing) might be responsible for the better recall on problems accompanied by gesture. Again there was no cause for concern—speakers produced the same number of words when gesturing as they did when not gesturing.

Of course, refraining from gesturing, even if it's done spontaneously (that is, without instruction from the experimenter), could add to a speaker's cognitive burden. However, if gesturing is so central to speaking that refraining from it adds to one's mental load, gesturing must be playing some sort of role in cognitive processing—which is the core of the argument I am making.

Taken together, the findings from this study suggest that gesturing reduces the cognitive load of explanation, freeing capacity that can be used on a memory task performed at the same time. Thus gesturing may not only reflect a speaker's cognitive state but may, by reducing cognitive load, also play a role in shaping that state.

The question that I am always asked at this point when I talk about this phenomenon is—do Italian speakers operate under less cognitive load because they gesture so much more than speakers of other languages? My response to this question is to question the assumption. Italian speakers produce more different types of emblems than speakers of other languages (Kendon 1992, 1995). But do they really gesture more? A recent study by Cornelia Mueller (2001) suggests that they may not. Mueller observed the gestures produced by speakers of Spanish (a language culturally and linguistically close to Italian), and compared them with the gestures produced by speakers of German (a language akin to English). Both groups were describing motion events. She found that the Spanish speakers gestured just as often as the German speakers. However, the Spanish speakers' gestures were "bigger" than the German speakers' gestures (they were produced by the forearm rather than by the hand, far away from the body rather than close, and from the upper trunk to the head and above rather than from the upper trunk to the center and below). Thus Spanish speakers' gestures may be more noticeable than German speakers' gestures, which could create the impression that Spanish speakers gesture more than German speakers. There may not be, in fact, large cultural differences in how often people gesture (see also Gulberg 1998, who found no differences in rate of gesture between French and Swedish speakers). But if there are—and if there turn out to be stable differences in how often individuals within a culture gesture—I think I would have to predict that those differences might well have an impact on the cognitive load of explanation.

Shifting the Burden or Lightening the Load?

How might gesture increase available cognitive resources? Up to this point, I have been assuming that gesturing reaps its cognitive benefits by actually lightening the speaker's load. An alternative possibility, however, is that rather than lightening cognitive load, gesturing shifts some of the load from one working memory store to another. In other words, effort isn't really saved, it's merely transferred in such a way that the task at hand is more easily accomplished.

This alternative view rests on the hypothesis, proposed by Baddeley (1986), that there are at least two distinct working memories, one that holds verbal material and one that holds visual or spatial material. These different working memories appear to be mediated by different cortical mechanisms (Smith and Jonides 1995). For example, systematically increasing demand on verbal working memory increases brain activity in left dorsolateral and left inferior prefrontal cortex; in contrast, increasing demand on visuo-spatial working memory increases brain activity in right parietal cortex (Jonides et al. 1993). Visuo-spatial working memory would seem to be ideal for storing information encoded in gesture.

In the speech-only explanations in our cognitive-load study (Goldin-Meadow et al. 2001), all of the information is expressed in speech and must be encoded in a verbal store. These representations compete for working memory capacity with the memory task (memory for words or letters), which is itself a verbal task. In contrast, in the speech-with-gesture explanations, some of the information is jointly expressed in speech and gesture. There is thus the possibility that this information can be encoded in a visuo-spatial store rather than a verbal store. In other words, information could be shifted from the verbal store it would have occupied had there been no gesture to a visuo-spatial store (which is now available because there is gesture). The effect of this shift is to remove some of the load from the verbal store, thus leaving more "room" and making it possible to remember more verbal material (the words or letters).

Note that under this view the load is shifted, not lightened. The load moves to a visuo-spatial store, which ought to then make it harder to remember spatial material. Thus if this view is correct, gesturing while speaking ought to make it harder to perform a second task if that task involves memory for spatial items. Susan Wagner tested this prediction by asking speakers to remember spatial (rather than verbal) items while explaining their solutions to the math problems. If gesturing is merely shifting cognitive load to a visuo-spatial store, memory for spatial items should be worse when speakers gesture than when they do not gesture simply because the shifted burden, combined with the to-be-remembered spatial items, overloads the visuo-spatial store. In this event, the pattern should be the reverse of the pattern we found for verbal items. If, however, gesture is truly lightening cognitive load, memory for spatial items should be better when speakers gesture than when they do not gesture—that is, the pattern should be the same for spatial items as it is for verbal items, and should resemble the patterns in Figures 19 and 20. Our findings support the second of these alternatives—gesturing is beneficial whether the speaker is asked to remember words or spatial items (Wagner, Nusbaum, and Goldin-Meadow n.d.). Gesturing seems to lift the speaker's cognitive burden rather than simply shift it.[3]

How Might Gesture Lighten the Load?

We now know that gesture lightens cognitive load rather than shifting it elsewhere. What might gesture be doing to reduce cognitive effort? In this section, I consider several non-mutually exclusive possibilities—in other words, all of the hypotheses might be correct.

---

3. The central issue here is whether gesturing while explaining *always* saves cognitive effort. The particular shifting-load hypothesis that we have just considered (and rejected) predicts that the answer to this question ought to be *no*. The lightening-load hypotheses that we consider in the next section are all compatible with a *yes* answer to this question and, in this sense, are distinct from our shifting-load hypothesis. Note, however, that there may well be other shifting-load hypotheses that are compatible with the lightening-load hypotheses considered next.

BOOSTING OVERALL ACTIVATION

Perhaps gesture lightens cognitive load by raising the overall activation level of the system so that words reach a firing level more quickly (Butterworth and Hadar 1989). Under this view, any movement would suffice to raise activation, and the beneficial effects of gesture would have nothing to do with its ability to convey meaning.

To test this hypothesis, we could restrain speakers from gesturing while allowing them to produce other movements (moving their head or feet). Alternatively, we could instruct people to move their hands rhythmically as they speak and explore the effects of real hand waving (as opposed to spontaneous gestures) on cognitive load.

There is, however, another way to test this hypothesis—one that allows us to use the data we have already collected. As we have come to expect, sometimes when the people in our study gestured, they conveyed the same information in their gesture as they conveyed in the accompanying speech—they produced gesture-speech matches. Other times, however, those very same speakers conveyed information in gesture that was different from the information conveyed in the accompanying speech—gesture-speech mismatches. If the mere act of moving one's hand is what reduces cognitive load, it shouldn't matter what the gestures mean and it therefore shouldn't matter whether the speaker's gestures are matches or mismatches. If, however, gesture reduces load because of the unique way in which it represents information, we might expect matches and mismatches to have different effects on cognitive load. Consider the following argument.

In a gesture-speech match, gesture and speech convey the same information and therefore can reinforce each other. Indeed, as described in the preceding section, gesture and speech might even share some of the representational load, which would then have a beneficial effect on load overall. In a gesture-speech mismatch, however, gesture conveys different information from speech, which means that the two cannot share the representational load. In fact, the load itself is heavier in a mismatch than in a match simply because there are two messages being conveyed—one in speech and another in gesture (see Nusbaum and Schwab 1986).

If the meaning of a gesture plays a role in its ability to reduce cognitive load, gesture ought to ease a speaker's cognitive burden more when it matches the speech it accompanies than when it doesn't—that is, speakers ought to remember more items on problems where their gestures match their speech than on problems where their gestures do not match their speech. This is precisely what we find when adults are asked to recall both verbal and spatial items (Wagner, Nusbaum, and Goldin-Meadow n.d.). Thus matches and mismatches are not equally good at easing a speaker's cognitive load, suggesting that the beneficial effects of gesture derive from meaning rather than from nonspecific movement. This is a comforting result, as all of the hypotheses described in the next sections assume that at least some of gesture's beneficial effects derive from its ability to represent information (rather than from its ability to add activation energy to the system overall).

FINDING THE RIGHT WORD

Rather than merely adding activation to the system, gesture might help speakers retrieve just the right word in their explanations (which would, in turn, save them cognitive effort so that they could perform better on the memory task). Gesture, particularly iconic gesture, might assist word finding by exploiting another route to the phonological lexicon, a route mediated by visual coding (Butterworth and Hadar 1989). There is, in fact, some evidence suggesting that gesture facilitates lexical recall. Butterworth and Beattie (1978) found that gestures can often be linked to a word in speech (for example, raising a hand during the utterance "when certain problems can be raised"), and that those gestures systematically precede the word in question (the hand raise is produced prior to the word "raised"). More recently, Morrel-Samuels and Krauss (1992) found a very precise relation in the timing of gesture to word—the more familiar the word, the smaller the gap between onset of gesture and onset of word. The assumption is that gesture primes the word and this priming effect is faster for familiar words than for unfamiliar words.

To test gesture's role in lexical access, Rauscher, Krauss, and Chen (1996) prevented speakers from gesturing and also made lexical access more difficult (they asked speakers to try to use as many obscure words as possible, or to avoid using words containing a specific letter). They found that preventing speakers from gesturing had the same effects as increasing the difficulty of lexical access by the other means. For example, speakers increased the number of speech errors they produced when they couldn't gesture, just as their errors increased when they were asked to use obscure words or to avoid words beginning with the letter "c." The only difference was that these effects were limited to speech with spatial content (for example, phrases containing words like "over," "under," "through") in the gesture-prohibition task but not in the other two tasks.

Rauscher, Krauss, and Chen (1996) suggest that gesture activates the semantic features (particularly the spatial features) used in the selection of a word, and therefore increases the likelihood that a speaker will come up with this particular word. One problem with this argument is that gesture often does not map neatly onto a single word (McNeill 1989). As McNeill (1992) has shown, gesture conveys its ideas globally, often mapping obliquely (or not at all, see Goldin-Meadow, Alibali, and Church 1993) onto the words it accompanies. How then can gesture be used to increase access to a sole lexical item?

Equally important, several studies designed to test gesture's role in lexical access have found negative results. The first two studies address the question by eliminating the need for lexical access—reasoning that if gesture is important to lexical access, it too ought to be eliminated (or at the least, decline). In the first, Beattie and Coughlan (1998) asked speakers to tell the same story on six consecutive trials. One would imagine that, at some point in the retellings, all of the words that the speaker might have had difficulty retrieving in the first telling would have been retrieved. The need for gesture (assuming that its function is to access words) ought then to decline. But gesture didn't decline over the six retellings. It stayed constant throughout. In the second study (which was described earlier in a different context), Alibali, Kita, and Young (2000) tested the lexical-access hypothesis by asking children to perform two tasks that did not differ in lexical access but did differ in conceptual difficulty—a description task and an explanation, both of which made use of precisely the same objects. The children used the same words across the two tasks, thus making it clear that lexical access did not differ across the tasks. If gesture's function is to access words, the children's gestures ought then to have been the same across tasks. But they weren't—they differed as a function of the conceptual demands of the task.

One last study took the opposite approach. Rather than manipulate the need for lexical access and observe the effects on gesture, Beattie and Coughlan (1999) manipulated gesture and observed the effects on lexical access. They gave speakers definitions of rare words and asked them to come up with the word that matched the definition. All of the words were rated high in imageability and thus ought to have been easy to gesture. Half of the speakers were free to gesture and the other half were instructed to fold their arms. The question was whether speakers who were allowed to gesture would come up with the missing word more often than speakers who were not allowed to gesture—they didn't. In fact, speakers who were free to gesture actually reached the target word less often than those who had their arms folded.

Gesturing may reflect the fact that a speaker is in the throes of searching for a word (or has completed such a search, see Christenfeld, Schachter, and Bilous 1991). But gesturing doesn't necessarily help the speaker find that word. Moreover, even when there seems to be little need to access a lexical item, speakers continue to gesture. Gesture may, of course, increase a speaker's access to a temporarily inaccessible lexical item on some occasions (my intuition is that there are times when gesture does just that). However, this function does not appear to be sufficiently widespread to account for gesture's beneficial effects on cognitive load. We explore two additional hypotheses in the next sections.

CONNECTING WORDS TO THE WORLD

Gesturing may make it easier to link a speaker's words to the world. Glenberg and Robertson (1999) argue that indexing, that is, linking words and phrases to real-world objects, is required for comprehension. Once a word is indexed to an object, the listener's knowledge of that particular object can guide his or her interpretation of the language. To test this hypothesis, Glenberg and Robertson gave adults background information on how to identify landmarks using a compass and a map. In addition to listening to a script describing how to use a compass, some of the adults saw a visual image of the compass and watched an actor's hand point to the compass's arrows (a deictic gesture) and turn its dial (a nonverbal demonstration, see Clark 1996) at the appropriate moments in the script. These adults, compared with others who did not see the actor's hand, read and followed new directions faster, referred to the background information less frequently, and performed the task using the compass and map more accurately. In other words, their understanding of the task was deeper and more usable than it would have been had they not seen the pointing gestures and demonstrations.

Glenberg and Robertson (1999) argue that comprehension is easier and better when the listener can make a link between the speaker's words and the world that those words map onto. Gesture is, of course, an ideal tool for making those links and listeners often make use of them (see Kelly et al. 1999). But the question is whether making these links is important, not only for listeners, but also for speakers. Does it ease the burden of production to index a word to an object? If so, this could explain how gesture reduces cognitive effort for the speaker.

Alibali and DiRusso (1999) explored the benefits of gestural indexing for the speaker. They asked preschool children to count objects. Sometimes the children were allowed to gesture while they counted and sometimes they weren't. The children counted more accurately when they gestured than when they didn't, which suggests that hooking word to world is easier for speakers when they can use their hands. Indeed, the children rarely made "coordination" errors (errors in coordinating the set of number words with the action of tagging each item) when they were allowed to gesture. Alibali and DiRusso also included a third condition—they asked children to count aloud while a puppet gestured for them. Here, too, the children counted more accurately than when there was no gesture at all. However, unlike on the self-gesturing trials, the errors that the children made on the puppet-gesturing trials tended to be coordination errors. Gesture helps speakers link words to the world, but only when the speakers themselves produce those gestures.

Note that the gestures in the Alibali and DiRusso study are what we might call "grounded"—they are oriented to objects in the world. Indeed, that's why these gestures serve the indexing function so well. The gestures in our cognitive-load study were, for the most part, also grounded (for example, children and adults pointed at numbers strung together in different ways to convey problem-solving strategies). What would happen if we redid our cognitive-load study using an explanation task that elicits nongrounded gestures (for example, metaphoric gestures or iconic gestures that are not produced near the objects to which they refer)?

If it is the indexing function of gesture that accounts for gesture's beneficial effects on cognitive load, then we would expect these effects to disappear when iconic or metaphoric (that is, nongrounded) gestures are used. In other words, producing iconic gestures ought not reduce cognitive load, and speakers ought to remember the same number of words when they produce iconic gestures as when they don't. If, however, speakers continue to remember more even when they produce iconic gestures, then the indexing hypothesis cannot be the sole explanation for gesture's ability to reduce cognitive load. No one has yet done this study, but I'm hoping someone soon will.

STRUCTURING SPATIAL INFORMATION

Gesturing may help speakers organize information, particularly spatial information, for the act of speaking and in this way ease the speaker's cognitive burden. Kita (2000) has argued that gesture helps speakers "package" spatial information into units appropriate for verbalization. If this hypothesis is correct, speakers should find it easier to convey spatial information when they gesture than when they don't.

Rimé, Schiaratura, Hupet, and Ghysselinckx (1984) conducted a study which provides some support for this hypothesis. Adults conversed naturally with the experimenter about a series of recent events in university life and about why they had not chosen to study psychology. For half the conversation, the adult spoke with total freedom of movement; for the other half, the adult's arms, hands, legs, and feet were restrained. The content of each adult's speech was analyzed by a computer program designed to quantify degree of imagery. The interesting result from our point of view was that the adults' speech contained less vivid imagery when their movements were restrained and they couldn't gesture than when their arms were free and they could.

Alibali, Kita, Bigelow, Wolfman, and Klein (2001) conducted a comparable study with children. They asked children to explain their answers to a series of conservation tasks under two conditions: when they could move their hands freely, and when their hands were placed in a muff and therefore restrained. As expected under the view that gesture helps speakers organize spatial information, the children produced more perceptual-based explanations when they were allowed to move their hands freely than when they weren't. Of course, it's possible that the children changed the content of their explanations for the listener, that is, they adjusted their speech to make up for the fact that the listener was or wasn't seeing gesture. However, in a second study, Alibali and her colleagues had a different set of children participate in the same task, with the exception that a curtain blocked the child's view of the listener and vice versa. The results were unchanged—children produced more perceptual-based explanations when they were allowed to gesture than when they weren't.

Although far from conclusive, these studies do suggest that gesture might play a role in helping speakers (as opposed to, or in addition to, listeners) organize spatial information into speech. This mechanism could well account for the beneficial effects that gesture has on a speaker's cognitive load. After all, the math tasks in our cognitive-load studies did call upon spatial skills. If gesture's help in packaging spatial information is what accounts for gesture's beneficial effects on cognitive load, then we would expect that these effects would disappear if the explanation task involved a nonspatial problem; for example, if speakers were asked to explain their reasoning on a moral dilemma rather than a math problem. It remains to be seen whether gesture reduces a speaker's cognitive load only when those gestures convey spatial information or, as I suspect, when the gestures convey nonspatial information as well.

Gesture-Speech Synergy

More than one, or even all, of the hypotheses that we've considered in this section might be correct. They are not mutually exclusive. Moreover, there is a theme that underlies all of them—that gesture and speech form an integrated and, indeed, synergistic system in which effort expended in one modality can (at times, but probably not always) lighten the load on the system as a whole.

So what have we learned about gesture's effect on the gesturer? We know that speakers tend to gesture more when the task becomes difficult. They appear to do so, not merely as a reflection of the cognitive effort they are expending, but as a way to reduce that effort. Giving an explanation while gesturing actually takes less cognitive effort than giving an explanation without gesturing. In addition, gesturing reduces cognitive load, not by shifting the load to a store that is not involved in the task at hand, but by actually lightening the load itself. The outstanding question is how—does gesture lighten the load because it's a motor act? because it can help us gain access to words or link those words to the world? because it organizes spatial information?

Whatever the mechanism, it's clear that gesturing can help free up cognitive resources that can then be used elsewhere. At the very least, we ought to stop telling people not to move their hands when they talk.

12

Gesturing Leads to Change

We have seen that gesturing can aid thinking by reducing cognitive effort. Gesturing saves effort on a task. That effort can then be used on some other task, one that would have been performed less well had the speaker not gestured on the first task. Gesturing thus allows speakers to do more with what they've got and, in this way, can lead to cognitive change.

But gesturing may contribute to cognitive change in other ways as well. Gesture offers a route, and a unique one, through which new information can be brought into the system. Because the representational formats underlying gesture make use of imagery and are not categorical, gesture permits speakers to represent ideas that lend themselves to these formats (for example, shapes, sizes, spatial relationships)—ideas that, for whatever reason, may not be easily encoded in speech. Take, for example, the child first described in Chapter 3 who expressed one-to-one correspondence in gesture but not in speech (see Figure 4B). This child may have found it relatively easy to focus on aligning the two rows of checkers in the visuo-spatial format gesture offers—at a time when he did not have sufficient grasp of the idea to express it in words. Gesture provides a format that makes it easy for the child to discover one-to-one correspondence, and thus allows this novel idea to be brought into his repertoire earlier than it would have been without gesture. Once brought in, the new idea can then serve as a catalyst for change.

The suggestion here is that gesture doesn't just reflect the incipient ideas that a learner has, but actually helps the learner formulate and therefore develop these new ideas. In other words, the course of cognitive change is different by virtue of the fact that the learner gestures.

This is a difficult hypothesis to test, and the evidence that we have for it is, for the most part, circumstantial. The argument that gesturing alters the course of cognitive change is most persuasively made when gesture conveys information that is not found in the learner's speech, that is, in gesture-speech mismatches, and it is there that we begin.

Reflecting a Second Idea

At some level, it seems completely obvious that when a speaker produces a gesture-speech mismatch, that person is expressing two ideas— one in speech and a second in gesture. Of course, this conclusion rests on our ability to demonstrate that the system we use to code gesture is reliable, and that our interpretations of those gestures are valid. For the most part, we've accomplished this goal (see Chapter 3 for a discussion of reliability and Chapter 5 for a discussion of validity). In this chapter, however, I take the argument one step further.

IN PROBLEM SOLVING

Speakers who produce gesture-speech mismatches have two ideas in mind when they produce the mismatch, that is, when they give their explanations of the task. But do they also have two ideas in mind when they solve the task, that is, when explanations are not involved at all? The data to address this question come from yet another cognitive-load study (Goldin-Meadow et al. 1993). We divided fourth-grade children into two groups on the basis of how many mismatches they produced when explaining their solutions to a series of mathematical equivalence problems: mismatcher children produced gesture-speech mismatches on three or more of their explanations (out of six); matcher children produced mismatches on fewer than three.

We then asked these same children to solve another set of math problems, but this time they did not have to explain their solutions. Instead, before solving each problem, the child was given a list of words to remember. After solving the problem, the child was asked to recall the list. As in our previous cognitive-load study, we took the number of correctly remembered words to be a measure of how much effort the child expended when solving the math problem. Note that this study differs from our other cognitive-load study in that it has nothing to do with effort expended while gesturing—gesture was not even involved in the cognitive-load portion of this study.

We gave the children two types of math problems, easy ones (4 + 7 + 3 + 5 = __) and hard ones (3 + 6 + 7 = __ + 8). We also gave them two types of word lists, easy ones (one-word lists) and hard ones (three-word lists). As expected, all of the children (both matchers and mismatchers) solved the easy math problems correctly and the hard math problems incorrectly (see the top graph in Figure 21). The issue, however, is the amount of effort the children expended in getting their wrong answers on the hard math problems. Our hypothesis was that the mismatchers entertained two problem-solving strategies simultaneously on the hard math problems, and thus expended more effort to get their wrong answers than the matchers.

Let's begin by thinking about how much effort the children expended on the easy math problems. All children (those in the matching group and those in the mismatching group) use gesture-speech matches when they explain problems of this type—in other words, they entertain only one problem-solving strategy in their explanations. If the way in which children explain their solutions to a math problem can be taken as an accurate reflection of how they solve problems of the same type, we should expect all of the children (both matchers and mismatchers) to activate only one problem-solving strategy when solving the easy math problems. The matcher and mismatcher children should then be expending the same amount of effort when solving these problems, and should remember precisely the same number of words—and they did (see the bottom graph in Figure 21; on the easy math problems, Matcher 1-word = Mismatcher 1-word and Matcher 3-word = Mismatcher 3-word).

But what about the hard math problems? By definition, the matcher children produced primarily gesture-speech matches when explaining their solutions to the hard math problems on the pretest prior to the cognitive-load task. Again, if the way in which children explain their solutions to a math problem reflects how they solve other problems of the same type, we should expect the matcher children to activate only one problem-solving strategy when they solve the hard math problems, just as they did when they solved the easy math problems. The matcher children should therefore expend the same amount of effort, and remember the same number of words, when solving the hard math problems as they expended when solving the easy math problems. Again, this prediction was confirmed (bottom graph in Figure 21; Matcher 1-word easy math problem = Matcher 1-word hard math problem, Matcher 3-word easy math problem = Matcher 3-word hard math problem).

We now turn to the mismatcher children, which is where our predictions start to get interesting. Recall that, by definition, the mismatcher children produced primarily gesture-speech mismatches when they explained their solutions to the hard problems—in other words, they entertained two distinct problem-solving strategies in their explanations of the hard problems. Assuming that the way in which children explain their solutions to a math problem is an accurate reflection of how they solve problems of the same type, we should expect these mismatcher children to activate two problem-solving strategies when they solve the hard math problems. Activating two strategies ought to take more effort than activating a single strategy. When the mismatcher children solve the hard math problems, they should therefore expend more effort and, as a result, have less effort left over to spend on the memory task than when they solve the easy math problems. Particularly when their memories are taxed (that is, on the three-word lists), they should then remember fewer words when solving the hard math problems than when solving the easy math problems (bottom graph in Figure 21; Mismatcher 3-word *hard* math problem < Mismatcher 3-word *easy* math problem). Moreover, they should remember fewer words when solving the hard math problems than the matcher children remembered when they solved the hard math problems (bottom graph in Figure 21; *Mismatcher* 3-word hard math problem < *Matcher* 3-word hard math problem). Both predictions were confirmed (Goldin-Meadow et al. 1993).

So what have we learned from this study? We now know that children who produce gesture-speech mismatches and thus activate two problem-solving strategies when explaining how they solved a task also

---

Figure 21 (facing page). The top graph (A) presents the proportion of easy and hard math problems that matchers and mismatchers solved correctly while simultaneously recalling one- versus three-word lists. The bottom graph (B) presents the proportion of word lists that the children recalled correctly. All of the children solved the easy problems correctly and the hard problems incorrectly (A). However, the mismatchers worked harder to arrive at their incorrect solutions on the hard math problems than the matchers. They were activating two problem-solving strategies on the hard problems and thus remembered less (Mismatcher 3-word, hard math problem, in (B)) than the matchers who were activating only one strategy (Matcher 3-word, hard math problem, in (B))—and less than they themselves remembered when solving the easy problems on which they activated only one strategy (Mismatcher 3-word, easy math problem, in (B)). The error bars indicate standard errors.

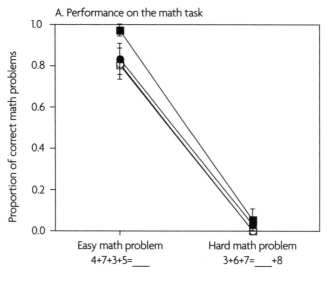

A. Performance on the math task

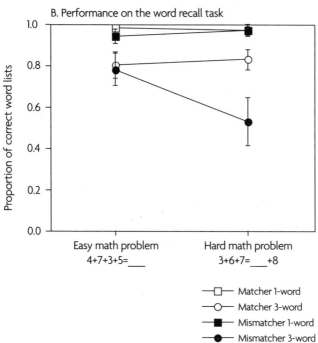

B. Performance on the word recall task

—□— Matcher 1-word
—○— Matcher 3-word
—■— Mismatcher 1-word
—●— Mismatcher 3-word

activate more than one strategy when actually solving that same task. The "second idea" reflected in the gestural component of a gesture-speech mismatch is, consequently, not there merely as a post hoc reconstruction of how the task was solved. Even when no explanations are required at all, that second idea consumes effort, which suggests that the idea is part of the solution process itself. Thus the insight that gesture gives us into a speaker's thoughts extends beyond the explanation task, which makes us that much more confident that gesture is an excellent tool for making inferences about thought. We are still amassing evidence, however, that gesture reflects thought rather than causes it.

AT A CHOICE POINT

Another way to establish that gesture-speech mismatches reflect the simultaneous activation of two ideas is to observe places where two ideas are likely to crop up at the same time. We would expect to see mismatches at just these points.

Take, for example, the Tower of Hanoi puzzle. The Tower of Hanoi has been extensively studied in cognitive psychology as an example of a problem-solving puzzle that involves subgoals (Egan and Greeno 1974; Kotovsky, Hayes, and Simon 1985). The task comes in many versions (see Hayes and Simon 1977) but a common one (and the one we used in our study) involves three vertical pegs and three disks of unequal sizes. In the initial state, all three disks are on a single peg, with the largest disk on the bottom, the medium-sized disk in the middle, and the smallest disk on the top. The task is to get all three disks onto another peg, stacked again from largest to smallest. The challenge is that only one disk can be moved at a time, and a larger disk can never be placed on top of a smaller disk. The solution involves setting up subgoals. If there are three disks, the optimal solution calls for establishing two subgoals; if there are four disks, the optimal solution calls for four subgoals. We reasoned that, in the transition to a subgoal, the problem solver is likely to be thinking about alternative paths (that is, more than one idea). Once having entered a subgoal, however, the die is cast and the problem solver is likely to think only about the next step along the already chosen path (that is, a single idea). Thus the problem solver ought to produce more mismatches when describing the transition to the subgoal than when describing all other moves.

We asked adults and children to solve the Tower of Hanoi problem and then describe how they solved it (Garber and Goldin-Meadow 2002). The children, who were nine years old, solved three 3-disk problems, and the adults solved three 4-disk problems. The standard 3-disk problem is difficult but not impossible for children aged six to twelve (Bidell and Fischer 1995; Borys, Spitz, and Dorans 1982; Byrnes and Spitz 1979), and the 4-disk problem is challenging for adults (Ewert and Lambert 1932; Gagne and Smith 1962). It turned out that everyone, adults and children alike, gestured when explaining their solutions to the problems. Indeed, almost every single move that was described contained gesture. And the adults and children produced both matches and mismatches (see Figure 22). For example, the adult shown in frame A in the figure gestured a path from peg 2 to peg 3 while describing precisely the same path in speech: "I moved the green one here." She thus produced a gesture-speech match. This same adult is shown in frames

Figure 22. Solving a Tower of Hanoi problem, the adult in frame A produces a gesture-speech match. She moves her right hand from the middle peg to the peg on the left side of the picture, while describing precisely the same trajectory in speech. In frames B1–B2, she produces a gesture-speech mismatch. She first moves her left hand from the middle peg to the peg on the right side of the picture, a trajectory that she does not mention in speech. She then holds her left hand shaped in a vertical "C" at the middle peg and moves her right hand from this middle peg to the peg on the left, a trajectory that she does describe in speech.

B1–B2 explaining a different step in the puzzle. In this explanation, she first gestured a path from peg 2 to peg 1, a path which she did not mention in speech. She then gestured the path from peg 2 to peg 3, which she did describe in speech: "I, uhm, moved the green disk here." She conveyed different paths in gesture and in speech, and thus produced a gesture-speech mismatch.

The question is—where did these mismatches occur? We hypothesized that the problem solvers would be particularly likely to produce gesture-speech mismatches when describing the first move of a subgoal which, in effect, is a "choice point" between alternative paths. And, in fact, we found that both children and adults were significantly more likely to produce gesture-speech mismatches at choice points than at nonchoice points (see Figure 23).

In this study, gesture often conveyed the path not taken—that is, the option that the problem solver considered but ultimately rejected. There are many situations, however, where the information conveyed in gesture predicts the speaker's next step—it's a harbinger of things to come.

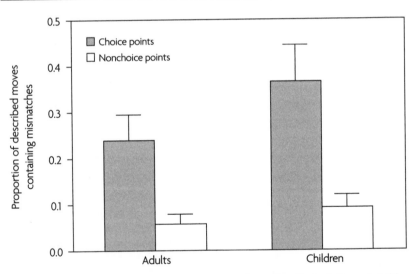

Figure 23. The proportion of moves containing mismatches that adults and children produced when explaining how they solved the Tower of Hanoi problem. Both groups produced more mismatches when describing choice points (where there was a choice between two paths) than when describing nonchoice points (where they were on a path and not likely to change). The error bars indicate standard errors.

If we want to argue that gesture is shaping thinking (and not just reflecting it), cases where gesture predicts the future seem particularly relevant. We consider some examples in the next section.

Predicting the Next Step

WHEN SOLVING A PROBLEM

One would assume that the way in which an adult represents a problem would influence his or her plans for solving that problem. We tested this rather obvious prediction but with one catch—we based our assessments of the adults' representation of the problem not only on what they said but also on what they gestured. We gave adults a series of word problems about constant change. The experimental protocol involved two sequential steps. We first asked adults to restate a word problem to a listener (a confederate). We then asked them to discuss how they would go about solving that problem (Alibali et al. 1999).

Two of the six problems depicted continuous change, two depicted discrete change, and two depicted change that could be construed as either continuous or discrete. The problems were reminiscent of those we all solved in grade school. An example of a problem depicting discrete change:

> A bookcase has 6 shelves and the number of books on each successive shelf increases by a constant number. If there are 15 books on the top shelf and 45 on the bottom, how many books total are there?

An example of a problem depicting continuous change:

> The speed of an airplane increases at a constant rate during a period of 12 minutes from 10 miles/minute to 34 miles/minute. What distance, in miles, will the plane travel during the 12-minute period?

An example of a problem depicting change that could be seen as either discrete or continuous:

> During the last 6 years, the rate of population growth in the town of Mudville increased steadily from 300 people/year to 1,500 people/year. How many people total were added to the population during the 6-year period?

In principle, all of the problems could be solved using either a discrete or a continuous problem-solving strategy. However, discrete formulations tended to elicit discrete problem-solving strategies and continuous formulations tended to elicit continuous problem-solving strategies, with the mixed formulations eliciting solutions somewhere in between.

We found that the adults often incorporated information about manner of change (that is, discrete versus continuous manner) into their spoken restatements of the problems and into their gestural restatements as well. We coded the speech and gesture in each restatement according to whether gesture conveyed the same information as speech (reinforcing) or not (neutral or conflicting). Interestingly, we found that the information an adult conveyed in gesture was often not the same as the information that adult conveyed in speech.

We then asked whether we could use an adult's restatement of a problem to predict how that adult would choose to solve the problem. To do so, we determined whether the adult's problem-solving strategy was compatible with that adult's spoken restatement of the problem. We found that adults were very likely to consider a problem-solving strategy that was compatible with their spoken restatement of a problem when their gestures reinforced that spoken restatement—significantly more likely than when their gestures were either neutral or conflicted with the spoken restatement of the problem. In other words, the adults proposed a solution that was compatible with their words most often when their gestures matched those words. Moreover, when their gestures conflicted with their words, the adults would often propose a solution strategy that was compatible with their gestures—just as often as they proposed a solution strategy compatible with their words.

Gesture thus appears to reflect ideas that adults have, but do not say, about the problem. Those ideas deflect the adults from solving the problem with the strategy that would have been predicted from their talk alone (often in favor of a strategy predicted from gesture alone). The bottom line is that the ideas displayed in gesture have an impact on how problems are solved.

WHEN LEARNING A TASK

We find the same pattern when children learn a new task—the gestures that the children produce prior to instruction predict the aspects of the task that they will learn after instruction.

For example, recall the training study described in Chapter 4 in which we instructed a group of children in conservation (Church and Goldin-Meadow 1986). None of the children was successful on conservation during the pretest. Some of the children, however, produced more gesture-speech mismatches when explaining their solutions to the pretest problems, and others produced more matches. As described earlier, the mismatchers were far more likely to profit from the instruction we gave them and to make progress on the post-test than the matchers. The important point for us here, however, is that we could predict which new conservation explanations the mismatchers added to their spoken repertoires after instruction on the basis of the gestural component of the mismatches the children produced prior to instruction. As an example, a child who produces one-to-one correspondence in gesture on the pretest (moving a pointing hand from each checker in one row to the corresponding checker in another row) would then add one-to-one correspondence to his spoken repertoire after instruction ("you can pair them up"). It's important to note that not all of the thoughts that the children conveyed in gesture were "smart"—that is, the children often conveyed information in gesture that was not useful in solving the problem at hand. However, when they did convey correct explanations in gesture prior to instruction, those explanations often cropped up in speech after instruction.

Similarly, in a parallel training study on mathematical equivalence also described in Chapter 4, we again found that children who produced many mismatches when explaining their solutions to the math problems were more likely to make progress on the post-test than children who produced few (Perry, Church, and Goldin-Meadow 1988). Moreover, when the mismatchers expressed correct strategies on the pretest, those strategies were expressed uniquely in gesture—that is, they could be found only in the gestural component of the mismatches that the children produced prior to instruction. The strategies expressed uniquely in gesture were the ones that the children acquired during instruction and led to success on the post-test.

Taken together, the findings from these studies suggest that gesture tells us which way the wind is blowing—it predicts the next step that a problem solver or a learner will take. When adults use gesture (but not speech) to describe a problem as one involving discrete change, they are more likely to solve that problem using a discrete approach than when they don't use gesture in this way. Children who express conservation explanations (or correct math strategies) uniquely in gesture are more likely to learn those explanations (or strategies) when given instruction than children who don't. We can therefore look at these individuals' gestures and predict where they will go next. The nagging question, however, is still whether gesture is reflecting the individual's cognitive course or playing a role in shaping it.

Reflecting Ideas or Creating Them?

How might gesture create ideas? McNeill (1992, 246–247) hypothesizes that gesture is part of the process of utterance formation, and that utterance formation is itself a continuous transformation of thought. According to McNeill, thought begins as an image that is idiosyncratic. When we speak, this image is transformed into a linguistic and gestural form (we can, of course, think without speaking and then this transformation would not occur). The speaker realizes his or her meaning only at the final moment of synthesis, when the linear-segmented and analyzed representations characteristic of speech are joined with the global-synthetic and holistic representations characteristic of gesture. The synthesis does not exist as a single mental representation for the speaker until the two types of representations are joined. The communicative act is consequently itself an act of thought. McNeill's (1992) meticulous observations of talk make it clear that gesture is a fully participating member in the communicative act. It is in this sense that gesture shapes thought.

One implication of this view is that thought would have been different had the speaker not gestured. To put this hypothesis to the test, we need a technique for assessing thought that is independent of gesture and speech; that is, we need a way to figure out whether thought has been altered that does not involve looking at either gesture or speech. At the moment, no studies have been designed with this particular goal in mind (but see the end of this section for some possibilities). We do, however, have examples of studies that explore gesture's effect on *talk*—studies in which gesture occurs spontaneously in talk and has an effect on subsequent talk, and studies in which gesture is manipulated (either discouraged or encouraged) and the manipulation then has an effect on talk.

SPONTANEOUS GESTURE

Is gesture determining the course of talk? One of the best places to explore gesture's role in talking is in teaching and learning situations. As described in Chapter 8, Crowder (1996) observed children participating in a science lesson on seasonal change, and found that the children expressed their views not only through talk but also through their hands. The telling observation from the point of view of this discussion is that, at times, the gestures a child produced seemed to alter that child's way of thinking about the problem. For example, Gail was trying to decide where the sun would shine most directly. She was representing the sun with her left fist, which she held at a distance from the globe, at the same time that she said the sun was shining "right about straight on the equator." She then gestured without speaking—she traced a line from her fist (her sun hand) to the globe. After finishing her gesture, which landed just below the equator on the globe, she revised her statement as follows: "No, right about *here*. More on the, . . . southern hemisphere. Shining directly about over, somewhere over here" (Crowder 1996, 190–191).

In this instance, Gail's gestures preceded her words and had a clear impact on those words—she altered her predictions as a direct result of the trajectory her hand took. In this way, gesture can help students reason and can encourage them to interrelate the components of an external model (in this case, the gestured sun and the globe). These components can then be internalized as mental imagery. At times, gesture can lead the thinker toward new ways of problem solving.

Note that in this example the student appeared to be aware of her gesture, perhaps not while producing it but certainly after its completion. In fact, she used her hand almost as she would a pencil, drawing a line between sun and earth. If asked, she might even have said that she changed her prediction because of the line she drew with her hand. In the next example, gesture again precedes speech but by the briefest of intervals, and its effect on speech is less likely to have been explicitly noticed by the speaker.

Emmorey and Casey (2001) asked adults to solve three spatial puzzles. The adults' task was to fill in a puzzle grid with all of the pieces, but they themselves were not allowed to touch the pieces—they had to tell the experimenter which blocks to move and where to move them. In a number of cases, the adults first produced a gesture conveying rotation; that gesture was then immediately followed by words expressing rotation. For example, the adult said, "and the red one [ ] like can you flip it over and then stick it in D, E, and then 3" (the puzzle grid was labeled with horizontal letter and vertical number coordinates). During the temporal window denoted by the empty brackets and just prior to describing rotation in words ("like can you flip it over"), the adult produced a rotation gesture (thumb and index finger twisted clockwise) which was accompanied by no words at all.

This sequence suggests that the speaker's words may have been primed by her gestures. Even more interesting, it's possible that these words would not have been expressed at all had the speaker not gestured (see also examples in Kita 2000, 172–175). Perhaps the speaker's gestures helped her visualize the rotation necessary to place the block within the puzzle and this visualization, in turn, led to her verbalization. It's possible, but our evidence is thin. In fact, we can't argue on the basis of spontaneous talk alone that *gesture* is crystallizing the rotation notion and increasing its chances of appearing in speech. It could well be that gesture and speech independently reflect the same underlying notion, and would do so whether or not the other was expressed. To determine whether gesture is an actual player in constructing thought, we need to be able to manipulate gesture and observe its effects.

MANIPULATING GESTURE

We considered some of the best evidence that gesture has an impact on thought when we examined gesture's role in packaging spatial information in Chapter 11. Recall that Rimé and his colleagues (1984) prevented speakers from gesturing and found that these speakers produced less visual imagery in their talk when they didn't gesture than when they did. Alibali, Kita, and their colleagues (2001) performed the same manipulation and found that their child speakers produced fewer perceptual-based explanations when they didn't gesture than when they did. The idea is that the act of gesturing promotes spatial thinking—and not gesturing inhibits it.

Both studies included design features that are important if we really want to claim that *gesture* is what's making the difference. In both studies, the design was within-subject (each subject participated in both the gesturing and the nongesturing conditions)—the speaker was first permitted to move his or her hands freely and only later was restrained. This design feature allowed the investigators to make sure that they were observing a decrement in gesture (if a speaker doesn't gesture in the first place, it hardly matters that gesture is suppressed). In addition, both studies made sure that time itself wasn't responsible for the changes found in talk. Rimé and his colleagues had the speaker talk freely for fifteen minutes, then talk with his or her hands and arms restrained for about twenty minutes, and then talk freely once again for fifteen minutes. They found no differences between the first fifteen minutes and the last, which successfully refutes the hypothesis that visual imagery in talk declines over time. Alibali and her colleagues took a different approach—they added a second group of children whose hands were not restrained during the latter half of the study. These children did not produce fewer perceptual-based explanations over time, suggesting that the decrease in perceptual-based explanations in the restrained group was, indeed, attributable to the decrement in their gesture.

Another way to approach this problem is to encourage gesturing in speakers and explore the effects on the content of speech. Wolff and Gutstein (1972) asked speakers to make a circular or linear movement with their hands while telling short stories. Speakers were asked to tell fictitious stories of two to three sentences with no time limitation (speakers were also asked to generate words in restricted categories, but no effects were found on word generation). Each speaker was taught to make a circular gesture (either a clockwise circular movement with the favored arm and hand; or two simultaneous circular movements, a clockwise motion with the right hand and a counterclockwise motion with the left) or a linear gesture (a repeated up-and-down movement with the favored arm and hand; or simultaneous up-and-down movements with both hands). A third of the speakers generated their stories while performing the assigned gesture with their eyes closed. Another third generated their stories while watching an experimenter perform the assigned gesture. The last third generated their stories with no accompanying gesture (they were taught either a linear or circular gesture but neither watched the experimenter gesturing nor produced the gesture on their own).

How could Wolff and Gutstein tell whether the gestures had influenced the stories that the speakers had generated? They relied on raters. Raters were told that one-third of the stories had been generated with accompanying circular gestures, one-third with linear gestures, and one-third with no gestures. The raters were shown the four possible gestures and were then instructed to judge the appropriateness of circular or linear gestures to each story using a seven-point scale. A mark in the middle of the scale was taken to mean that neither gesture type was appropriate or that both gesture types were equally appropriate. A positive mark indicated linear influence; a negative mark indicated circular influence. Raters were also asked to underline the segments of the story that gave them the linear or circular impression.

There were, in fact, large and reliable effects of gesture. Speakers who produced linear gestures created stories that were judged more linear than the stories created by speakers who produced circular gestures. Interestingly, speakers who watched linear gestures also created stories that were judged more linear than the stories created by speakers who watched circular gestures. The third, control group, which was taught either a linear or a circular gesture, did not use or see that gesture when producing their stories. Predictably, there were no differences among the ratings of the stories generated by these speakers.

As examples, the first story that follows was generated by a speaker circling his hands, and the second was generated by a speaker making linear movements (Wolff and Gutstein 1972, 286). In both stories, the italicized segments indicate the portions that gave the rater the impression that the story was circular or linear.

> *The moon is circling the earth* as the *day wears on,* hopefully. As the day wears on Bill *gets older;* as Bill *gets older,* so does his family.

> I was riding *down the highway* and I was moving very fast *passing all the cars along the side* and looking out into the distance and trying to see *how straight the highway goes into the distance.*

These results suggest that waving your hands about in prescribed ways can affect what you're going to say. The segments that the raters underlined included single words (both nouns and verbs) but also phrases and clauses. The impact of gesture was not restricted to a single linguistic category. Moreover, the impact of gesture was not restricted to speakers who produced gesture. Its impact was felt even by those speakers who merely witnessed others' hand movements, a finding that confirms the conclusion we came to in the second part of this book— gesture does have an impact on listeners.

One elegant aspect of the Wolff and Gutstein study is that the speakers who produced gestures did so with their eyes closed. Thus they felt their gestures but did not see them. It is consequently very clear that seeing versus feeling hand movements can have separable effects on the content of talk. The effects could, of course, be additive—had the speakers been allowed to both see and feel their own gestures (which is, after all, what typically happens when speakers talk), the content of their stories might have been that much more skewed. Alternatively, feeling one's own gestures may be such a powerful stimulus that little is added by watching them. Moreover, the perspective we have on our own gestures is distinctly different from the perspective we have on others' gestures. We may get something out of watching other speakers' gestures, but little out of watching our own. This is an area where many questions remain.

In general, much more needs to be done to explore the effects of gesture on thinking. Note that we have looked at two types of studies that manipulate gesture. The first, exemplified by the Rimé et al. (1984) and the Alibali, Kita et al. (2001) studies, manipulated gesture by discouraging it. But we could also encourage speakers to move their hands while they talk. If gesture has an impact on visuo-spatial thinking, speakers ought to have more visual imagery, and more perceptual-based explanations, when we encourage them to increase their rate of gesturing. The effects found thus far for gesture have all been in the spatial domain. However, we do find gesture in tasks that are not spatial—for example, both children and adults gesture while explaining their reasoning behind moral dilemmas (Church et al. 1995). Should we expect effects on the content of talk if gesture is either discouraged or encouraged in these speakers? Are the benefits of gesturing limited only to spatial domains? These are important questions that await future research.

In the second type of study, Wolff and Gutstein (1972) did more than manipulate the presence of gesture—they dictated which gestures the speakers were to produce. The experimenters could therefore make specific predictions about the kinds of ideas that ought to infiltrate the stories accompanied by gesture. The Wolff and Gutstein findings are striking because the gestures were completely unrelated to the story-telling task. From an educational (or even a conversational) point of view, however, it would be worth exploring the effects on thinking of movements that are more directly related to the task.

For example, what would happen if we asked a child who did not know how to solve the mathematical equivalence problem $4 + 5 + 3 = \_\_ + 3$ to produce a V-hand under the 4 and the 5 and to point at the blank while solving the problem? This gesture represents the "grouping" strategy—group 4 and 5 together, add them, and put the sum in the blank. Another child could be asked to indicate the two 3's with her hands—the "equal addends" strategy upon which the grouping strategy is predicated. If the actions that the children are required to produce do, in fact, influence their thinking, we might expect them to produce more correct solutions on these problems than children who are not required to make these movements—or even more telling, more correct solutions than children who are required to make other, less-targeted movements.

To explore the effect of feeling one's own gestures versus watching one's own or another's gestures, the ideal study ought to include three conditions—the two Wolff and Gutstein used plus a third. Some children should watch another person producing the gestures while they themselves solve the problem (watching another's gestures). Some should produce the gestures on their own and keep their eyes closed (feeling one's own gesture). And some should produce the gestures on their own and keep their eyes open (feeling and watching one's own gestures). Such a study would begin to address the impact that watching gesture versus feeling gesture versus feeling-and-watching gesture can have on thought. In addition, if we look at how children solve the problems rather than at how they explain them, we will be tapping thought using a technique that is independent of both gesture and speech—an essential step if our goal is to determine whether gesture's effects on thought extend beyond thinking-for-speaking (see Slobin 1996).

Why Does Gesture Promote Cognitive Change?

Gesture is clearly implicated in cognitive change. It is, of course, possible that gesture is nothing more than an epiphenomenon of change, associated with it but not in any way central to its causes. Evidence is mounting, however, that gesture may be involved in the process of change itself, communicating "silent" aspects of the learner's cognitive state to potential agents of change, or helping more directly to ease the learner's cognitive burden. Why might gesture be particularly well suited to fostering cognitive change?

AN ALTERNATIVE WAY TO REPRESENT INFORMATION

We all know that you don't really understand something until you are able to explain it to someone else. Indeed, researchers have found that asking people to explain their responses to a problem has a beneficial effect on learning (for example, Chi et al. 1989; Siegler 1997). Being forced to come up with an explanation encourages learners to articulate their, perhaps previously unexamined, presuppositions and to put their ill-formed ideas into words. This self-examination may be what's important in eliciting explanations from learners. But requesting explanations may also be effective because it elicits gesture from the learner. Gesture offers the opportunity to explain in another modality, one that has representational demands and possibilities that are very different from those of speech.

As described in the first part of this book, McNeill (1992) has argued that gesture and speech form complementary components of a single integrated system, with each modality best suited to expressing its own set of meanings. Gesture reflects a global-synthetic image. It is idiosyncratic and constructed at the moment of speaking—it does not belong to a conventional code. In contrast, speech reflects a linear-segmented, hierarchical linguistic structure, utilizing a grammatical pattern that embodies the language's standards of form and drawing on an agreed-upon lexicon of words. Consider, for example, a speaker who is describing the seating arrangement of a group of friends. One well-formed gesture can do much more to convey the nuances of the arrangement (who's sitting closer to whom, and with what orientation) to a listener than even the best-chosen set of words. Gesture thus allows speakers to convey thoughts that may not easily fit into the categorical system that their conventional language offers (Goldin-Meadow and McNeill 1999). Taken together, gesture and speech offer the possibility of constructing multiple representations of a single task, and these multiple perspectives may prove useful, particularly in learning certain complex tasks.

In fact, gesture itself can allow for the construction of two different types of representations—visuo-spatial representations and motor representations. Gesture is seen. Each hand forms a configuration and, if two hands are used, together they form yet another shape. Moreover, the hands move in space, thus carving out trajectories. These shapes and movements are meaningful—both to experimenters who have been taught to code gesture, and to ordinary listeners and speakers who have not. Gesture evokes visual images, either concrete images (for example, a wrist rotating several times to represent opening a jar) or metaphoric images (for example, a pointing finger circling continuously to represent continuity) that are seen by both speaker and listener.

But gesture is also felt. Speakers move their hands through space and thus, in a very concrete sense, embody their thoughts in action. Gesture may therefore not only evoke visual images; it may also evoke motor images, thereby broadening the representational possibilities for the speaker. In addition, there may be a sense in which gesture can be felt by listeners. So-called mirror neurons are motor neurons that are activated not only when performing an activity oneself but also when observing another perform that activity (Rizzolatti and Arbib 1998). In this way, mirror neurons may allow the observer to experience the actions performed by the observed. If, in fact, mirror neurons exist for gesturing, we may find that we construct motor representations not only when gesturing ourselves but also when observing others gesture.

Gesture thus expands the set of representational tools available to speakers and listeners. It can redundantly reflect information represented through verbal formats, or it can augment that information, adding nuances possible only through visual or motor formats. By bringing unique information into the system, gesture may help to change the balance and thus bring about change.

NO MONITORING INVOLVED

Gesture may have an advantage over speech in that it can bring new ideas in without disrupting the current system. Because gesture is not regulated by an acknowledged codified system, the notions that are expressed in this modality can easily go unchallenged. Rarely are speakers criticized for their gestures (unless, of course, those gestures are emblems with unprintable meanings). The same message that elicits disapproval when expressed in speech may go without comment (though probably not without notice) when expressed in gesture.

Not only are the notions conveyed in gesture likely to go unchallenged by others, but they are also likely to go unchallenged by the self. A speaker can "sneak in" an idea, perhaps an ill-formed one, in gesture that doesn't cohere well with the set of ideas expressed in speech. Gesture may be an ideal place to try out inchoate, untamed, and innovative ideas simply because those ideas don't have to fit. Much experimentation may take place, and remain, in gesture, never reaching the conventionally shared spoken system.

As an example, recall the study described in Chapter 5 in which a group of mismatching children appeared to be making no progress at all on the mathematical equivalence task (Alibali 1994; Goldin-Meadow and Alibali 1995). In fact, these children were constantly revamping their repertoires of problem-solving strategies—adding new strategies and abandoning old ones (see Figure 13). They maintained the same number of strategies throughout the study, but the particular strategies they entertained differed at each point. Moreover, and importantly, all of the experimentation that the children were doing was taking place in gesture, and though new, the children's experimental ideas were often wrong. It may be easier to experiment (and be wrong) in gesture than in words simply because no one is watching critically. Gesture may be the place where we can expect to see children's worst guesses about how a task works. But the experimentation itself may be useful, and perhaps even necessary, for cognitive change.

A HALFWAY HOUSE

Gesture is not subject to the same standards of approval as speech simply because it is not an explicit representational system in the way speech is. However, gesture is symbolic in its own right. Gesturing about a procedure is not the same as enacting that procedure—although gesture does look (and feel) much more like the enactment than whatever words we use to describe the same procedure. Gesture reflects knowledge that, in a sense, is halfway between performing a procedure and describing that procedure using a conventional linguistic code. A growing group of researchers have come to believe that linguistic meaning is itself grounded in bodily action (Barsalou 1999; Glenberg and Kaschak 2002; Glenberg and Robertson 1999)—that meaning derives from the biomechanical nature of bodies and perceptual systems and, in this sense, is embodied (Glenberg 1997). If so, gesture may be an overt depiction of the action-meaning embodied in speech, and a halfway point in this sense. At times, we can even see individuals moving through this halfway point.

For example, Schwartz and Black (1996) asked adults to solve simple gear problems. They found that adults initially used depictive models to solve the problems and, over time, switched to a more abstract rule. The interesting observation from our point of view is that the adults' depictive models were reflected in their hand gestures. Moreover, these hand gestures were particularly frequent just prior to the moment when the adults stated the rule for the first time, and dropped in frequency shortly thereafter. The types of gestures also changed over time. Initially, the adults used rotating gestures—rotating motions depicting the gear dynamics—and then switched to ticking gestures—motions that indicated the sequence of the gear chain without including the dynamic properties of the scene (for example, raising or pointing the fingers, without rotating them, to indicate the successive gears). At the end of the set of problems, the adults used no gestures at all, suggesting that they were no longer relying on an external model but had progressed to an abstract rule. Schwartz and Black (1996, 464) suggest that hand movements are physical instantiations of the speaker's mental model, and that these movements are a way station on the path to abstract rules.

As another example, recall the study described in Chapter 4 in which we taught children mathematical equivalence and observed their progress over the course of instruction. Although many children were able to articulate equivalence explanations by the end of the study, only a subset were able to generalize their understanding of equivalence to multiplication, and to maintain that understanding on a follow-up test two weeks later. That subset included only those children who went through a period in which their newest ideas were expressed exclusively in gesture (see Figure 9). Here again, gesture appears to be an important stepping-stone along the path to learning.

Gesture may also serve as a way station at the group level. Individual speakers use their hands to construct external representations. Because these representations are visible to all, they can help achieve common ground within the group. This common ground, in turn, can serve as the starting point for change. Gesture may thus function as an external touchstone, available to all participants in the conversation. As an example, Schwartz (1995) observed dyads attempting to solve the gear problems together, and found that the members often openly discussed their gestural representations. For example, one dyad member asked, "Is that the third or fourth gear?" while pointing at the other member's hands (Schwartz 1995, 332). Interestingly, by the second or third gear problem, the hand motions of the dyad members began to mirror one another, suggesting that the members had indeed achieved some sort of common ground, and that the hands had literally had a hand in this achievement.

Expressing knowledge in gesture may therefore represent an important step in the learning process for individuals and for groups. Karmiloff-Smith (1992) lays out a process of redescription in which action representations are continuously redescribed into different representational formats. The process culminates in a verbal format that brings with it explicit awareness. Because gesture supports a variety of representational formats that are distinct from those on which speech relies, gesture may play a unique role in this process of redescription and, as a result, a unique role in fostering cognitive change.

With and without Speech

We have come to the end of Part III. We now know that gesture not only has a communicative function for listeners but also has a function for speakers. Speakers gesture even when no one is watching, and for good reason. Gesturing can lighten a speaker's cognitive load, thus saving effort to expend on other tasks. Moreover, gesturing may even affect the course of thought, making some ideas salient and others not. We may be changing what we think just by moving our hands.

The hypothesis that gesture is causally involved in thinking could use more evidence. One point, however, is beyond question—gesturing is an integral part of the speaking process. Even speakers who are blind from birth and have never seen anyone gesture move their hands when they talk. The question to which we turn in Part IV is "what happens to gesture when there is no talk? when gesture itself must assume the full burden of communication?" Take, for example, congenitally deaf children whose profound hearing losses prevent them from acquiring the spoken language that surrounds them, and whose hearing parents have not yet exposed them to a conventional sign language. Spontaneously created gesture is the only accessible means of communicating that these children have, and they use it. We might guess that gesture in these children would assume the same form that it assumes when produced with speech. But this guess would be wrong.

In fact, gesture looks quite different when it is produced without speech and is forced to assume the full burden of communication on its own, as opposed to when it is produced with speech and shares with it the burden of communication. As we have seen, when produced along with speech, gesture is framed by that speech. It takes on a global and holistic form that is interpretable only within the framing that speech provides. In contrast, when produced on its own, gesture assumes the discrete and segmented form characteristic of all linguistic systems. It becomes languagelike. Thus gesture changes its form as it changes its context and its function.

In the remaining chapters, I explore this transformation over a number of timespans—historical time (for example, sign languages developed by deaf cultures, Chapter 13), ontogenetic time (for example, gesture systems invented by deaf children lacking exposure to sign language, Chapter 14), and momentary time (for example, gestures produced on the spot by hearing individuals asked to use their hands and not their mouths to communicate, Chapter 15). By examining gesture when it is produced without speech, we develop a more complete understanding of the forms and functions it assumes when it is produced with speech.

part four

When There Is Only Gesture

13

Gesture within a Community

The gestures that accompany speech share the burden of communication with that speech. They convey meaning but do so only in conjunction with the words that accompany them and frame them. These gestures assume a global and imagistic form created on the fly to capture the meaning of the moment. They are thus very different from speech, which has an established lexicon, codified rules of combination, and arbitrary standards of form.

The question that occupies us in Part IV is whether an imagistic form is inevitable in the manual modality (the modality of the hands rather than of the mouth). Does the manual modality assume this form whenever it is used in communication situations? What happens, for example, when speech is removed and gesture must do all of the communicative work on its own? Although gesture might retain its global and imagistic properties, it is just as likely that it will take on new properties better suited to its expanded role. When gesture accompanies speech, it is framed by that speech and is meaningful only within the framing. Removing the speech frame ought to have some effect on gestural form. And indeed it does.

In this chapter I describe a well-known situation in which the manual modality assumes the full burden of communication—deaf communities that develop sign languages which are then passed down from generation to generation. Although technically not gesture in the sense that I have been using the term in this book, sign languages are relevant to our discussion simply because they flesh out what we know about communication in the manual modality. We will find that, when called upon to assume the functions of language, the manual modality takes on the forms of language. Sign languages thus look quite different from the gestures that accompany speech. This transformation underscores the fact that communication using the manual modality does not have to be global and imagistic in form. When we do find that gesture assumes a global and imagistic form (as it does when it accompanies speech), we can be certain that this form is not an inevitable outgrowth of the manual modality and may instead reflect pressures on the thinking and talking process itself.

Linguistic Structure on the Hands

Perhaps the clearest example of the resilience of language comes from the fact that language is not tied to the mouth and ear but can be processed by the hand and eye. Deaf individuals around the globe use sign languages as their primary means of communication. These sign languages assume all of the functions of spoken languages. They are used to communicate not only about the here and now but also about worlds that are not present. They are used to direct, to advise, to declare, to joke, to pun—any functions that spoken languages serve can be, and are, filled by sign language.

Equally striking, sign languages assume the structural properties characteristic of spoken languages. At one point in their history, sign languages were thought to be nothing more than pantomimic systems lacking all linguistic structure. In 1960 William Stokoe began to challenge this view with the publication of *Sign Language Structure*. Stokoe argued that the signs of American Sign Language (ASL) are not global pantomimic wholes, but rather are composed of discrete meaningless units, akin to phonemes. The decades since Stokoe wrote have seen a steady stream of research on the structure of sign language, with a clear conclusion—sign languages have the same types of grammatical properties as spoken languages, and those properties are very different from those that characterize the gestures that accompany speech.

SIGNS: ARBITRARY STANDARDS OF FORM

Sign languages are autonomous systems that are not based on the spoken languages of hearing cultures (Bellugi and Studdert-Kennedy 1980; Klima and Bellugi 1979; Lane and Grosjean 1980). Thus the structure of ASL is distinct from the structure of English. Indeed, the structure of

American Sign Language is distinct from the structure of *British* Sign Language (BSL)—an observation which dramatically underscores the point that sign languages are not derivative from spoken languages.[1]

The fact that sign languages are not borrowed from spoken languages makes it that much more striking that they share many attributes with spoken languages. Like spoken languages, but unlike the gestures that accompany speech, sign languages adhere to standards of form. For example, the ASL sign for "candy" is made by rotating the tip of the index finger on the cheek. I cannot arbitrarily choose to, say, rotate the knuckle of my index finger on my cheek to mean "candy." In fact, if I do use my knuckle, I produce the sign for "apple." If I use my middle finger instead of my index finger, I produce no sign at all. It is easy to produce an incorrect sign, but it doesn't even make sense to talk about an incorrect gesture.

Indeed, the way in which a gesture is produced often varies across speakers. For example, three speakers described Sylvester's ascent up a drainpipe and gestured along with their descriptions. The first flicked a flat palm upward to denote the ascent. The second wiggled the two fingers of a "V" handshape as he moved his hand upward. The third produced a basketlike handshape and moved it upward (McNeill 1992, 125–126). Each of the three speakers used a different handshape (palm, "V," basketlike shape)—clearly there is more than one way to represent an ascending Sylvester in gesture. Note, however, that the three speakers did use the same motion in their gestures. McNeill (1992, 106) argues that the upward path found in all three gestures is there, not because of a recognized gestural lexicon, but because an upward path is the obvious motion to use to represent ascent—indeed, it's hard to imagine a gesturer producing anything other than an upward motion in this context. Thus gestures are rarely completely identical even when they are produced in the same context or to explain the same event. And when

1. There is a form of sign language that is derived from spoken language, but that form is not what I'm describing here. American educators of the deaf invented a variety of sign systems (Signing Essential English, Seeing Essential English, Signing Exact English, Signed English; Lou 1988) which, as a group, are referred to as Manually Coded English. These systems borrow signs from ASL and syntactic structure from English, and were created so that profoundly deaf children could learn the structure of English through the manual modality. Unfortunately, MCE systems are difficult to process (Marmor and Petitto 1979) and difficult to learn (Gee and Goodhart 1985; Goodhart 1984; Livingston 1983; S. Supalla 1991; Suty and Friel-Patti 1982). They are thus quite different from a natural sign language such as ASL or BSL.

they do share aspects of form it's because the gesturers have represented the same aspect of the scene in their gestures and have done so using the most obvious, often iconic, representation.

In contrast, one ASL signer's "candy" is always the same as another's, not by chance, but because there is a lexicon that the signers must adhere to if they wish to communicate with others in the ASL community. Thus unlike the gestures that accompany speech (but like all spoken languages), sign languages have established lexicons—a store of items with set meanings and forms that are arbitrarily paired. One of the best ways to demonstrate that the form-meaning pairings in a given sign language are arbitrary is to examine two different sign languages. Take, for example, American Sign Language and Chinese Sign Language (CSL). Klima and Bellugi (1979) have identified signs whose forms are the same in the two languages but whose meanings differ. As an example, bringing two fists together at chest level has the meaning "with" in ASL but "friend" in CSL. Even more striking, the subtle way in which the fist handshape is produced differs across the two languages. When an ASL signer produces a fist handshape, she holds her fingers loosely curved as they close against her palm with the back of her thumb touching her fingers and not protruding beyond them. In contrast, a CSL signer folds her fingers further onto her palm, creating a more rigid and angular shape and forcing her thumb to protrude beyond her fingers (Klima and Bellugi 1979).

Looking at other aspects of the lexicon, we find systematic distinctions of form that signers make, but that gesturers don't. For example, a gesturer can produce the same kind of gesture in a noun context and in a verb context—a twisting motion produced along with *jar* in "There's a jar over there" or along with *open* in "Can you open this please?" (see Goldin-Meadow et al. 1994; Petitto 1992). In other words, there is no formal distinction between nouns and verbs in gesture. However, there is such a distinction in sign. In ASL, for example, there are signs in which the noun form and the verb form resemble one another but, importantly for the point I am making here, are not completely identical. There are subtle—and systematic—distinctions between noun forms and verb forms. As an instance, the noun "chair" is produced by moving the index and middle fingers, slightly bent, of one hand down onto the index and middle fingers, also slightly bent, of the other hand; the motion is made with a tight and restrained manner and repeated several times. In contrast, the verb "sit" is produced with precisely the same handshapes; however, the downward motion is made with a longer and more fluid motion that is produced only once and ends in an abrupt stop (Supalla and Newport 1978). In general, the nouns are made with restrained manner, the verbs are not. There are standards of well-formedness that dictate how these and other signs should be produced, and native signers (like native speakers) know and adhere to those standards.

SIGNS: ICONICITY EASILY SACRIFICED

One of the most salient features of the manual modality is its potential for iconic representation—it's easy to represent opening a jar just by miming the action. Gesturing takes advantage of this potential. Indeed, its ability to convey information to listeners (and researchers) depends on it. The question is whether sign languages also exploit the potential for iconic representation offered by the manual modality.

As the examples in the preceding section illustrate, signs can be arbitrary pairings between form and meaning—there is nothing about an index finger rotating on the cheek that would call "candy" to mind in someone who did not already know the ASL sign. Many, indeed most, of the signs of ASL are arbitrary in this way. But there are signs in ASL that do have an iconic base. For example, in the sign for "bird," the index finger and thumb are held at the mouth and are moved together and apart several times. The sign looks like a bird's beak as it opens and closes.

The presence of iconicity in even a subset of signs seems, at least at first blush, to highlight the ties between gesture and sign language. But the interesting point about iconicity in sign is that, unlike iconicity in gesture, it is easily sacrificed. For example, the sign for "slow" in ASL is made by moving one hand across the back of the other hand. One could easily imagine that the sign for "very slow" would just be a sloweddown version of the original sign—moving the hand even more slowly across the back of the other hand. Surprisingly, however, when "slow" is modified to mean "very slow," the movement is actually made more rapidly, not more slowly. This is because the particular modification in ASL that indicates intensification involves an increase in motion, not a decrease (Klima and Bellugi 1979). Although the manual modality offers the potential for a relatively iconic mapping between form and meaning, in this instance, the rules of ASL do not permit the signer to take advantage of this potential. And the rules win—the sign for "very slow" is produced quite rapidly. In contrast, a gesture meaning "very slow" must be enacted slowly, else it will not convey its intended meaning.

There is evidence that iconicity is sacrificed in ASL over both historical and developmental time. For example, Frishberg (1975) examined changes that ASL has undergone over historical time, and found that there is a strong tendency for signs to become more arbitrary. In general, the changes sacrifice transparency in order to bring about internal consistency within the system. As an example, the old sign for "compare" was made by holding two flat hands, palms facing the signer, one hand to the signer's right, the other to the signer's left. The signer moved his or her eyes from one hand to the other, then brought the two hands together in the center of the body and focused on both hands at once—a relatively transparent rendition of comparing. In the modern-day sign, however, the two hands simply rotate around the wrists, either in alternation or in unison (Klima and Bellugi 1979, 71). The sign has assumed a less transparent shape, one that is easier to produce and more consistent with the principles that dictate good form in ASL.

We also see the relative unimportance of iconicity over developmental time. Children learning sign language from their deaf parents are exposed to both iconic and noniconic signs. If iconicity plays a large role in how sign languages are learned, we might expect children to acquire signs whose forms are transparently related to their meanings before they acquire signs whose forms are arbitrarily related to meaning. Indeed, when hearing adults learn ASL as a second language, they are often captivated by the iconicity of the language. Signs like "drink" (a cupped hand moved up at the mouth) or "tree" (the forearm extended vertically) are easy to remember and are very often the first signs these adult learners acquire. However, children don't seem to notice—or, at least, they fail to take advantage of—the iconicity in the signs they are learning. Only one-third of the first signs that children produce are iconic (Bonvillian and Folven 1993), and this third doesn't seem to change the nature of their early vocabularies. Their vocabularies are identical in size and scope to those developed by hearing children learning spoken languages that have no iconicity to speak of (Newport and Meier 1985).

All sign languages have some transparent signs and, in this sense, capitalize on the potential for iconic representation offered by the manual modality. Iconicity does not seem to be essential to sign language, however, as it is often sacrificed in the construction of signs and ignored in their acquisition. In this way, sign languages differ from the speech-accompanying gestures whose ability to convey meaning often depends crucially on iconicity.

SIGNS: PART OF A COMBINATORIAL SYSTEM

As described in Chapter 3, speech segments and linearizes meaning. What might be an instantaneous thought is divided up and strung out through time. A single event, say, a spider climbing up the wall, must be conveyed in segments—the spider, the movement, the direction, the wall. These segments are organized into a hierarchically structured string of words. The total effect is to transform what had been a single picture into a string of segments.

The gestures that accompany speech convey meaning without undergoing segmentation or linearization. Unlike spoken sentences in which lower constituents combine into higher constituents, each gesture is a complete expression of meaning unto itself. Thus a speaker who describes a spider climbing up the wall can produce a single gesture that incorporates all of the segments that must be strung out in speech—for example, extending the hand toward the wall and wiggling the fingers as the hand moves upward. Gestures as a whole are meaningful—they are not composed of meaningful parts and, in turn, do not combine to create larger wholes.

Segmentation and linearization are essential characteristics of all spoken languages. The question is whether they are also essential characteristics of sign languages, which, like gesture, have the potential to represent meaning more globally and simultaneously.

It turns out that sign languages, like spoken languages, are characterized by segmentation, and there are rules that dictate how those segments must be combined at each of the levels important to language—at the sentence level (that is, syntactic structure: Liddell 1980; Lillo-Martin 1986), at the word/sign level (that is, morphological structure: Klima and Bellugi 1979; Padden 1983; T. Supalla 1982), and at the level of meaningless units (that is, "phonological" structure: Lane, Boyes-Braem, and Bellugi 1976; Liddell 1984; Liddell and Johnson 1986; Sandler 1986; Wilbur 1986). As pointed out above, although all sign languages are structured, they (like spoken languages) differ in the particular structures they display. Thus ASL differs from Finnish Sign Language or Japanese Sign Language just as English differs from Finnish or Japanese.

Let's take as an example the way in which signs are constructed in ASL (that is, morphological structure). In English, we can construct words out of parts, or morphemes. For example, the verb "distrust" is composed of two morphemes—*dis-* and *trust*. Do signs have this kind of internal structure? Originally, all of the mimetic signs in ASL were assumed to have no structure whatsoever. They were thought to be built on an analog use of movement and space with movement mapped in a continuous, rather than discrete, fashion (Cohen, Namir, and Schlesinger 1977; DeMatteo 1977). In other words, mimetic signs were thought not to be divisible into component parts, but rather were considered unanalyzable lexical items that mapped, as wholes, onto events in the world—they were thought to be no different from gestures. Subsequent research, however, has found that these mimetic signs are indeed composed of combinations of a limited set of discrete morphemes (McDonald 1982; Newport 1981; Schick 1987; T. Supalla 1982). For example, to describe a drunk's weaving walk down a path, an ASL signer would not represent the idiosyncrasies of the drunk's particular meandering, but would instead use a conventional morpheme representing random movement (that is, a side-to-side motion) in conjunction with a conventional morpheme representing change of location (for example, a linear path).

What evidence do we have that these mimetic signs really are composed of smaller units in the minds of signers? One type of evidence comes from looking at how children approach signs of this sort at the early stages of learning ASL. They could treat these signs like pictures with essentially no internal structure. If so, they ought to acquire these complex multimorphemic forms relatively early—after all, in their eyes, the signs wouldn't be complex at all. If, however, children ignore the iconicity in these signs and approach them as complex combinations composed of smaller units, they should acquire these signs relatively late.

In fact, at no point during the ASL acquisition process do deaf children seem to consider multimorphemic signs to be unanalyzed pictorial representations. Rather, they treat multimorphemic signs as just that—combinations of discrete and separable morphemes. Thus children do find mimetic signs difficult, and they produce them correctly relatively late in development. Moreover, they deal with the complexity of these signs by unpacking the multiple morphemes within a sign (Newport 1981; T. Supalla 1982). Children begin by producing only one of the morphemes in a complex sign. For example, they move their hand in a linear path or they move it side to side, but not both. As they develop, the children continue to add morphemes to their signs, sometimes even producing the morphemes sequentially rather than simultaneously. For example, they might move their hand forward in a linear path followed by a side-to-side motion, rather than producing the two motions at the same time (moving the hand side to side as it goes forward). Only after several years do the children produce the adult sign, with manner and path conflated.

In sum, morphemes in sign are frequently produced simultaneously and are thus not easy to separate from one another. This makes them look like global gestures, but they really aren't—as even young deaf children just learning the language seem to know.

We have discovered that the manual modality is versatile—probably more versatile than the oral modality (a point to which we return at the end of Chapter 15). The manual modality can take on linguistic properties when it needs to, segmenting meanings into units and combining those units into larger wholes. But it can also eschew linguistic properties and assume a global and imagistic form when it is used in conjunction with speech. One nagging question remains—when the manual modality takes on linguistic properties, what happens to the functions typically served by gesture? Are they also served by the manual modality? In other words, do signers gesture?

Do Signers Gesture?

It's easy to distinguish the gestures speakers produce from their words—words come out of the mouth, and gestures come out of the hands. It's less easy to identify a signer's gestures. The key to distinguishing sign from gesture is the fact that signs belong to an acknowledged conventional system—gestures do not. Nevertheless, it's still not an easy matter to tell when a signer has produced a gesture. It's certainly not the case that any novel construction must automatically be considered a gesture. After all, speakers make up new words all the time; for example, someone made up "smurf" to refer to small purple creatures and "smurfing" to refer to their activities. Signers too make up new signs. How then can we tell that these new constructions are signs and not gestures?

In order to count as a sign (rather than as a gesture), novel constructions must conform to the rules of the particular sign language. Thus, for example, when a deaf child traces the shape of a suspension bridge after signing "I saw bridge there" (Marschark 1994), the trace is considered a gesture and not a sign because it does not adhere to the rules for constructing traces in ASL (tracing movements in ASL start with both hands together in one place; one hand moves away in one direction or both hands move in opposite directions, T. Supalla 1982; see also Emmorey and Casey 1995). The question is whether signers make clear-cut distinctions between gestures and signs. Emmorey (1999) suggests that they might, and gives pointing as an example. Points may be constructed differently when they serve as signs versus as gestures. Sign-points function as pronouns and are characterized by a single motion made with the index finger toward a person or location in space (Emmorey 1999, 148). In contrast, gesture-points can contain short, repeated motions and can be made with any part of the hand. In addition, sign-points occur in rule-governed positions within a sentence where gestures are not typically found (Emmory 1999, 149). We don't yet know how completely signers adhere to this distinction. For example, do signers avoid using an index finger in a single motion when they gesture, reserving the form for their signs? If so, they may have a completely unambiguous way of marking the distinction between gesture-points and sign-points. Distinctions of this sort would be useful, as they would make it relatively easy to separate sign from gesture.

Are the gestures that signers produce comparable to those produced by speakers? Emmorey (1999) suggests that in many ways they are not. First of all, signers do not gesture while they're signing. They can't—their hands are already occupied. What they do instead is stop signing in order to gesture. For example, a signer is describing a scene in which a boy peers over a log and gestures to his dog to be quiet and come over; the two then creep over to the log. He signs "look" and then "legged-creatures-move." In between the two signs, he produces a series of gestures: come-on, shh, come-on, thumb-point (in the same direction that the "look" sign pointed), what? (two hands flip over ending with the palms up), come-on. The sign "look" remains loosely articulated on one hand while the signer produces the gestures with the other (Emmorey 1999, 146). This may be as close as signers can come to gesturing while signing—but the signs and gestures are hardly cotemporal productions.

In fact, the gestures that accompany sign are closer to what McNeill (1992), following Kendon, calls "language-like gestures" than to "gesticulation" (or what I have been calling plain old gesture). Gesticulation almost never occurs in the absence of speech. In contrast, language-like gestures substitute for words and thus do not co-occur with them (Slama-Cazacu 1976). For example, the speaker says, "The parents were all right, but the kids were . . ." and finishes his sentence with a "crazy" gesture (winding his finger in circles near his temple; McNeill 1992, 37).

As another example, Clark and Gerrig (1990, 782) describe a speaker who says, "I got out of the car and I just . . ." and finishes the sentence by demonstrating turning around and bumping his head on an invisible telephone pole. In these cases, gesture is filling a grammatical slot, adjective in the first example, verb in the second. It is not co-occurring with speech—it is replacing it.

In addition, the gestures that signers produce do not depend on their surrounding signs for their meaning. Indeed, they are often more conventional than the gestures that speakers produce and thus do not require the framing context that speech typically provides. In the above example, "come-on," "shh," and "what?" are all emblems (Ekman and Friesen 1969; see Chapter 1)—gestures that are recognizable forms with specified meanings within American culture. They would be understandable whether or not they were accompanied by signs. Indeed, Emmorey (1999, 148) predicts that if viewers were shown a signer's gestures isolated from the surrounding signs (akin to studies described in Chapter 6), they would be much more accurate in assigning meanings to those gestures than if asked to assign meanings to gestures that had been isolated from their accompanying speech. If she's right, the gestures that accompany sign are less dependent on their host linguistic system than the gestures that accompany speech. Does this matter?

In one sense, no. The gestures that accompany signs are still able to serve one of the important functions that speech-accompanying gestures serve—they fill in gaps, giving signers freedom to express notions that they seem unable (for whatever reason) to express in their conventional language. But the gestures that accompany sign may not be able to serve all of the functions served by speech-accompanying gestures. Signers are more likely to be aware of their gestures than speakers are of theirs—signers have to stop signing to gesture and the gestures they produce are often relatively conventional. Because they may be more deliberate, the gestures that signers produce may not have access to their implicit thoughts, that is, the thoughts that they don't even know they have. For example, a young signer explaining how she solved a mathematical equivalence problem may not be able to express one problem-solving strategy in sign and another in gesture—in other words, she may not be able to use gesture to express thoughts that she cannot yet articulate in sign. If so, the gestures that accompany sign would lack what may be one of the most important functions gesture serves. This question is, of course, subject to empirical testing, and the results would be very interesting either way.

Before deciding this question one way or the other, however, we need to make sure that we have fully explored all of the forms that gesture in sign can take. For example, Liddell and Metzger (1998) suggest that gesture can be incorporated into the signs themselves and thus need not be produced only when sign isn't. As an instance, the verb "give" in its dictionary form is produced by directing the sign away from the body. However, when used in a sentence, the sign is directed toward the "givee." If that person happens to be on the scene, the "give" sign will be directed toward him or her; if the person is not there, a locus will be established that stands for this person and the sign will be directed toward that locus. In this way, the sign incorporates into its own form information that, according to Liddell and Metzger, is conveyed gesturally.

In general, the argument is that signs are constructed in space and the signer's use of space conveys a great deal of information. There is no disagreement among researchers that signers use space to convey information. There is disagreement, however, as to whether this use of space is grammatical or gestural. For example, Padden (1983) suggests that the directionality of these so-called inflecting verbs reflects agreement of the verb with its subject or object, in the same way that a verb in English "agrees with" its subject; in particular, the inflecting verb is said to agree with whether the subject is singular or plural (if the subject is singular, the verb is "gives"; if it's plural, the verb is "give"). Verbs in ASL agree with the person (I, you, he/she/it) of their subject or object. The first-person affix places the sign near the signer's body; the second-person affix places the sign in the direction of the addressee; and the third-person affix places the sign at the locus assigned to that entity. Under this view, the variations in sign placement are part of the linguistic system of ASL and are grammatically controlled (see also Fischer 1975, Lillo-Martin and Klima 1990, and Liddell and Johnson 1989 for other accounts that are also grammatically based).

One argument against the view that these spatial displacements are gestural is that they are obligatory on certain signs—they must be there in order for a sign to be considered well formed. However, Liddell (2000) points out that, at times, gestures can be obligatory too. Take, for example, the sentence "I'll take one of those." In order to be comprehensible, this sentence must be accompanied by a deictic gesture of some sort indicating the desired object. I have not really focused in this book on deictic gestures of this sort—gestures that speakers know they are producing. I have focused on the gestures that slip out of speakers' hands without their really noticing. In this sense, the spatial displacements found in ASL, be they gestural or grammatical, are distinct from the gestures that have occupied us in this book. They seem to be under relatively conscious control and thus are not likely to be able to capture a signer's implicit thoughts.

There are, however, other parts of the body at work besides the hands when signers communicate. Take, for example, the eyes. Where the eyes are directed can convey information, as in the example of a signer narrating a Garfield cartoon described by Liddell and Metzger (1998). The cat is sitting and watching TV in the cartoon and the signer produces a "look-at" gesture. While doing so, he gazes outward as if watching something. According to Liddell and Metzger, the signer's eye gaze indicates where the TV was relative to the cat—had the TV been higher, the signer would have elevated his gaze to convey that information. Thus if a signer's eyes gaze upward when describing a conversation between two participants, the listener might infer that one of the participants is much taller than the other. Undoubtedly, the signer knows of the unequal heights between the conversational partners, but he may have had no intention of conveying that information to the listener. In other words, information conveyed by eye gaze might be under less conscious control than information conveyed by placement of the hands (although see Bahan 1996, who suggests that eye gaze in ASL is also under grammatical control and marks object agreement). In this sense, eye gaze might qualify as a gesture for signers (one interesting question, of course, is whether eye gaze is gestural in the sense I have been using the term for speakers as well as for signers).

Several years ago, David McNeill and I, convinced of the importance of gesture to all human languages, including sign languages, speculated that mouth movements might be serving a gestural function for signers (Goldin-Meadow and McNeill 1999). Although such movements had often been observed in fluent signers (see Padden 1990), at the time no work had been conducted to investigate whether these behaviors serve for sign the function that gesture serves for speech. It turns out that our speculation may have been correct. Signers may gesture with their mouths.

Sandler (2003) described the way the mouth works in Israeli Sign Language (ISL). The mouth serves several functions in ISL that are clearly not gestural. For example, a small number of lexical signs in ISL require a mouth shape or movement of some kind—without the mouth, the sign is incorrect. As a second example, mouth movements can function as grammatical morphemes in ISL, for example, a rapidly repeated tongue flap co-occurring with a verb indicates that the activity described by the verb is distributed in time or place. But the mouth is also used for gestures in ISL. Unlike the linguistic mouth units, the mouth gestures are independent of the grammatical system. Moreover, they vary from signer to signer, as do the gestures that accompany speech.

For example, one signer in Sandler's (2003) study produced a sentence translated as "he emptied the water out of the pool." While signing, he passed air through his constricted lips, thus creating friction and representing how the water drained through a small opening. Like the manual gestures that accompany speech, this mouth gesture complements the message conveyed in sign, adding information about the way in which the water was emptied from the pool. Another signer produced a sentence translated as "he loaded the wagon with grass." While signing, she first puffed out her right cheek and then both of her cheeks. As the wagon filled, the puffing spread from one cheek to two, thus conveying the gradual accretion of grass not explicitly mentioned in her signs. Even more striking, a third signer produced a sentence translated as "he carried a suitcase," while puffing out his right cheek (he was signing with his right hand). The signer thus indicated that the suitcase was full with his mouth gesture, and only with his mouth gesture—a phenomenon reminiscent of the gesture-speech mismatches we find in speakers.

My assumption here is that the signers were not as aware of their mouth movements—and the information that those movements conveyed—as they were of their hand movements. The mouth movements were not obligatory and indeed had no grammatical role whatsoever. Mouth movements thus have the potential to capture a signer's unsigned thoughts much as gestures do for speakers.

It's even possible that a signer's use of space might serve this same function if it's done unwittingly. Emmorey (1999, 155) recounts an anecdote told by Elisabeth Engberg-Pedersen which suggests that signers can indeed use space meaningfully and unknowingly. The signer was videotaped describing a yearly meeting of the National Association of the Deaf. The signer indicated that the same group of people always came to these meetings, but that this year was different in that many "ordinary" deaf people attended. When this tape was shown to a group of deaf people, they laughed at just this point. When asked why, they all said that the signer had displayed her true opinion of this year's conference participants, and had done so by using a very low spatial location when referring to them. In this example, signing space carried meaning beyond identifying a referent. It metaphorically conveyed a sense of low status (see Lakoff and Johnson 1980), and thus seemed to reveal the speaker's inner thoughts—thoughts she may well have preferred to keep hidden.

Time, and more research, will tell whether signers frequently produce gestures that unwittingly convey information not found in their signs. If so, the next question is whether these gesture-sign mismatches function in the same way that gesture-speech mismatches do. Do they reveal information that the signer does not know she knows? Are they a signal— to researchers and to ordinary signers—that the signer has an unstable understanding of what she's describing and thus is ready to make progress on it? Do the gestures that the signer produces help her think? I'd guess yes, but at this point the verdict is far from clear.

14

Gesture by a Child

At this point, we know that the manual modality can, if necessary, rise to the occasion and take on the forms and functions of language—it can support a sign language. Sign languages are fully functioning linguistic systems that assume the full burden of communication. I have suggested that it is this communicative burden that causes sign languages to look quite different from the gestures that accompany speech. However, sign languages differ from speech-accompanying gestures in at least one other respect—they are systems that have histories and are passed down from one generation of users to the next. They are thus codified in a way that speech-accompanying gestures are not.

In this chapter, we take a look at noncodified gesture over developmental time, focusing on children who for one reason or another are limited in their use of speech and thus must turn to gesture. We ask about the roles that gesture assumes when speech falters, and we do so by observing children in three different situations:

- Children at the earliest stages of language learning, when they have to break into the spoken system and often use gesture to help them do it;

- Children who are having difficulty acquiring spoken language and often turn to gesture as a supplement or alternative;

- Children whose hearing losses prevent them from acquiring spoken language and whose hearing parents have not yet exposed them to a conventional sign language—they too turn to gesture.

We will see that, even when noncodified, the manual modality rises to the occasion. Gesture can fill in for speech, and when it does, it often assumes languagelike properties. Gesture takes on the functions of language and also its forms, particularly when the full burden of communication falls on its shoulders, as it does for the deaf children. In this situation, gesture is once again structurally closer to sign languages than it is to speech-accompanying gestures.

When Speech Is Just Beginning

At a time when children are limited in what they can say, there is another avenue of expression open to them, one that can extend the range of ideas they are able to express. Children can gesture—and they do. For example, in a group of twenty-three children learning Italian, all twenty-three used gestures, whereas only twenty-one used words. Moreover, the children's gestural vocabularies, on average, were twice the size of their speech vocabularies (11 gestures versus 5.5 words; Volterra and Iverson 1995). Strikingly, even deaf children acquiring sign language produce gestures and, at the earliest stages of language learning, they produce more gestures than signs (Capirci, Montanari, and Volterra 1998).

Beginning around ten months, children produce gestures that indicate an interest in objects—holding an object up for an adult's inspection, pointing at an object to draw an adult's attention to it, reaching for an object to indicate to an adult that they want it (Bates 1976; Bates et al. 1979). For some children, these gestural overtures precede their first spoken words by several months. Note that these early gestures are unlike nouns in that they rely heavily on context. An adult has to follow the pointing gesture's trajectory to its target in order to figure out which object the child means to indicate. Despite their reliance on the here-and-now, these gestures constitute an important early step in the development of symbols and pave the way for learning spoken language.

Take, for example, a study that we conducted on five children at the earliest stages of language learning (Iverson et al. 2000). We first looked at how many objects a child referred to using speech-only ("ball"), gesture-only (point at ball), or both ("ball" and point at ball, produced either at the same time or at any time during our observations). The children referred to a surprisingly small percentage of objects in speech-only, and an even smaller percentage in both speech and gesture. Over half of the objects the children mentioned were referred to in gesture-only. This pattern is consistent with the view that gesture serves a "bootstrapping" function in lexical development—it provides a way for the child to refer to objects in the environment without actually having to produce the appropriate verbal label.

Does this same pattern arise with respect to individual lexical items? In other words, does a lexical item enter a child's repertoire first in gesture, and then over time transfer to speech? To explore this question, we looked across a child's observation sessions and noted any time that the child referred to an object in more than one session. We then noted whether the references were all in the same modality, or switched from one modality to another (Iverson et al. 2000). We found that children used a single modality to refer to an object across sessions about a third of the time—and, as we have now come to expect, over 80 percent of this third were in gesture, not speech. The interesting cases are the ones where the child began referring to the object using one modality and then switched to the other, or began using both modalities. We found that, for the majority of objects, children indicated the object first in gesture (point at ball) and only in a later session indicated that object in speech ("ball"). Children referred to an object for the first time using both modalities relatively rarely, and referred to an object for the first time using speech-only even less often. Thus children not only use pointing and holding-up gestures as a class before they use words, but they frequently use these gestures to indicate a particular object prior to using a word for that very object. Gesture either reflects the child's interest in learning the name for a particular object, or it may even be paving the way for the child to learn that name.

At some point in development, of course, this pattern changes. As adults, we are certainly capable of introducing a word into our vocabularies in speech without a gestural precursor, and we often do so. But at the very beginning of language learning, simple pointing gestures appear to serve as a stepping-stone on the path toward acquiring particular vocabulary items.

In addition to pointing gestures, many children produce what McNeill (1992) calls iconic gestures. For example, a child might open and close her mouth to represent a fish, or flap her hands to represent a bird (Acredolo and Goodwyn 1985; Iverson, Capirci, and Caselli 1994). Unlike a pointing gesture, the form of an iconic gesture captures aspects of its intended referent—its meaning is consequently less dependent on context. These gestures therefore have the potential to function like words and, according to Goodwyn and Acredolo (1998, 70), they do just that. Children use their iconic gestures to label a wide range of objects (tractors, trees, rabbits, rain). They use them to describe how an object looks (big), how it feels (hot), and even whether it's there (all gone). They use them to request objects (bottle) and actions (out). And they combine these gestures with other gestures, and even with other words.

In a sense, these gestures have become words. Interestingly, however, there are differences across children, not only in how often they use iconic gestures, but also in whether they use these gestures when they cannot yet use words. Goodwyn and Acredolo (1993) compared the ages at which children first used words and iconic gestures symbolically. They found that the onset of words occurred at the same time as the onset of gestures for only thirteen of their twenty-two children. The other nine began producing gestural symbols at least one month before they began producing verbal symbols—some even began three months before. Importantly, none of the children produced verbal symbols before they produced gestural symbols. In other words, none of the children found words easier than gestures, but some did find gestures easier than words.

Not surprisingly, children drop their reliance on symbolic gestures over time. They use fewer gestural symbols once they begin to combine words with other words, whether the language they are learning is English (Acredolo and Goodwyn 1985, 1988) or Italian (Iverson, Capirci, and Caselli 1994). There thus appears to be a shift over developmental time—the young child seems to be willing to accept either gestural or verbal symbols; as the child ages, she begins to rely uniquely on verbal symbols. Indeed, Namy and Waxman (1988) have found experimental support for this developmental shift. They tried to teach eighteen- and twenty-six-month-old children novel words and novel gestures. Children at both ages learned the words, but only the *younger* children learned the gestures. The older children had already figured out that words, not gestures, carry the communicative burden in their worlds.

Thus children exploit the manual modality at the very earliest stages of language learning. Perhaps they do so because the manual modality presents fewer burdens. It certainly seems easier to produce a pointing gesture to indicate a bird than to articulate the word "bird." It may even be easier to generate a wing-flap motion than to say "bird"—children may need more motor control to make their mouths produce words than to make their hands produce gestures. Whatever the reason, gesture does seem to provide an early route to language learning, at least for some children.

What then happens to gesture over development? Gesture never really disappears, as is clear from the preceding chapters. However, gesture does seem to change its relation to speech. In very young children, gesture takes the place of speech, standing in its stead presumably because the child is not yet able to master the complexities of the spoken word. In contrast, later in childhood and in adulthood, gesture does not replace words but rather works alongside them, complementing speech so that the two modalities together provide a wealth of meaning that neither modality could provide on its own. The question is, when in development does gesture begin to assume this more adultlike function? The answer awaits future research.

When Speech Goes Awry

Some children have more than the usual amount of difficulty in breaking into the spoken-language system. Their progress may even be slow enough for them to be considered language delayed. Do these children, for whom the acquisition of speech has gone awry, turn to gesture?

Thal, Tobias, and Morrison (1991) observed a group of children in the one-word stage of language acquisition who were in the lowest 10 percent for their age group in terms of size of productive vocabulary. They characterized the children's verbal and gestural skills at the initial observation session when the children ranged in age from eighteen to twenty-nine months, and then observed each child again one year later. They found that some of the children were no longer delayed at the one-year follow-up—they had caught up to their peers. The interesting point about these so-called late bloomers is that they had actually shown signs of promise a year earlier—and they showed this promise in gesture. The late bloomers had performed significantly better on a series of gesture tests taken during the initial observation session than did the children who, a year later, were still delayed. Indeed, the late bloomers' gesture performance was no different from normally developing peers. Thus children whose language development was delayed but whose gestural development was not had a better prognosis than children who were delayed in both language and gesture. At the least, gesture seems to reflect skills that can help children recover from language delay—it may even be able to serve as one of those skills.

What happens to children who continue to be delayed at later stages of development? Some children fail to acquire age-appropriate language skills yet seem to have no other identifiable problems (that is, no emotional, neurological, visual, hearing, or intellectual impairments). Children who meet these criteria are diagnosed as having Specific Language Impairment (SLI). Evans, Alibali, and McNeil (2001) studied a group of SLI children ranging in age from seven to nine and a half years. They asked each child to participate in a series of Piagetian conservation tasks, and compared his or her performance with that of a group of normally developing children who were matched to the SLI children on the number of correct judgments they gave on the tasks. The task-matched normally developing children turned out to be somewhat younger (seven to eight) than the children with SLI (seven to nine and a half).

The question that Evans and her colleagues asked was whether the children with SLI would turn to gesture to alleviate the difficulties they had with spoken language. They found that the SLI children did not use gesture more often than the task-matched children without SLI—the rate of gestures per 10 words was comparable in both groups (2.40 and 2.14, respectively). However, the SLI children did display their competence in gesture, and did so more often than the task-matched children. The children with SLI were far more likely than the task-matched children to express information in their explanations that could only be found in gesture (in other words, to produce gesture-speech mismatches). For example, when asked whether the amount of water changes after it's poured from a tall thin glass into a short wide dish, an SLI child might indicate the height of the glass in words ("it's different because this one's taller"), while at the same time indicating its width in gesture.

Indeed, the children with SLI were likely to express relatively advanced reasoning when *both* their gestures and their speech were considered—more likely than the task-matched children without SLI. The two groups of children did not differ at all in the number of conserving explanations they gave in speech. When the children's gestures were coded along with their speech, however, the children with SLI ended up producing significantly more conserving explanations than the task-matched children without SLI. Note that, in the example given above, if we take both gesture and speech into account, the SLI child has expressed the essential components of a conserving explanation—the glass is not only taller than the dish but it is also thinner (the two dimensions can compensate for each other). The SLI children were older than the task-matched children and thus might be expected to know more about conservation—and, in fact, they did. However, all of their "extra" knowledge was in gesture. The children seemed to be using gesture as a way around their difficulties with speech.

Throughout development, speakers seem to be able to use gesture to detour around whatever roadblocks prevent them from expressing their ideas in words. These detours may not always be obvious to the ordinary listener, to the researcher, or even to the clinician. They may reside, not in how much a speaker gestures, but in the type of information the speaker conveys in those gestures. It is important to note that the gestures the SLI children produced did not form a substitute system replacing speech. Rather, the children's gestures seemed no different from the gestures that any speaker produces along with talk. As far as I can tell, the children with SLI were exploiting the gesture-speech system that all speakers employ, and using it effectively to work around their language difficulties.

When Speech Is Impossible

We turn, finally, to a situation in which children are unable to acquire spoken language. It's not, however, because they can't acquire language—it's because they can't hear. It turns out to be extremely difficult for deaf children with profound hearing losses to acquire spoken language. But if these children are exposed to sign language, they learn that language as naturally and effortlessly as hearing children learn spoken language (Lillo-Martin 1999; Newport and Meier 1985).

The problem is that most deaf children are not born to deaf parents who can provide them with input from a sign language from birth. Rather, 90 percent of deaf children are born to hearing parents (Hoffmeister and Wilbur 1980). These parents typically do not know sign language and would prefer that their deaf children learn the language that they and their relatives speak—in America, that's usually English. As a result, a number of profoundly deaf children of hearing parents are sent to oral schools for the deaf—schools that focus on developing a deaf child's oral potential, using visual and kinesthetic cues and eschewing sign language to do so. Unfortunately, most profoundly deaf children do not achieve the kind of proficiency in spoken language that hearing children do. Even with instruction, deaf children's acquisition of speech is markedly delayed when compared either with the acquisition of speech by hearing children of hearing parents or with the acquisition of sign by deaf children of deaf parents. By age five or six, and despite intensive early training programs, the average profoundly deaf child has only a very reduced oral linguistic capacity (Conrad 1979; Mayberry 1992; K. Meadow 1968).

Over the last two decades, my colleagues and I have studied deaf children who have not succeeded at mastering spoken language despite intensive oral education. In addition, at the time of our observations, these children had not been exposed to a conventional sign language by their hearing parents. The question we asked was whether deaf children in this situation turn to gesture to communicate with the hearing individuals in their worlds. If so, do the children use gestures in the same way that the hearing speakers who surround them do (that is, as though they were accompanying speech), or do they refashion their gestures into a linguistic system reminiscent of the sign languages of deaf communities?

It turns out that deaf children who are orally trained often communicate using their hands (Fant 1972; Lenneberg 1964; Mohay 1982; Moores 1974; Tervoort 1961). These hand movements even have a name— "home signs." It may not be all that surprising that these deaf children exploit the manual modality for the purposes of communication—after all, it is the only modality that is accessible to them, and they are likely to be seeing gesture used in communicative contexts when their hearing parents talk to them. It is surprising, however, that the deaf children's gestures turn out to be structured in languagelike ways (see Goldin-Meadow 2003).

Like hearing children at the earliest stages of language learning, deaf children who have not yet been exposed to sign language use both pointing gestures and iconic gestures to communicate. The difference, however, is that as they get older, the deaf children continue using their gestures as a primary communication system—the hearing children do not. Early on, hearing children use gesture on its own without any speech at all, just as the deaf children do. Over time, however, hearing children begin to fashion a single system out of gesture and speech— they produce gesture more often with speech than without it, and those gesture-speech combinations form integrated wholes in terms of both timing and meaning (see, for example, the Butcher and Goldin-Meadow 2000 study described in Chapter 2). In contrast, the deaf children continue to produce gesture on its own, and those gestures blossom in two ways. They take on the functions, and the forms, that are typically assumed by conventional language, either spoken or signed.

HOME SIGN ASSUMES THE FUNCTIONS OF LANGUAGE

Like hearing children learning spoken languages, the deaf children of hearing parents request objects and actions from others, but they do so using gesture. For example, Karen pointed at a nail and gestured "hammer" to ask her mother to hammer the nail. Moreover, and again like hearing children, these deaf children comment on the actions and attributes of objects and people in the room. For example, Chris gestured "march" and then pointed at a wind-up toy soldier to comment on the fact that the soldier was, at that very moment, marching.

Among language's most important functions is making reference to objects and events that are not perceptible to either the speaker or the listener—displaced reference (see Hockett 1960). Displacement allows us to describe a lost hat, to complain about a friend's slight, and to ask advice on college applications. Just like hearing children learning spoken languages, the deaf children communicate about nonpresent objects and events (Butcher, Mylander, and Goldin-Meadow 1991; J. Morford and Goldin-Meadow 1997). For example, David indicated that, in preparation for setting up the cardboard chimney for Christmas, the family was going to move a chair downstairs. He produced the following gesture sentences (the child neither paused nor broke the flow of movement within each gesture sentence):

He points at the chair and gestures "move-away."

He points at the chair and then points downstairs.

He gestures "chimney" in neutral space, "move-away" near the chair, and "move-here" near the chimney.

The deaf children also use their gestures to make generic statements (Goldin-Meadow, Gelman, and Mylander, n.d.). Generic statements ("birds fly") refer to an entire category of objects (all birds, not just the bird in my living room) and highlight qualities of that category that are essential, enduring, and timeless (flying, as opposed to having a broken wing). As an example, David produced a "fly" gesture to identify a picture of a bird that could not fly (the bird had its wings grasped firmly on the handlebars of the bicycle it was riding). David was using gesture to highlight a property that is true of the class of birds but is not true of the particular bird to which he was referring. The deaf children use their gestures to make generic statements about animals more often than artifacts. This same animacy bias is found in the generic statements that hearing adults (Gelman and Tardif 1998) and hearing children (Goldin-Meadow, Gelman, and Mylander n.d.) make with their words. The bias seems to reflect the essential difference between animals and artifacts—animals are natural kinds, concepts with many similarities in common that promote rich inferences and can lead to generic statements; artifacts are not (Gelman 1988). Thus the deaf children use gesture to talk not only about individual objects right in front of them but also about classes of objects that need to be constructed.

The deaf children even use their gestures to tell stories (Phillips, Goldin-Meadow, and Miller, 2001). They tell stories about events they or others have experienced in the past, events they hope will occur in the future, and events that are flights of imagination. For example, in response to a picture of a car, Marvin produced the following two-sentence narrative:

He gestures "break" (two fists breaking apart in the air), gestures "away" (hand arcs away from the body), points at his dad, and then gestures "car-goes-onto-truck" (flat right hand glides onto back of flat left hand).

He gestures "crash" and then gestures "away."

Roughly translated, these gesture sentences mean, "Dad's car broke and went onto a tow truck. It crashed." Note that, in addition to producing gestures to describe the event itself, Marvin produced an "away" gesture, which we have called a narrative marker (J. Morford and Goldin-Meadow 1997). Marvin recognized that he was not talking about an event that was taking place in the here-and-now. Rather, he was describing a real event that happened in another time and place. He indicated this stance with his "away" gesture. The "away" gesture marks a piece of gestural discourse as a narrative in the same way that "once upon a time" is often used to signal a story in spoken discourse.

In addition to using their gestures to communicate with others, the deaf children also use their gestures for a number of the other, more exotic functions that language serves. For example, we occasionally caught a deaf child using his gestures when he thought no one was paying attention, as though "talking" to himself. David and his hearing sister were sitting side by side playing with clay and not with each other. David needed a plastic knife to cut the clay. He got up, looked around, and without making eye contact with any of the people in the room, produced a "where" flip and then a point at his chest, as though asking himself where the object that belonged to him was.

Another important use of language is its metalinguistic function—using language to talk about language. Occasionally, the deaf children used gesture to refer to their own gestures. For example, to request a Donald Duck toy that an adult held behind her back, David pursed his lips, thus referring to the Donald Duck toy. He then pointed at his own pursed lips and pointed toward the Donald Duck toy. When the adult offered him a Mickey Mouse toy instead, he shook his head, pursed his lips and pointed at his own pursed lips once again (Goldin-Meadow 1993). The point at his own lips is roughly comparable to the words "I say," as in "I say 'Donald Duck.' " It therefore represents a communicative act in which gesture is used to refer to a particular act of gesturing and, in this sense, is reminiscent of young hearing children's quoted speech (see Miller and Hoogstra 1989).

Finally, the deaf children also used gesture to comment on the gestures of others. For example, David and his hearing sister were, in turn, responding to videotaped scenes of objects moving in space. David was using his home sign system to describe the scenes, and his sister was inventing gestures on the spot (see Singleton, Morford, and Goldin-Meadow 1993 and also Chapter 15). David considered his sister's response to be inappropriate on a number of the items, and he used his own gestures to correct her gestures. On one scene, the sister extended her index finger and thumb, as though holding a small object, to describe a tree. Reacting to her choice of handshape, David teased his sister by reproducing the handshape, pretending to gesture with it, and finally completely ridiculing the handshape by using it to poke himself in the eye. His sister then shrugged and said, "okay, so what should I do?"—a reaction that both acknowledged the fact that there was a system of which David was the keeper, and admitted her ignorance of this system. David then indicated that a point handshape would be a correct way to respond to this item (a point handshape is, in fact, an appropriate handshape for straight thin objects, and therefore an appropriate handshape for a tree in David's gesture system; see Goldin-Meadow, Mylander, and Butcher 1995). Thus not only did the deaf child produce gestures that adhered to the standards of his system, but he also used his gestures to impose those standards on the gestures of others.

In sum, unlike hearing children who rely on speech to fulfill language's many functions, the deaf children use gesture. In addition to calling upon gesture for the well-known communicative functions that language serves, the deaf children extend their use of gesture to the functions that give language its uniqueness (talking about things that aren't there, talking to oneself, talking about talk). The children are able to distance themselves from their own and others' gestures and treat them as objects to be reflected on and referred to. They therefore exhibit in their self-styled gesture systems the very beginnings of the reflexive capacity that is found in all languages and that underlies much of the power of language (see Lucy 1993).

HOME SIGN ASSUMES THE FORMS OF LANGUAGE

As mentioned earlier, pointing gestures are not words. The pointing gesture directs a communication partner's gaze toward a particular person, place, or thing, but doesn't specify anything about that entity. Despite this fundamental difference, pointing gestures function for the deaf children in our studies as object-referring words (nouns and pronouns) do for hearing children. They do so in three ways:

- The deaf children use their pointing gestures to refer to precisely the same range of objects that young hearing children refer to with their words—and in precisely the same distribution (Feldman, Goldin-Meadow, and Gleitman 1978, 380).
- The deaf children combine their pointing gestures with other points and with iconic gestures just as hearing children combine their object-referring words with other words (Goldin-Meadow and Feldman 1977; Goldin-Meadow and Mylander 1984).
- The deaf children use their pointing gestures to refer to objects that are not visible in the room just as hearing children use words for this function. For example, a deaf child points at the chair at the head of the dining room table and then gestures "sleep"; this chair is where the child's father typically sits, and the child is telling us that his father (denoted by the chair) is currently asleep in another room (Butcher, Mylander, and Goldin-Meadow 1991).

Iconic gestures also differ from words. The form of an iconic gesture captures an aspect of its referent. The form of a word does not. Interestingly, as I noted in Chapter 13, although iconicity is present in many of the signs of ASL, deaf children learning ASL do not seem to notice. Most of their early signs are either not iconic (Bonvillian, Orlansky, and Novack 1983) or, if iconic from an adult's point of view, not recognized as iconic by the child (Schlesinger 1978). In contrast, the deaf children in our studies are forced by their social situation to create gestures that not only begin transparently but remain so. If they didn't, no one in their worlds would be able to take any meaning from the gestures they created (remember that the children's hearing parents were interested in having their children learn to talk, not learn to gesture; they therefore paid little or no explicit attention to their children's gestures).

Although unlike conventional languages in terms of the importance of iconicity, the deaf children's gestures resemble conventional languages in that they have a stable store of lexical items. The deaf children could, of course, create each gesture anew every time they use it, as hearing speakers seem to do (McNeill 1992). If so, we might expect some consistency in the forms the gestures take simply because the gestures are iconic and iconicity constrains the set of forms that can be used to convey a meaning. However, in this event, we might also expect a great deal of variability around a prototypical form—variability that would crop up simply because each situation is a little different, and a gesture created specifically for that situation is likely to reflect that difference. In fact, it turns out that there is relatively little variability in the set of forms a deaf child uses to convey a particular meaning. The child tends to use the same form, say, two fists breaking apart in a short arc, to mean "break" every single time that child gestures about breaking, no matter whether it's a cup breaking, or a piece of chalk, or a car (Goldin-Meadow et al. 1994). Thus the deaf child's gestures adhere to standards of form, just as a hearing child's words do. The difference is that the deaf children's standards are idiosyncratic to that child rather than shared by a community of language users.

One of the biggest differences between the deaf children's gestures and those that hearing children use is that the deaf children often combine their gestures into sentencelike strings. For example, David combined a point at a toy grape with an "eat" gesture to comment on the fact that grapes can be eaten, and at another time combined the "eat" gesture with a point at me to invite me to lunch with the family. The deaf children even combine their gestures into sentences that convey more than one proposition; that is, they produce complex gesture sentences. Take, for example, David, who was looking at a picture of a shovel stuck in sand. Inspired by this picture, he used gesture to describe what you do with a snow shovel. Without pausing or breaking the flow of his motion, he produced the following complex gesture sentence (Figure 24):

> He gestures "dig," points at a picture of a shovel, gestures "pull-on-boots," points outside, points downstairs, points at the shovel picture, gestures "dig," and gestures "pull-on-boots."

The child has strung a series of gestures together to convey several propositions about the snow shovel: how it's used (to dig), when it's used (when boots are worn), where it's used (outside), and where it's kept (downstairs).

Moreover, and equally important, the deaf children's gesture combinations function like the spoken sentences that hearing children produce in a number of respects.

- They convey the meanings that young hearing children learning spoken languages typically convey with both their single-proposition and their multiproposition sentences (Goldin-Meadow and Mylander 1984).

- They are structured at underlying levels just like the early sentences of hearing children (Goldin-Meadow 1985). For example, the framework underlying a gesture sentence about giving contains three arguments—the giver (actor), the given (patient or object acted upon), and the givee (recipient). In contrast, the framework underlying a sentence about eating contains two—the eater (actor) and the eaten (patient).

- They are structured at surface levels, containing many of the devices to mark "who does what to whom" that are found in the early sentences of hearing children (Goldin-Meadow and Mylander, 1984, 1998; Goldin-Meadow et al., 1994).

In terms of structure at the surface level, the deaf children use three distinct devices to indicate objects that play different thematic roles—in other words, to indicate who is the doer and who is the done-to in a gesture sentence:

- The children preferentially produce (as opposed to omit) gestures for objects playing particular roles (for example, they point at the drum, the patient, as opposed to the drummer, the actor).

- The children place gestures for objects playing particular roles in set positions in a gesture sentence (for example, they produce the gesture for the patient, "drum," before the gesture for the act, "beat").

- The children displace verb gestures toward objects playing particular roles (for example, they produce the "beat" gesture near the patient, the drum).

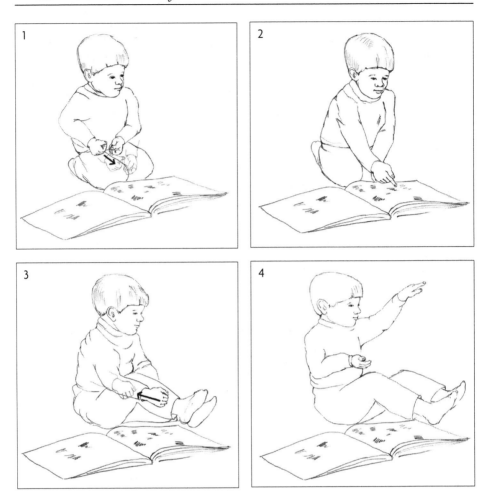

Figure 24 (above and on facing page). A deaf child producing a complex gesture sentence in home sign. This child uses gesture as his only means of communication. In this example, he produces a "dig" gesture (frame 1), points at a picture of a shovel (frame 2), produces a "pull-on-boots" gesture (frame 3), points outside where shovels are used (frame 4), points downstairs where shovels are kept (frame 5), and then repeats the point at shovel (frame 6), "dig" (frame 7), and "pull-on-boots" (frame 8) gestures. The child produced all of these gestures without breaking the flow of movement, and thus conveyed several propositions within the bounds of a single gesture string.

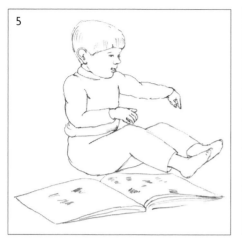

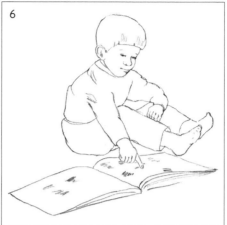

The gesture sentences therefore adhere to rules of syntax, albeit simple ones.

On this basis, the deaf children's gesture combinations warrant the label "sentence." And consequently the deaf children's gestures seem to resemble hearing children's *words*—not their gestures. The deaf children's gestures are distinct from hearing children's gestures in having a set of elements (gestures) that combine systematically to form novel larger units (sentences).

What further distinguishes the deaf children's gestures is the fact that this combinatorial feature is found at yet another level—the gestures that combine to form sentences are themselves composed of parts (morphemes). For example, on one occasion, I was being deliberately obtuse with David, who had produced the following (perfectly understandable) gesture to ask me to put a penny down flat (I had put the penny on its edge so that it stood vertically in the slot of a bank rather than horizontally)—David had formed his index finger and thumb into an O-shape indicating the round penny and moved the O downward in a short arc as though placing it flat. Disgusted with my apparent inability (or unwillingness) to understand his gesture, David then broke his gesture into two distinct parts—he produced the pennylike O-shape, holding it still in the air; he then changed his handshape to a flat palm and moved his palm downward in an arc. The gesture had decomposed into its handshape (O) and motion (short arc) parts right before my eyes. It is very likely that David altered his original gesture because it didn't achieve the results he wanted. The fact that he used a "breaking-gestures-into-parts" strategy when frustrated, however, suggests that his gestures do have parts.

Indeed, in systematic analyses of the iconic gestures produced by four deaf children, we found that each child had developed his or her own morphological system that could account for almost all of the gestures the child produced (Goldin-Meadow, Mylander, and Butcher 1995). Each gesture is composed of a handshape component (for example, the O-handshape representing the roundness of a penny) and a motion component (for example, the short arc motion representing a putting-down action). The meaning of the gesture as a whole is simply a combination of the meanings of its parts ("round-put-down").

There is one final characteristic of the deaf children's gestures that distinguishes them from hearing children's gestures—gestures serving nounlike functions are different in form from gestures serving verblike functions. For example, if a deaf child using home signs were to use his "twist" gesture as a noun to mean "jar," he would abbreviate the form (producing only one rotation rather than several) and would place it at chest level (rather than near the jar itself). In contrast, if he were to use the same "twist" gesture as a verb to mean "twist open," he would produce the full form of the gesture (with all of its rotations) and would place it near the jar. Not only does the way in which the gesture is produced vary as a function of its use as a noun or a verb, but where the gesture appears in a sentence also varies. If the "twist" is used as a noun, it is likely to be placed in first position, before the point at the jar.

If, however, the "twist" is used as a verb, it is likely to be placed in the second position of a two-gesture sentence, that is, after a point at the jar (Goldin-Meadow et al. 1994).

Thus the deaf children's gestures resemble conventional languages, both signed and spoken, in having a stable lexicon, having combinatorial regularities at both the sentence and the word levels, and having a noun-verb distinction. The deaf children have invented gesture systems that contain many of the basic properties found in all natural languages. It is important to note, however, that the deaf children's gesture systems are not full-blown languages—they are not ASL and for good reason. The children in our studies are inventing their gesture systems on their own without a community of communication partners (the deaf children's hearing parents never learn their children's gesture systems; see the next section). Indeed, when home sign children are brought together into a community (as they were in Nicaragua after the first school for the deaf was opened in the late 1970s), their sign systems begin to cohere into a recognized and shared language. That language becomes increasingly complex, particularly after a new generation of deaf children learns the system as a native language (Kegl, Senghas, and Coppola 1999; Senghas 1995, 2000; Senghas et al. 1997). The manual modality can take on linguistic properties, even in the hands of a young child not yet exposed to a conventional language model. But it grows into a full-blown language only with the support of a community that can transmit the system to the next generation.

GESTURES: DEAF CHILDREN'S VERSUS THEIR PARENTS'

The deaf children in our studies had not been exposed to a conventional sign language and thus could not have fashioned their gesture systems after such a model. They were, however, exposed to the gestures that their parents used when they talked to them. Although we know that the gestures hearing speakers typically produce when they talk are not characterized by languagelike properties, it is possible that the gestures produced by the hearing parents of these deaf children were not typical. Perhaps the deaf children's hearing parents introduced languagelike properties into their own gestures. If so, these gestures could have served as a model for the structure in their deaf children's gestures.

Hearing parents gesture when they talk to young children (Bekken 1989; Iverson et al. 1999; Shatz 1982), and the hearing parents of our deaf children were no exception. The children's parents were committed to teaching them to talk and therefore talked to their children as often as they could. And when they talked, they gestured. The question is whether these gestures displayed the languagelike properties found in the deaf children's gestures, or whether they looked just like any hearing speaker's gestures.

To find out, we selected six deaf children whose mothers were captured on the videotapes we took of their children's play sessions. We analyzed the gestures these mothers produced when they addressed their children. In each case, the mother was the child's primary caretaker. We used the analytic tools developed to describe the deaf children's gestures to describe the mothers' gestures. We turned off the sound and coded the mothers' gestures as though they had been produced without speech. In other words, we attempted to look at the gestures through the eyes of a child who cannot hear.

Not surprisingly, we found that all six mothers used both pointing and iconic gestures when they talked to their children. Moreover, the mothers used pointing and iconic gestures in roughly the same distribution as their children. However, the mothers' use of gestures did not resemble their children's along many dimensions.

The mothers produced fewer different types of iconic gestures than their children, and they also used only a small subset of the particular iconic gestures that their children used (Goldin-Meadow and Mylander 1983, 1984).

In addition, the mothers produced very few gesture combinations—that is, like most English speakers (McNeill 1992), they tended to produce one gesture per spoken clause and rarely combined several gestures into a single, motorically uninterrupted unit. Moreover, the very few gesture combinations that the mothers did produce did not exhibit the same structural regularities as their children's combinations (Goldin-Meadow and Mylander 1983, 1984). The mothers thus did not appear to have structured their gestures at the sentence level.

Nor did the mothers structure their gestures at the word level. Each mother used her gestures in a more restricted way than her child, omitting many of the handshape and motion morphemes that the child produced (or using the ones she did produce more narrowly than the child), and omitting completely a very large number of the handshape/motion combinations that the child produced. Indeed, there was no evidence at all that the mothers' gestures could be broken into meaningful and consistent parts (Goldin-Meadow, Mylander, and Butcher 1995).

Finally, the deaf child's iconic gestures were stable in form and meaning over time; the hearing mother's gestures were not. Moreover, the deaf child introduced into his gesture system a consistent distinction between gestures serving a noun role and gestures serving a verb role; the mother did not (Goldin-Meadow et al. 1994).

So did the deaf children learn to structure their gesture systems from their mothers? Probably not—although it may have been necessary for the children to see hearing people gesturing in communicative situations in order to get the idea that gesture can be appropriated for the purposes of communication. But in terms of how the children structured their gestured communications, there is no evidence that this structure came from the children's hearing mothers. The hearing mothers' gestures do not have structure when looked at with the tools that we use to describe the deaf children's gestures (although they do when looked at with the tools used to describe hearing speakers' gestures, that is, when they are described in relation to speech).

The hearing mothers interacted with their deaf children on a daily basis. We therefore might have expected that their gestures would eventually have come to resemble their children's gestures (or vice versa). But they didn't. Why not—why didn't the hearing parents display languagelike properties in their gestures?

It should be clear from the arguments made throughout this book that, in a very real sense, the deaf children's hearing parents did not have the option of altering their gestures. The parents were interested in teaching their deaf children to talk, not gesture. They therefore produced all of their gestures with talk—in other words, their gestures were speech-accompanying gestures and had to behave accordingly. The gestures had to fit, both temporally and semantically, with the speech they were produced with. As a result, the hearing parents' gestures were not "free" to take on languagelike properties.

In contrast, the deaf children had no such constraints on their gestures. They had no productive speech and thus always produced gesture on its own, without talk. Moreover, because gesture was the only means of communication open to these children, it had to take on the full burden of communication. The result was languagelike structure. Although the deaf children may have used their hearing parents' gestures as a starting place, they went well beyond that point. They transformed the speech-accompanying gestures they saw into a system that looks very much like language.

Throughout my observations of deaf children inventing their own gesture systems, I constantly had the feeling that if the children's hearing parents had merely refrained from speaking as they gestured, their gestures would have become more languagelike in structure. They would have begun to assume the segmented and combinatorial form characteristic of the children's gestures. In other words, the mothers might have been more likely to use gestures that mirrored their children's if they kept their mouths closed. The next chapter constitutes an experimental test of this hunch.

15

Gesture on the Spot

When the manual modality is asked to carry the full burden of communication, it not only behaves like a language, it looks like one. And it looks like language whether it is being used by a community of signers over generations or by a single deaf child in early childhood. The question now is whether the manual modality assumes linguistic properties even over very short timespans. What if we prevented speakers from using the oral modality and asked them to communicate on the spot using only their hands? Would these speakers-turned-signers continue to use their hands in a global and imagistic fashion, or would they begin to introduce linguistic properties into their gestures?

Situations That Make Speech Impossible

There are times when speech is impossible—when noise makes it difficult to hear, when the rules require silence, or when no one shares a common spoken language. Under circumstances of this sort, speakers sometimes turn to their hands; they develop sign systems (Wundt [1900] 1973). These speech surrogates have been called "alternate sign languages" (Kendon 1990), although they are not, in fact, as morphologically or syntactically complex as sign languages developed by deaf communities. They are sign systems developed by people already in full command of speech to serve some of the functions of speech. In each case, a core of signs is developed to fill a particular need. Once developed, that core is extended to serve other purposes.

Let's look first at the effect of noise. Interestingly, sign systems do not arise in all noisy situations, but they do crop up in sawmills (Meissner and Philpott 1975). The operations of a sawmill are so noisy that spoken conversation among workers is impossible. There are times, however, when information needs to be transmitted from one workstation to another, and a system of hand signals has grown up so that this information can be exchanged. The system began with a list of number signs, standardized for use in mills throughout British Columbia (number signs indicate how many inches the log is to be moved forward for the next cut). This list is the official part of the language, and all that is recognized by management. The actual system, however, includes signs for many other technical terms—signs for major pieces of equipment, for specific operations, and for specific people (identified by number, job, or ethnicity—for example, drawing a circle above the head to indicate a Sikh turban). The system can therefore be used for a variety of purposes, problem control among them. For example, the head sawyer in a mill once gave a light signal that would have resulted in sending a work piece to the wrong destination. The sawyer gestured to the setter, "I push-button wrong tell lever man." The setter then gestured to the lever man and the piece was retrieved and sent to the right place—all in a matter of seconds (Meissner and Philpott 1975, 297).

The system is also used to discuss topics not likely to be sanctioned by management. For example, the sign for "a little bit" (rubbing index finger and thumb together) tells the setter to advance the log a little more. In its extended use, it refers to sexual intercourse, as in "I think I go home get a-little-bit" (Meissner and Philpott 1975, 299). To meet an array of uses, new signs are created and old signs are combined to create new meanings. For example, "knocked-up" means "pregnant" and is formed by two simple and obvious signs, "knock" and "up." A worker who gets fired gets his walking papers, and the signs are "walk" and "paper" (Meissner and Philpott 1975, 300). Thus although there is a set of items that constitute the "lexicon" of the sawmill sign system, the system is not constrained by that lexicon or, for that matter, by any apparent rules at all. It is open to instant innovation—any sign is admissible as long as it works, where "works" is defined as being understood.

Talk can be curtailed not only by the physical layout, but also by the social world. For example, Benedictine monastic orders (including the Cluniacs, Cistercians, and Trappists) follow a rule of silence as an essential part of their religious observance. Although not allowed to talk, the monks have always been allowed a minimal amount of communication using their hands (Umiker-Sebeok and Sebeok 1987). Indeed, lists of permitted signs were first drawn up in the tenth century, although signs were almost certainly in use in monasteries even before these lists were made (Kendon 1990). The lists served two purposes—to standardize the signs in use and to specify the topics that the monks were permitted to sign about. However, as in the sawmills, the official sign lists were only the beginning. Unofficial, and very different, signs cropped up in each monastery and were combined creatively. Signers simply put together as many signs as were needed to convey a given meaning; for example, "Easter" can be signed as "God + up + day," "literature" as "read + all + beautiful + writing" (Kendon 1990, 321). The resulting sign systems ended up being so varied that visiting brothers often found they could not easily communicate beyond officially sanctioned topics using sign.

Central desert Australian Aboriginal women, who are not permitted to talk when in mourning, are a second example of a social constraint on speaking. These women are, however, permitted to communicate, and they do so using their hands (Kendon 1988). Here again, the signs constructed for this ritual use have been extended to nonritual contexts—when speech is difficult, when the speaker is angry, or when the discussion involves matters that are private or deserve respect. Interestingly, these signs differ from the sawmill and monastic signs in that they are more dependent on spoken language. Perhaps because the Aboriginal sign system can be used along with speech (although during periods of mourning, of course, it is not), it has adopted forms reminiscent of that speech. The signs are ordered in the same way within signed discourse as are words within spoken discourse, and many of the signs are derived from spoken lexical items (Kendon 1990). For example, the spoken word for "understand" is *pina ja-nta,* which is a compound composed of two forms: *pina,* meaning "ear" and *ja-nta,* meaning "stand"; the sign is similarly composed of two forms: the index and little fingers directed toward the ear ("ear") and an upright index finger moved forward slightly ("stand"). Thus, rather than create a visual representation that captures the meaning "understand," Aboriginal signers often create signs that borrow from the structure of their words.

A final example is the sign language of the Plains Indians of North America (Mallery [1881] 1972). This system arose as a form of communication among groups of Indians who did not share a spoken language. Although this sign system too has a stable store of lexical items, there are also strategies available for making up new signs. Interestingly, of all the alternate sign systems, this is the one that is least closely tied to spoken language and has the greatest number of features reminiscent of sign languages created by deaf communities (Kendon 1990).

These examples of alternate sign systems underscore once again that when communication is prevented from coming out of the mouth, it manages to come out of the hands. And when it does, it seems the first order of business is to construct words. It is, however, difficult to know whether the words in these alternate sign systems really constitute a system—that is, whether they are part of anything like a grammar—because most of the analyses that have been done on these sign systems have focused on vocabulary and have not looked carefully at how signs are combined to form sentences. Moreover, although I have put forth these alternate sign systems as examples of inventions over the short term (and for the individual users, there does seem to be a great deal of on-the-spot creativity involved), these systems do have histories—in some cases, very long histories. If we are interested in figuring out whether the manual modality can take on linguistic properties over the short term, we may have to create the situations we need experimentally—ask people to use their hands, rather than their mouths, to communicate.

Experiments That Make Speech Impossible

As we have seen, hearing speakers routinely use gesture when they talk, and those gestures are not languagelike in structure. The question we ask here is whether these gestures immediately become languagelike when speech is prevented and the gestures themselves must assume the full burden of communication. To address this question, we asked adult English speakers to describe scenes both with and without speech, and then compared the gestures the adults produced in each situation. We were interested in knowing whether the gestures the adults produced without speech would be segmented and combined into sentencelike strings. In other words, would they be distinct from the gestures that these same adults produced when describing the scenes with speech?

SEGMENTATION AND COMBINATION APPEAR IMMEDIATELY

Only English speakers who had no knowledge of sign language participated in the study (Goldin-Meadow, McNeill, and Singleton 1996). We showed the adults videotaped vignettes of objects and people moving in space taken from the test battery designed by Supalla, Newport, and their colleagues (n.d.) to assess knowledge of ASL. Half the scenes contained only one moving object (for example, a porcupine wandering across the screen); the other half contained one moving object and one stationary object (for example, a girl jumping into a hoop; a donut-shaped object rising out of an ashtray). The adults were asked to describe each event depicted on the videotape twice, first using speech and then, in a second pass through the scenes, using only their hands. We examined whatever gestures the adults produced in their first pass through the events (the gesture + speech condition) and compared them with the gestures they produced in their second pass (the gesture condition). As predicted, we found differences in the gestures produced in the two conditions—gesture changes its form as soon as it is asked to change its function.

As we would expect from the descriptions of speech-accompanying gestures presented in earlier chapters, in the gesture + speech condition, the adults produced gestures that represented actions and objects, but they used those gestures as representations for global wholes rather than as segmented building blocks for larger units. In contrast, in the gesture condition, although the gestures that the adults produced also represented actions and objects, those gestures were easily segmentable (with crisp handshapes and demarcated motions) and were often combined with one another into strings of connected gestures (the adult's hands did not return to a resting position between gestures but were in constant motion). Moreover, and most important, the gesture strings that the adults produced in the gesture condition were reliably ordered, with gestures for certain semantic elements occurring in particular positions in the string.

As an example, consider Figure 25. Frame A displays one of the videotaped vignettes that the adults in this study saw—a donut-shaped object rising on its own in an arc out of an ashtray and landing nearby on the table. When asked to describe the scene in words, the adult said, "a crooked circular donut shape moved from out . . . from within a yellow ashtray." He produced several gestures along with his verbal description, but the gestures were not connected to one another—that is, he produced a single gesture and then returned his hands to a resting state before producing another single gesture. His first gesture was a small arcing motion away from his body made with his left hand in no particular shape (= arc; frame B1). He paused, returning his hands to his lap (frame B2), and then made a larger arcing motion that crossed space, this time with his hand in a loose "O" shape (= arc-out; frame B3). He paused again (frame B4), and then pointed toward the spot where his arc had begun and rotated his hand twice in the air (= ashtray; frame B5).

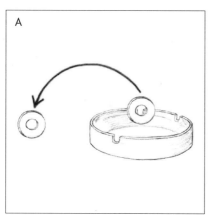

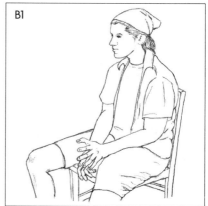

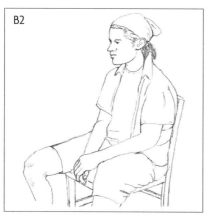

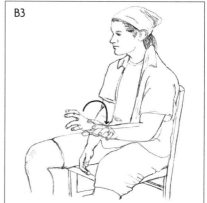

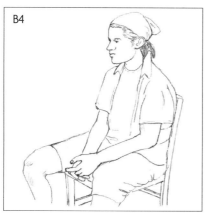

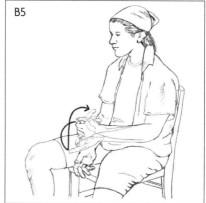

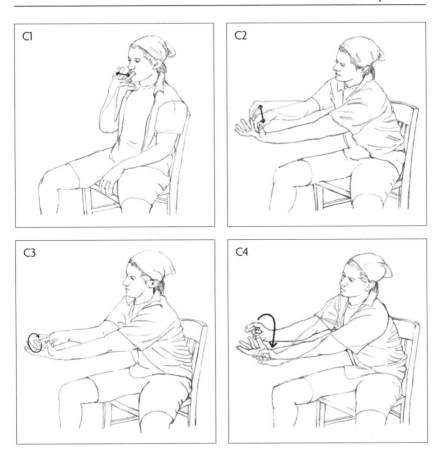

Figure 25 (above and on facing page). Describing a donut-shaped object arcing out of an ashtray (frame A) in speech, the adult in frames B1–B5 produces gestures that are separated by pauses (frames B2 and B4) and thus do not form a single gesture string. In addition, the handshapes he uses are loosely formed and sloppy. In frames C1–C4, the adult describes the event using only his hands and no words. He now produces a string of gestures without breaking his flow of movement, and his handshapes become crisp and clearly articulated.

In contrast, consider the gestures that this adult produced when he was prevented from talking, displayed in the C frames in Figure 25. The gestures produced in this condition were crisp (clearly formed handshapes and motions), segmented, and connected within a single string. The adult first mimed smoking a cigarette with his right hand held to his lips in a "V" (frame C1); he then cupped his left hand in the shape of a dish and mimed stubbing out a cigarette with his right hand (= ashtray; frame C2). While still holding his left hand in the shape of a dish, he drew a circle in the air with his right hand (= donut-shaped object; frame C3). He then formed his right hand into an "O" shape and arced it out of his left, still in the shape of the dish (= arc-out; frame C4).

Were the adults in the gesture-without-speech condition fashioning their gesture strings after English? In other words, did they, like the Australian Aboriginal mourners, use their spoken language as a model for the gesture sentences they created? The answer, very simply, is no. The gesture order that the adults used in the gesture condition did not follow typical English word order. For example, to describe a girl jumping into a hoop, the adults gestured "hoop girl jump," putting the stationary object first, the moving object second, and the action last—rather than putting their gestures in an order more typical of English ("the *girl jumps* into the *hoop*"; Goldin-Meadow, McNeill, and Singleton 1996, see also Goldin-Meadow, Yalabik, and Gershkoff-Stowe 2000).

As another example, look again at the C frames in Figure 25. The adult gestures "ashtray donut arc-out," thus following the "stationary object—moving object—action" order, rather than the "moving object—action—stationary object" order more typical of English ("the *donut arcs-out* of the *ashtray*"). The English order was, in fact, the order that this particular adult did use in speech when describing the scene in the gesture + speech condition—"a crooked circular *donut* shape *moved* from out . . . from within a yellow *ashtray*." The adults in our study may have borrowed the idea of using consistent order from English, but they certainly didn't borrow the order itself.

The imagistic information that gesture conveys when it accompanies speech is an important part of the communicative act. However, the findings presented in this chapter and the others that make up Part IV make it clear that, when gesture is called upon to carry the full burden of communication, it is no longer purely driven by imagery. Rather, gesture takes on the segmented and combinatorial form typically assumed by speech—and it does so right away.

A SYSTEM OF CONTRASTS?

The emergence of segmentation and combination (including ordering) in our experimental paradigm underscores gesture's versatility. With no time for reflection, the adults in our study constructed a set of gestures characterized by segmentation and combination and, in this sense, introduced structure at the sentence level into their gestures. Did they also introduce structure at the word level? Did their gestures display morphological structure?

In fact, they did not. When the hearing adults generated a gesture, their goal was to produce a handshape that adequately represented the object, and their choice of handshapes appeared to be constrained only by their imaginations and the physical limitations imposed by their hands (gesture-to-world relations). For example, a hearing adult might produce a different handshape for each of the five airplanes that appeared in our videotaped vignettes, with each handshape capturing an idiosyncratic property of the airplane pictured in that event. The adults' gestures were not systematically organized into a system of internal contrasts, that is, into a morphology.

It's important to recall here that a gesturer *can* invent morphological structure—indeed, the deaf children did so in their home sign systems (Goldin-Meadow, Mylander, and Butcher 1995; see also Chapter 14). Unlike the adults, when the home signers generated a gesture, their choice of handshapes was guided not only by how well the handshape captured the features of the object (gesture-to-world relations) but also by how well that handshape fit into the set of handshapes allowed in their individual gesture systems (gesture-to-gesture relations). Thus the deaf children used the same handshape for all airplanes (indeed, for all vehicles), regardless of their individual idiosyncrasies, and this handshape contrasted with the handshape used to represent, say, curved objects (Singleton, Morford, and Goldin-Meadow 1993).

The adults did not develop a system of internal contrasts, but they did introduce segmentation and combination into their gestures right away—some properties of language seem to crop up as soon as the manual modality assumes the full burden of communication, others do not. It may, in fact, take time for the manual modality to adopt a system of internal contrasts. Continued experience with a set of gestures may be required for a morphological system of this sort to emerge. Moreover, although we know that children can introduce a system of internal contrasts into the manual modality if given enough time and experience with their own gestures (Goldin-Meadow, Mylander, and Butcher 1995), it's not clear at the moment whether adults can do the same. Indeed, it's possible that the gesture creator must be a child in order for a system of contrasts to emerge. We are going to need long-term studies of the sort described here in order to determine whether the generation of certain linguistic properties in gesture depends on the age of the gesture creator.

DOES THE COMMUNICATION CONTEXT MATTER?

The adults in our study were actually communicating in a very restricted sense. The experimenter was the communication partner for all of the adults, and experimenter and adult watched each videotaped scene together. After the scene, the adult produced gestures to represent the event that the experimenter and adult had both witnessed. Thus the adults were not really conveying new information to the experimenter—they were merely commenting on an event that they and the experimenter had both witnessed, much as mothers and young children do when they comment on events in the here and now, or as friends do when they watch a sporting event together. We wondered what effect a naive communication partner would have on the gesture combinations the adults constructed.

To satisfy our curiosity and to explore the effect that the communication context might have on the adults' gesture combinations, we asked adults to gesture to a naive partner under a variety of communication conditions (Gershkoff-Stowe and Goldin-Meadow 2002):

- We varied whether the partner was permitted to give the gesturer feedback;

- We varied whether the information to be communicated was present in the context that gesturer and partner shared (that is, did they both watch the videotape or not?);

- We varied whether the gesturer switched off and assumed the role of gesture receiver as well as gesture producer.

We then looked at the gesture combinations that the adults created under each condition. Surprisingly, we found that none of the communication variables we explored mattered—the adults used a consistent ordering of semantic elements in all contexts. Even more impressive, they used the same non-English order in all contexts. Word order or, in this case, gesture order appears to be a robust aspect of languagelike communication.

To summarize, speakers who rely on talk to communicate are perfectly capable of abandoning their verbal system and turning to gesture. Moreover, as soon as they begin to gesture without speech, their gestures change in form. The speakers-turned-gesturers no longer represent scenes with a global and unanalyzed gesture. Rather, they create separate gestures for the elements in the scene and string those gestures together into sentencelike units. The sentences that the gesturers create are characterized by ordering patterns (gestures representing certain elements occupy particular positions in the string) and, strikingly, the particular ordering patterns the gesturers use are not typical of English. The gesturers are not merely borrowing a pattern from their spoken language, but are inventing a new one.

Once again, we see that the manual modality is capable of taking on linguistic properties, here over a very short time scale. Given how easily the manual modality can assume a linguistic role, it makes sense to ask why it doesn't do so more often.

Why Don't the Hands Take On Linguistic Structure More Often?

Sign languages (as well as our gesture creation data in children and adults) make it clear that the manual modality can assume a segmented and combinatorial form. Why then did language become the province of the oral modality? Why is speech the most common form of linguistic behavior in human cultures when it could just as easily have been sign?

David McNeill and I (Goldin-Meadow and McNeill 1999) have gone out on a limb and proposed an (undoubtedly untestable) hypothesis to explain this situation. We speculate that having segmented structure in the oral modality, as we currently do, leaves the manual modality free to co-occur with speech and to capture the mimetic aspects of communication *along with* speech. Thus our current arrangement allows us to retain, along with a segmented representation and in a single stream of communication, the imagistic aspects of the mimetic that are so vital to communication.

We argue that the alternative arrangement—in which the manual modality serves languagelike functions and the oral modality serves the mimetic functions—won't work because it forces the oral modality to be unnaturally imagistic in form (although see Haiman 1985 for evidence that the oral modality does exhibit some iconic properties). To recall an example first presented in Chapter 3, Huttenlocher (1973, 1976) points out that a verbal description of the shape of the east coast of the United States is likely not only to be very cumbersome, but also to leave out important information about the coastline—information that we suggest could easily be captured in a mimetic gesture tracing the outline of the coast.

Because the manual modality allows one to represent an image as a whole without breaking it into parts, gesture offers a better vehicle for encoding imagistic information than does speech. The manual modality is therefore the natural choice to encode mimetic information, leaving information that is better captured in a discrete and segmented form to the oral modality.

Under this scenario, speech did not become the predominant medium of human language because it is so well suited to the linear and segmented requirements of symbolic human communication—the manual modality is equally suited to the job. Rather, speech became the medium of human communication because it is not particularly good at capturing the imagistic components of human communication—a task at which the manual modality excels. Language is the province of speech because it's the only job the oral modality can do well.

Note also that the scenario we have proposed leads naturally to the hypothesis with which we began Part IV—that the functions gesture serves are so important that all communicators must do it, even signers. And in Chapter 13 we found evidence that signers do indeed gesture.

So where are we? We have discovered just how versatile the manual modality is. It can take on linguistic properties when called upon to do so, and it can assume the global and imagistic form that is its trademark when accompanied by speech. This versatility was important for us to discover. We now know that when gesture does assume a global and imagistic form, it does so by choice. The form is not required by the manual modality—quite the contrary, it seems to be required by the functions gesture serves, and thus has the potential to inform us about those functions. If our goal is to fully understand how we think and talk, we cannot afford to ignore the unique view that gesture provides.

Conclusion: Talking and Thinking with Gesture

It should be clear by now what it might mean to "hear gesture." Gesture is an integral part of talk, processed by both speakers and listeners. The message that moves between speaker and hearer includes not only what comes out of the mouth and goes into the ear but also what comes out of the hands and goes into the eyes—we can't avoid "hearing" gesture as we hear speech (unless, of course, we close our eyes).

Comes with Talk

When people talk, they gesture. You don't have to be taught to gesture. Strikingly, you don't even have to have arms to feel yourself gesturing. Ramachandran and Blakeslee (1998) describe a young woman, armless from birth, who should know nothing of gesturing firsthand—but she does. Mirabelle was born with two short stumps dangling from her shoulders, but could feel the arms she never had. She had what are known as "phantom limbs." People typically experience a phantom limb after it has been removed. But Mirabelle never had a limb to lose, and Ramachandran was skeptical. When he asked her how she knew that she had phantom limbs, she replied:

> "Well, because as I'm talking to you, they are gesticulating. They point to objects when I point to things, just like your arms and hands . . . When I walk, doctor, my phantom arms don't swing like normal arms, like your

arms. They stay frozen on the side, like this." She stood up, letting her stumps drop straight down on both sides. "But when I talk," she said, "my phantoms gesticulate. In fact, they're moving now as I speak." (Ramachandran and Blakeslee 1998, 41)

Gesturing is part of talking. We don't need to think about gesturing in order to do it. All we need to do is think about talking, and gesturing comes for free. The most striking example is IW (Cole 1991). IW suffered an illness of unknown etiology when he was nineteen years old; he is now in his forties. The illness affected the nerves of his spinal cord and resulted in loss of the sense of touch and proprioception below the neck and loss of all motor control that depends on proprioceptive feedback. Over time and with great effort, IW learned to control his arm and leg movements using visual attention. He has thus regained control over his posture and movement but can exercise that control only when he can see his limbs. In the dark, he cannot move. Our question, of course, is whether IW gestures and, if so, whether he gestures in the dark.

Gallagher, Cole, and McNeill (2001) showed IW the infamous Tweety Bird cartoon and asked him to narrate the story to a listener. He did so twice, once with free vision and once with his arms and hands hidden under a blind. Surprisingly (or perhaps by now, not so surprisingly), IW gestured under both conditions, when he could see his hands and when he could not. Thus IW is able to move his unseen hands when he talks despite the fact that he is unable to move his unseen hands when asked, for example, to pick up a block. Gesturing is clearly not just moving your hands—it's part of the act of talking, and an inseparable part at that.

There remain, however, many questions about which aspects of gesturing are bound to speech. For example, we know that speakers of all languages gesture, but we also know that there are subtle differences in the gestures these speakers produce (Kita and Özyürek 2003; McNeill and Duncan 2000; Özyürek and Kita 1999). My first guess would be that you learn these subtle differences from watching speakers of your language gesture. But maybe you don't. Perhaps learning Spanish is enough to make you gesture like a Spanish speaker, just as learning Turkish would be enough to make you gesture like a Turkish speaker.

The best way to explore this issue is to observe congenitally blind speakers around the globe. We know that individuals who are blind from birth gesture when they talk (Iverson and Goldin-Meadow 1998; see Chapter 10), but do they gesture like natives? If exposure to gesture is necessary to be able to gesture like a native, congenitally blind speakers across the globe shouldn't be able to do it—they should all gesture alike since, under this hypothesis, they lack the input that would create differences across their gestures. If, however, you learn to be a native gesturer by becoming a native speaker, congenitally blind speakers of a given language should look like every other gesturer who speaks that same language—they should produce gestures that look no different from the gestures produced by sighted speakers of that language.

Individuals who are blind from birth are gesturers against all odds, as are Mirabelle and IW. They have taught us much about the deep relation between gesture and talk, and they have more to tell us still.

A Unique Window on Thought

The gestures that we produce when we talk are not just hand waving. They convey substantive ideas. Moreover, those ideas are related to, but are often different from, ideas expressed in the accompanying speech. The manual modality offers a representational format that is distinct from the format used by speech. This format makes it relatively easy to convey visuo-spatial information in gesture; often it is much easier than conveying the same information in speech. As a result, speakers can at times express information in gesture that they are, at that moment, unable to express in speech.

I have argued that these so-called gesture-speech mismatches can be remarkably informative to researchers who pay attention to them. They can tell us who is most likely to profit from instruction—who is ready to learn. And they can reveal knowledge that is not found anywhere in a learner's speech, thus offering unique insight into that learner's thoughts. There are two aspects of these findings that deserve mention and further research.

First, in our explorations of children learning either a math or a conservation task, we have found that children typically express correct ideas first in gesture, and only later in speech. This pattern is not all that surprising, given that math and conservation both involve spatial reasoning. Hadamard (1945) argues that mathematical thinking, particularly innovative mathematical thinking, is conducted not in words but rather in spatial images. These images are likely to be more easily translated into the global-synthetic representation characteristic of gesture than into the linear-segmented representation characteristic of speech. As a result, advances in mathematical reasoning are very likely to come first in gesture—and they do.

The question is whether this phenomenon is a general one. Do new ideas always come first in gesture, regardless of domain? It is certainly possible that speech could anticipate gesture in other, less spatial domains. For example, Church, Schonert-Reichl, and their colleagues (1995) have found that gesture and speech do not always match when children and adults respond to moral reasoning tasks. Moral reasoning is more culturally and socially bound than mathematical reasoning. As a result, talk might be essential for acquiring moral concepts in a way that it may not be for mathematical concepts. If so, gesture might not have privileged access to initial insights into the moral domain, and advances in reasoning might appear first in speech and only later in gesture. Church and Schonert-Reichl are conducting the relevant studies and should know soon.

Second, the ideas speakers express uniquely in gesture are often ideas that the speakers themselves don't even know they know. It may be the very unconsciousness of gesture that gives it its special access to nascent ideas. One question that is of both theoretical and practical concern is "how important is unconsciousness to gesturing?" For example, if I made a speaker aware of her own gestures, would she still be able to express implicit thoughts in gesture (that is, thoughts of which she is not consciously aware)? Would gesture still function to lighten the speaker's cognitive load? In other words, how important is it that we not be aware of what we're gesturing? I'm of two minds about this issue. On the one side, I can easily imagine that making the act of gesturing conscious could fundamentally change that act, perhaps even stripping it of some of its most beneficial features.

On the other side, I'm not at all sure how conscious speakers can ever be of their own gestures. We can tell someone to gesture and the obedient speaker will concentrate on making sure that his hands are in motion. But how much control will that speaker have over precisely what his hands do when in motion? My hunch is that speakers cannot directly control what they do with their hands—their speech does the controlling. Thus, in the end, asking people to gesture may be an excellent way to increase how much they gesture, and may be just the right strategy to use to explore whether gesture really does play a role in thinking (see Chapter 12).

But my hunch may be wrong—and, if so, we need to be cautious not only about the way we conduct our studies but also about what we tell the world, particularly the educational world, about gesture. Should we tell teachers to pay attention to their own gestures? What about students? Should they be told to pay attention to their gestures? to their teachers' gestures? My guess is that they should pay attention to both, but gesture seems to be functioning very effectively in teacher-student exchanges at the moment without any intervention from us (see Chapters 8 and 9). We need much more experimental work before we tamper with a system that appears to be already working.

An Unwitting Part of the Communicative Act

We know that gesture can reveal thoughts that we don't even know we have. Researchers armed with videotape and patience can discover those thoughts and use them to predict who will learn and what they will learn. But the thoughts expressed in gesture are there for the taking. Anyone who is able to understand gesture has access to them, and what we've discovered is that everyone can understand gesture—children, adults, teachers, students. Gesture reading is not a skill that must be taught. We all do it, and are moderately good at it (although we can get better, Kelly et al. 2002; see also Chapter 8).

What this means is that an underground conversation can potentially be taking place every time we talk. Speakers are not always aware of the ideas they express in gesture. Listeners pick up on these ideas, but may themselves not be aware of having done so. An entire exchange can take place without either speaker or listener being consciously aware of the information passed between them.

The teachers described in Chapter 9 are a good example. They were asked to instruct children individually in mathematical equivalence after watching each child participate in a pretest on the task. The children varied in whether they produced gesture-speech mismatches, and the question was whether the teachers noticed and altered their instruction accordingly. The answer was clearly yes. During the instruction period, teachers gave children who produced mismatches more variable input (more different kinds of problem-solving strategies and more of their own gesture-speech mismatches) than they gave to children who did not produce mismatches. The teachers had paid attention to the children's gestures and changed their instruction because of those gestures.

But the underground conversation didn't stop there. Children who received variable input (the variability involved gesture as well as speech) noticed, and profited from that input. In other words, they profited from the instruction that they themselves (via their gestures) had elicited from the teachers. My guess is that all of this happened without anybody, either teacher or student, explicitly noticing gesture.

Again, we need to ask how general this phenomenon is. Does gesture play the same role in other school domains—history, literature, science—or is it limited to math? Does gesture play this role in other communication situations? I suggested in Chapter 8 that gesture might play this same underground role in clinical settings or legal interviews. Indeed, gesture is very likely to provide an undercurrent of conversation in any setting in which there is talk. It is, of course, possible that there are individual differences in how well people pick up on these cues, although we haven't found any yet. It's also possible that there are cultural differences in how much attention is paid to gesture across the globe, although again we've no evidence on this point. But, by and large, it seems very clear that gesture is part of most communicative acts, albeit an unwitting part.

Part of Thinking

Not only is gesture an integral part of communication, but it may also be an integral part of thinking. One of the striking facts about gesturing is that we do it even when no one is watching—on the telephone, when talking to ourselves, when our listener's back is turned. Of course, we might gesture when we're alone out of habit—we're used to moving our hands when we talk and it's hard to stop just because no one is there to appreciate the movements. But this argument won't work for blind speakers who have never seen anyone gesture or react to gesture. They can't have developed a lifelong habit of gesturing for others. Yet blind speakers do gesture when they talk, even when talking to blind listeners (Iverson and Goldin-Meadow 1998). It's hard to get around the fact that, at times, we do seem to be gesturing for ourselves.

Why do we do it? Perhaps gesturing is a vestige of the evolutionary process that gave us speech. It's a hanger-on that accompanies the act of speaking but plays no active role in how we speak or think. If so, gesture would be of interest for what it could reveal to us about the process of speaking or thinking, but it would have no influence on the process itself. This is the least we can say about gesture.

But I believe that the evidence is mounting in favor of the view that gesture does more than just reflect thought—it may shape it as well. We know, for example, that gesturing can lighten a speaker's cognitive load so that the speaker (child or adult) then has more effort left over to perform other tasks (Goldin-Meadow et al. 2001; Chapter 11). We know that children who produce gestures that "mismatch" their speech at a certain point during their acquisition of a math concept arrive at a deeper and longer-lasting understanding of that concept than children who don't (Alibali and Goldin-Meadow 1993b; Chapter 4). What could gesture be doing?

One possibility is that gesture creates instability, and does so over both the short term (speaking at the moment) and the long term (learning over time). For example, McNeill (1992; see also Chapter 12) has proposed that there are moments of instability as we speak (moments that he has called "growth points"), and that gesture has a hand in creating these moments. As described in Chapter 12, gesture facilitates representation of notions very different from what speech facilitates. Growth points form at moments of speaking when there is great disparity between the notions expressed in gesture and speech. Resolution of this disparity propels talk forward toward its next growth point, and thus energizes the system. One circumstantial piece of evidence for this hypothesis comes from the fact that we are most likely to find gesture at moments of greatest ambiguity in speech (that is, when it is most difficult to predict which word will come next; Beattie and Shovelton 2000).

Gesture may also have a hand in creating points of instability during learning over longer time periods. The "mismatch" between gesture and speech defines periods of instability in a child's acquisition of a concept. If provided with instruction, a mismatching child will profit from that instruction and move forward to a stable, correct state. If not given instruction, the mismatching child will again move to a stable state but typically to an incorrect one (Chapter 4). The hypothesis here is that by facilitating the representation of ideas that are different from those expressed in speech, gesture is helping to create an unstable state. That unstable state requires resolution and thus leads to change (not always to progress, but to some sort of movement). We are still far from proving to everyone's satisfaction (even my own) that gesture has a hand in creating instability rather than merely reflecting it. Yet it is a viable hypothesis that deserves our future attention.

If we find, as I suspect we will, that gesture is causally involved in change, gesture's effect is likely to be widespread. As we have seen, gesture is pervasive, appearing in all sorts of situations and over all ages and cultures. Gesture is ever present, and we notice it even though we typically don't know we're noticing it. The time seems ripe to look beyond speakers' words to the secrets that, until now, have been locked in their hands.

References / Credits / Index

References

Acredolo, C., and O'Connor, J. 1991. On the difficulty of detecting cognitive uncertainty. *Human Development, 34,* 204–223.

Acredolo, L. P., and Goodwyn, S. W. 1985. Symbolic gesture in language development: A case study. *Human Development, 28,* 40–49.

——— 1988. Symbolic gesturing in normal infants. *Child Development, 59,* 450–466.

Alibali, M. W. 1994. Processes of cognitive change revealed in gesture and speech. Ph.D. dissertation, University of Chicago.

——— 1999. How children change their minds: Strategy change can be gradual or abrupt. *Developmental Psychology, 35,* 127–145.

Alibali, M. W., Bassok, M., Olseth, K. L., Syc, S. E., and Goldin-Meadow, S. 1999. Illuminating mental representations through speech and gesture. *Psychological Sciences, 10,* 327–333.

Alibali, M. W., and DiRusso, A. A. 1999. The function of gesture in learning to count: More than keeping track. *Cognitive Development, 14,* 37–56.

Alibali, M. W., Flevares, L., and Goldin-Meadow, S. 1997. Assessing knowledge conveyed in gesture: Do teachers have the upper hand? *Journal of Educational Psychology, 89,* 183–193.

Alibali, M. W., and Goldin-Meadow, S. 1993a. Modelling learning using evidence from speech and gesture. *Proceedings of the 15th Annual Conference of the Cognitive Science Society,* 203–208.

——— 1993b. Gesture-speech mismatch and mechanisms of learning: What the hands reveal about a child's state of mind. *Cognitive Psychology, 25,* 468–523.

Alibali, M. W., Heath, D. C., and Myers, H. J. 2001. Effects of visibility between speaker and listener on gesture production: Some gestures are meant to be seen. *Journal of Memory and Language, 44,* 1–20.

Alibali, M. W., Kita, S., Bigelow, L. J., Wolfman, C. M., and Klein, S. M. 2001. Gesture plays a role in thinking for speaking. In *Oralité et gestualité: Interac-*

tions et comportements multimodaux dans la communication, ed. C. Cavé, I. Guaïtella, and S. Santi, 407–410. Paris: L'Harmattan.

Alibali, M. W., Kita, S., and Young, A. J. 2000. Gesture and the process of speech production: We think, therefore we gesture. *Language and Cognitive Processes, 15,* 593–613.

Allen, R., and Shatz, M. 1983. 'What says meow?' The role of context and linguistic experience in very young children's responses to *what*-questions. *Journal of Child Language, 10,* 14–23.

Andersen, R. A. 1995. Coordinate transformations and motor planning in posterior parietal cortex. In *The cognitive neurosciences,* ed. M. S. Gazzaniga, 519–532. Cambridge: MIT Press.

Argyle, M. 1975. *Bodily communication.* New York: International Universities Press.

Baddeley, A. D. 1986. *Working memory.* Oxford: Oxford University Press.

Baggett, P. 1984. Role of temporal overlap of visual and auditory material in forming dual media associations. *Journal of Educational Psychology, 76,* 408–417.

Bahan, B. 1996. Non-manual realization of agreement in American Sign Language. Ph.D. dissertation, Boston University.

Barsalou, L. W. 1999. Perceptual symbols systems. *Behavioral and Brain Sciences, 22,* 577–660.

Bates, E. 1976. *Language and context: The acquisition of pragmatics.* New York: Academic Press.

Bates, E., Benigni, L., Bretherton, I., Camaioni, L., and Volterra, V. 1979. *The emergence of symbols: Cognition and communication in infancy.* New York: Academic Press.

Bavelas, J. B. 1994. Gestures as part of speech: Methodological implications. *Research on Language and Social Interaction, 27,* 201–221.

Bavelas, J. B., Chovil, N., Lawrie, D. A., and Wade, A. 1992. Interactive gestures. *Discourse Processes, 15,* 469–489.

Beattie, G., and Coughlan, J. 1998. Do iconic gestures have a functional role in lexical access? An experimental study of the effects of repeating a verbal message on gesture production. *Semiotica, 119,* 221–249.

———— 1999. An experimental investigation of the role of iconic gestures in lexical access using the tip-of-the-tongue phenomenon. *British Journal of Psychology, 90,* 35–56.

Beattie, G., and Shovelton, H. 1999a. Do iconic hand gestures really contribute anything to the semantic information conveyed by speech? An experimental investigation. *Semiotica, 123,* 1–30.

———— 1999b. Mapping the range of information contained in the iconic hand gestures that accompany spontaneous speech. *Journal of Language and Social Psychology, 18,* 438–462.

———— 2000. Iconic hand gestures and the predictability of words in context in spontaneous speech. *British Journal of Psychology, 91,* 473–491.

Behr, M., Erlwanger, S., and Nichols, E. 1980. How children view the equal sign. *Mathematics Teaching, 92,* 13–15.

Bekken, K. 1989. Is there "Motherese" in gesture? Ph.D. dissertation, University of Chicago.

Bellugi, U., and Studdert-Kennedy, M., eds. 1980. *Signed and spoken language: Biological constraints on linguistic form.* Deerfield Beach, Fla.: Verlag Chemie.

Berger, K. W., and Popelka, G. R. 1971. Extra-facial gestures in relation to speech-reading. *Journal of Communication Disorders, 3,* 302–308.

Bidell, T. R., and Fischer, K. W. 1992. Beyond the stage debate: Action, structure, and variability in Piagetian theory and research. In *Intellectual development,* ed. R. Sternberg and C. Berg, 100–140. New York: Cambridge University Press.

—— 1995. Developmental transitions in children's early on-line planning. In *The development of future-oriented processes,* ed. M. M. Haith, J. B. Benson, R. J. Roberts, Jr., and B. F. Pennington. Chicago: University of Chicago Press.

Bonvillian, J. D., and Folven, R. J. 1993. Sign language acquisition: Developmental aspects. In *Psychological perspectives on deafness,* ed. M. Marschark and M. D. Clark, 229–265. Hillsdale, N.J.: Erlbaum.

Bonvillian, J. D., Orlansky, M. O., and Novack, L. L. 1983. Developmental milestones: Sign language acquisition and motor development. *Child Development, 54,* 1435–1445.

Borys, S. V., Spitz, H. H., and Dorans, B. A. 1982. Tower of Hanoi performance of retarded young adults and nonretarded children as a function of solution length and goal state. *Journal of Experimental Child Psychology, 33,* 87–110.

Broaders, S., and Goldin-Meadow, S. n.d. Misleading the child by the hand. In preparation.

Butcher, C., and Goldin-Meadow, S. 2000. Gesture and the transition from one-to two-word speech: When hand and mouth come together. In *Language and gesture,* ed. D. McNeill, 235–257. New York: Cambridge University Press.

Butcher, C., Mylander, C., and Goldin-Meadow, S. 1991. Displaced communication in a self-styled gesture system: Pointing at the non-present. *Cognitive Development, 6,* 315–342.

Butterworth, B., and Beattie, G. 1978. Gesture and silence as indicators of planning in speech. In *Recent advances in the psychology of language: Formal and experimental approaches,* ed. R. N. Campbell and P. T. Smith. New York: Plenum.

Butterworth, B., and Hadar, U. 1989. Gesture, speech, and computational stages: A reply to McNeill. *Psychological Review, 96,* 168–174.

Byrnes, M. M., and Spitz, H. H. 1979. Developmental progression of performance on the Tower of Hanoi problem. *American Journal of Mental Deficiency, 81,* 561–569.

Capirci, O., Montanari, S., and Volterra, V. 1998. Gestures, signs, and words in early language development. In *The nature and functions of gesture in children's communications,* ed. J. M. Iverson and S. Goldin-Meadow, 45–60. New Directions for Child Development, no. 79. San Francisco: Jossey-Bass.

Ceci, S. J. 1995. False beliefs: Some developmental and clinical considerations. In *Memory distortion: How minds, brains, and societies reconstruct the past,* ed. D. L. Schacter, 91–125. Cambridge: Harvard University Press.

Chi, M. T. H., Bassok, M., Lewis, M. W., Reimann, P., and Glaser, R. 1989. Self-explanations: How students study and use examples in learning to solve problems. *Cognitive Science, 13,* 145–182.

Christenfeld, N., Schachter, S., and Bilous, F. 1991. Filled pauses and gestures: It's not coincidence. *Journal of Psycholinguistic Research, 20,* 1–10.

Church, R. B. 1999. Using gesture and speech to capture transitions in learning. *Cognitive Development, 14,* 313–342.

Church, R. B., Ayman-Nolley, S., and Estrada, J. n.d. The effects of gestural instruction on bilingual children. *International Journal of Bilingual Education and Bilingualism.* In press.

Church, R. B., and Goldin-Meadow, S. 1986. The mismatch between gesture and speech as an index of transitional knowledge. *Cognition, 23,* 43–71.

Church, R. B., Schonert-Reichl, K., Goodman, N., Kelly, S. D., and Ayman-Nolley, S. 1995. The role of gesture and speech communication as reflections of cognitive understanding. *Journal of Contemporary Legal Issues, 6,* 123–154.

Clark, H. 1996. *Using language.* Cambridge: Cambridge University Press.

Clark, H., and Gerrig, R. 1990. Questions as demonstrations. *Language, 66,* 764–805.

Cohen, A. A., and Harrison, R. P. 1973. Intentionality in the use of hand illustrators in face-to-face communication situations. *Journal of Personality and Social Psychology, 28,* 276–279.

Cohen, E., Namir, L., and Schlesinger, I. M. 1977. *A new dictionary of Sign Language.* The Hague: Mouton.

Cole, J. 1991. *Pride and a daily marathon.* London: Duckworth.

Conrad, R. 1979. *The deaf child.* London: Harper & Row.

Crowder, E. M. 1996. Gestures at work in sense-making science talk. *Journal of the Learning Sciences, 5,* 173–208.

Crowder, E. M., and Newman, D. 1993. Telling what they know: The role of gesture and language in children's science explanations. *Pragmatics and Cognition, 1,* 341–376.

DeMatteo, A. 1977. Visual imagery and visual analogues in American Sign Language. In *On the other hand: New perspectives on American Sign Language,* ed. L. Friedman, 109–136. New York: Academic Press.

De Ruiter, J.-P. 1998. Gesture and speech production. MPI Series in Psycholinguistics, no. 6. Max Planck Institute for Psycholinguistics, Nijmegen, The Netherlands.

Dienes, Z., and Perner, J. 1999. A theory of implicit and explicit knowledge. *Behavioral and Brain Sciences, 22,* 735–80.

Duffy, R. J., and Duffy, J. R. 1981. Three studies of deficits in pantomimic expression and pantomimic recognition in aphasia. *Journal of Speech and Hearing Research, 46,* 70–84.

Duffy, R. J., Duffy, J. R., and Pearson, K. L. 1975. Pantomime recognition in aphasics. *Journal of Speech and Hearing Research, 18,* 115–132.

Efron, D. 1972. *Gesture, race, and culture.* The Hague: Mouton. Originally published in 1942 under the title *Gesture and environment,* by King's Crown Press, Morningside Heights, N.Y.

Egan, D. E., and Greeno, J. G. 1974. Theory of rule induction: Knowledge acquired in concept learning, serial pattern learning, and problem solving. In *Knowledge and cognition*, ed. L. W. Gregg. Hillsdale, N.J.: Erlbaum.

Ekman, P., and Friesen, W. 1969. The repertoire of nonverbal behavioral categories. *Semiotica, 1,* 49–98.

—— 1972. Hand movements. *Journal of Communication, 22,* 353–374.

Ekman, P., Friesen, W., and Ellsworth, P. 1972. *Emotion in the human face.* New York: Pergamon Press.

Emmorey, K. 1999. Do signers gesture? In *Gesture, speech, and sign,* ed. L. S. Messing and R. Campbell, 133–159. Oxford: Oxford University Press.

Emmorey, K., and Casey, S. 1995. A comparison of spatial language in English and American Sign Language. *Sign Language Studies, 88,* 255–288.

—— 2001. Gesture, thought, and spatial language. *Gesture, 1,* 35–50.

Evans, J. L., Alibali, M. W., and McNeil, N. M. 2001. Divergence of embodied knowledge and verbal expression: Evidence from gesture and speech in children with Specific Language Impairment. *Language and Cognitive Processes, 16,* 309–331.

Evans, M. A., and Rubin, K. H. 1979. Hand gestures as a communicative mode in school-aged children. *Journal of Genetic Psychology, 135,* 189–196.

Ewert, P. H., and Lambert, J. F. 1932. The effect of verbal instructions upon the formation of a concept. *Journal of General Psychology, 6,* 400–413.

Fant, L. J. 1972. *Ameslan: An introduction to American Sign Language.* Silver Springs, Md.: National Association of the Deaf.

Feldman, H., Goldin-Meadow, S., and Gleitman, L. 1978. Beyond Herodotus: The creation of language by linguistically deprived deaf children. In *Action, symbol, and gesture: The emergence of language,* ed. A. Lock, 351–414. New York: Academic Press.

Feyereisen, P. 1983. Manual activity during speaking in aphasic subjects. *International Journal of Psychology, 18,* 545–556.

Feyereisen, P., and de Lannoy, J.-D. 1991. *Gestures and speech: Psychological investigations.* Cambridge: Cambridge University Press.

Feyereisen, P., van de Wiele, M., and Dubois, F. 1988. The meaning of gestures: What can be understood without speech. *Cahiers de Psychologie Cognitive/European Bulletin of Cognitive Psychology, 8,* 3–25.

Fischer, K. W. 1980. A theory of cognitive development: The control and construction of hierarchies of skills. *Psychological Review, 87(6),* 477–531.

Fischer, S. 1975. Influences on word order change in American Sign Language. In *Word order and word order change,* ed. C. Li, 1–25. Austin: University of Texas Press.

Flevares, L. M., and Perry, M. 2001. How many do you see? The use of nonspoken representations in first-grade mathematics lessons. *Journal of Educational Psychology, 93,* 330–345.

Frishberg, N. 1975. Arbitrariness and iconicity: Historical change in American Sign Language. *Language, 51,* 696–719.

Gagne, R. M., and Smith, E. C. 1962. A study of the effects of verbalization on problem solving. *Journal of Experimental Psychology, 63,* 12–18.

Gallagher, S., Cole, J., and McNeill, D. 2001. The language-thought-hand system. In *Oralité et gestualité: Interactions et comportements multimodaux dans la com-*

munication, ed. C. Cavé, I. Guaïtella, and S. Santi, 420–424. Paris: L'Harmattan.

Garber, P., Alibali, M. W., and Goldin-Meadow, S. 1998. Knowledge conveyed in gesture is not tied to the hands. *Child Development, 69,* 75–84.

Garber, P., and Goldin-Meadow, S. 2002. Gesture offers insight into problem-solving in adults and children. *Cognitive Science, 26,* 817–831.

Geary, D. C. 1995. Reflections of evolution and culture in children's cognition: Implications for mathematical development and instruction. *American Psychologist, 50,* 24–37.

Gee, J. P., and Goodhart, W. 1985. Nativization, linguistic theory, and deaf language acquisition. *Sign Language Studies, 49,* 291–342.

Gelman, R., and Gallistel, C. R. 1978. *The child's understanding of number.* Cambridge, Mass.: Harvard University Press.

Gelman, S. A. 1988. The development of induction with natural kind and artifact categories. *Cognitive Psychology, 20,* 65–95.

Gelman, S. A., and Tardif, T. 1998. A cross-linguistic comparison of generic noun phrases in English and Mandarin. *Cognition, 66,* 215–248.

Gershkoff-Stowe, L., and Goldin-Meadow, S. 2002. Is there a natural order for expressing semantic relations? *Cognitive Psychology, 45,* 375–412.

Gershkoff-Stowe, L., and Smith, L. B. 1997. A curvilinear trend in naming errors as a function of early vocabulary growth. *Cognitive Psychology, 34,* 37–71.

Ginsburg, H. 1977. *Children's arithmetic.* New York: Van Nostrand.

Glenberg, A. M. 1997. What memory is for. *Behavioral and Brain Sciences, 20,* 1–55.

Glenberg, A. M., and Kaschak, M. P. 2002. Grounding language in action. *Psychonomic Bulletin and Review, 9,* 558–565.

Glenberg, A. M., and Robertson, D. A. 1999. Indexical understanding of instructions. *Discourse Processes, 28,* 1–26.

Goffman, E. 1976. *Gender advertisements.* New York: Harper & Row.

Goldin-Meadow, S. 1985. Language development under atypical learning conditions: Replication and implications of a study of deaf children of hearing parents. In *Children's language,* vol. 5, ed. K. Nelson, 197–245. Hillsdale, N.J.: Erlbaum.

—— 1993. When does gesture become language? A study of gesture used as a primary communication system by deaf children of hearing parents. In *Tools, language, and cognition in human evolution,* ed. K. R. Gibson and T. Ingold, 63–85. New York: Cambridge University Press.

—— 2003. *The resilience of language: What gesture creation in deaf children can tell us about how all children learn language.* New York: Psychology Press.

Goldin-Meadow, S., and Alibali, M. W. 1994. Do you have to be right to redescribe? *Behavioral and Brain Sciences, 17,* 718–719.

—— 1995. Mechanisms of transition: Learning with a helping hand. In *The psychology of learning and motivation,* vol. 33, ed. D. Medin, 115–157. New York: Academic Press.

—— 1999. Does the hand reflect implicit knowledge? Yes and no. *Behavioral and Brain Sciences, 22,* 766–767.

—— 2002. Looking at the hands through time: A microgenetic perspective on learning and instruction. In *Microdevelopment: Transition processes in develop-*

ment and learning, ed. N. Granott and J. Parziale, 80–105. New York: Cambridge University Press.

Goldin-Meadow, S., Alibali, M. W., and Church, R. B. 1993. Transitions in concept acquisition: Using the hand to read the mind. *Psychological Review, 100,* 279–297.

Goldin-Meadow, S., and Butcher, C. 2003. Pointing toward two-word speech in young children. In *Pointing: Where language, culture, and cognition meet,* ed. S. Kita, 85–107. Hillsdale, N.J.: Erlbaum.

Goldin-Meadow, S., Butcher, C., Mylander, C., and Dodge, M. 1994. Nouns and verbs in a self-styled gesture system: What's in a name? *Cognitive Psychology, 27,* 259–319.

Goldin-Meadow, S., and Feldman, H. 1977. The development of language-like communication without a language model. *Science, 197,* 401–403.

Goldin-Meadow, S., Gelman, S. A., and Mylander, C. n.d. Expressing generic concepts with and without a language model. Under review.

Goldin-Meadow, S., Kim, S., and Singer, M. 1999. What the teacher's hands tell the student's mind about math. *Journal of Educational Psychology, 91,* 720–730.

Goldin-Meadow, S., and McNeill, D. 1999. The role of gesture and mimetic representation in making language the province of speech. In *The descent of mind,* ed. Michael C. Corballis and Stephen Lea, 155–172. Oxford: Oxford University Press.

Goldin-Meadow, S., McNeill, D., and Singleton, J. 1996. Silence is liberating: Removing the handcuffs on grammatical expression in the manual modality. *Psychological Review, 103,* 34–55.

Goldin-Meadow, S., and Mylander, C. 1983. Gestural communication in deaf children: The non-effects of parental input on language development. *Science, 221,* 372–374.

———— 1984. Gestural communication in deaf children: The effects and non-effects of parental input on early language development. *Monographs of the Society for Research in Child Development, 49,* 1–121.

———— 1998. Spontaneous sign systems created by deaf children in two cultures. *Nature, 91,* 279–281.

Goldin-Meadow, S., Mylander, C., and Butcher, C. 1995. The resilience of combinatorial structure at the word level: Morphology in self-styled gesture systems. *Cognition, 56,* 195–262.

Goldin-Meadow, S., Nusbaum, H., Garber, P., and Church, R. B. 1993. Transitions in learning: Evidence for simultaneously activated strategies. *Journal of Experimental Psychology: Human Perception and Performance, 19,* 92–107.

Goldin-Meadow, S., Nusbaum, H., Kelly, S. D., and Wagner, S. 2001. Explaining math: Gesturing lightens the load. *Psychological Science, 12,* 516–522.

Goldin-Meadow, S., and Sandhofer, C. M. 1999. Gesture conveys substantive information about a child's thoughts to ordinary listeners. *Developmental Science, 2,* 67–74.

Goldin-Meadow, S., and Singer, M. A. 2003. From children's hands to adults' ears: Gesture's role in the learning process. *Developmental Psychology, 39,* 509–520.

Goldin-Meadow, S., Wein, D., and Chang, C. 1992. Assessing knowledge through gesture: Using children's hands to read their minds. *Cognition and Instruction, 9,* 201–219.

Goldin-Meadow, S., Yalabik, E., and Gershkoff-Stowe, L. 2000. The resilience of ergative structure in language created by children and by adults. *Proceedings of Boston University Conference on Language Development, 24,* 343–353.

Goodglass, H., and Kaplan, E. 1963. Disturbance of gesture and pantomime in aphasia. *Brain, 86,* 703–720.

Goodhart, W. 1984. Morphological complexity, ASL and the acquisition of sign language in deaf children. Ph.D. dissertation, Boston University.

Goodwyn, S. W., and Acredolo, L. P. 1993. Symbolic gesture versus word: Is there a modality advantage for onset of symbol use? *Child Development, 64,* 688–701.

———— 1998. Encouraging symbolic gestures: A new perspective on the relationship between gesture and speech. In *The nature and functions of gesture in children's communications,* ed. J. M. Iverson and S. Goldin-Meadow, 61–73. New Directions for Child Development, no. 79. San Francisco: Jossey-Bass.

Graham, J. A., and Argyle, M. 1975. A cross-cultural study of the communication of extra-verbal meaning by gestures. *International Journal of Psychology, 10,* 57–67.

Graham, J. A., and Heywood, S. 1975. The effects of elimination of hand gestures and of verbal codability on speech performance. *European Journal of Social Psychology, 2,* 189–195.

Graham, T. A. 1999. The role of gesture in children's learning to count. *Journal of Experimental Child Psychology, 74,* 333–355.

Griffin, P., and Cole, M. 1985. Current activity for the future: The zo-ped. In *Children's learning in the "zone of proximal development,"* ed. B. Rogoff and J. V. Wertsch, 45–64. New Directions for Child Development, no. 23. San Francisco: Jossey-Bass.

Gulberg, M. 1998. *Gesture as a communication strategy in second language discourse: A study of learners of French and Swedish.* Lund, Sweden: Lund University Press.

Hadamard, J. 1945. *The psychology of invention in the mathematical field.* New York: Dover Publications.

Haiman, J. 1985. *Iconicity in syntax.* Amsterdam: John Benjamins.

Haviland, J. 1993. Anchoring, iconicity, and orientation in Guugu Yimithirr pointing gestures. *Linguistic Anthropology, 1,* 3–45.

———— 2000. Pointing, gesture spaces, and mental maps. In *Language and gesture,* ed. D. McNeill, 13–46. Cambridge: Cambridge University Press.

Hayes, J. R., and Simon, H. A. 1977. Psychological differences among problem isomorphs. In *Cognitive theory, 2,* ed. N. J. Castellan, D. B. Pisoni, and G. R. Potts, 21–41. Hillsdale, N.J.: Erlbaum.

Heath, C. C. 1992. Gesture's discrete tasks: Multiple relevancies in visual conduct in the contextualization of language. In *The contextualization of language,* ed. P. Auer and A. di Luzio, 102–127. Amsterdam: John Benjamins.

Hockett, C. F. 1960. The origin of speech. *Scientific American, 203(3),* 88–96.

Hoffmeister, R., and Wilbur, R. 1980. Developmental: The acquisition of sign language. In *Recent perspectives on American Sign Language*, ed. H. Lane and F. Grosjean. Hillsdale, N.J.: Erlbaum.

Horobin, K., and Acredolo, C. 1989. The impact of probability judgments on reasoning about multiple possibilities. *Child Development, 60,* 183–200.

Huttenlocher, J. 1973. Language and thought. In *Communication, language, and meaning: Psychological perspectives,* ed. G. A. Miller, 172–184. New York: Basic Books.

—— 1976. Language and intelligence. In *The nature of intelligence,* ed. L. B. Resnick, 261–281. Hillsdale, N.J.: Erlbaum.

Iverson, J. M. 1999. How to get to the cafeteria: Gesture and speech in blind and sighted children's spatial descriptions. *Developmental Psychology, 35,* 1132–1142.

Iverson, J. M., Capirci, O., and Caselli, M. C. 1994. From communication to language in two modalities. *Cognitive Development, 9,* 23–43.

Iverson, J. M., Capirci, O., Longobardi, E., and Caselli, M. C. 1999. Gesturing in mother-child interaction. *Cognitive Development, 14,* 57–75.

Iverson, J. M., and Goldin-Meadow, S. 1997. What's communication got to do with it: Gesture in blind children. *Developmental Psychology, 33,* 453–467.

—— 1998. Why people gesture as they speak. *Nature, 396,* 228.

—— 2001. The resilience of gesture in talk: Gesture in blind speakers and listeners. *Developmental Science, 4,* 416–422.

Iverson, J. M., Tencer, H. L., Lany, J., and Goldin-Meadow, S. 2000. The relation between gesture and speech in congenitally blind and sighted language-learners. *Journal of Nonverbal Behavior, 24,* 105–130.

Jancovic, M. A., Devoe, S., and Wiener, M. 1975. Age-related changes in hand and arm movements as nonverbal communication: Some conceptualizations and an empirical exploration. *Child Development, 46,* 922–928.

Jecker, J. D., Maccoby, N., and Breitrose, H. S. 1965. Improving accuracy in interpreting nonverbal cues of comprehension. *Psychology in the Schools, 2,* 239–244.

Jonides, J., Smith, E. E., Koeppe, R. A., Awh, E., Minoshima, S., and Mintun, M. A. 1993. Spatial working memory in humans as revealed by PET. *Nature, 363,* 623–625.

Karmiloff-Smith, A. 1986. From meta-processes to conscious access: Evidence from children's metalinguistic and repair data. *Cognition, 232,* 95–147.

—— 1992. *Beyond modularity: A developmental perspective on cognitive science.* Cambridge: MIT Press.

Kegl, J., Senghas, A., and Coppola, M. 1999. Creation through contact: Sign language emergence and sign language change in Nicaragua. In *Language creation and language change: Creolization, diachrony, and development,* ed. M. DeGraff, 179–237. Cambridge: MIT.

Keil, F. C. 1984. Mechanisms of cognitive development and the structure of knowledge. In *Mechanisms of cognitive development,* ed. R. J. Sternberg, 81–100. New York: W. H. Freeman and Co.

Kelly, S. D. 2001. Broadening the units of analysis in communication: Speech and nonverbal behaviours in pragmatic comprehension. *Journal of Child Language, 28,* 325–349.

Kelly, S. D., Barr, D., Church, R. B., and Lynch, K. 1999. Offering a hand to pragmatic understanding: The role of speech and gesture in comprehension and memory. *Journal of Memory and Language, 40,* 577–592.

Kelly, S. D., and Church, R. B. 1997. Can children detect conceptual information conveyed through other children's nonverbal behaviors? *Cognition and Instruction, 15,* 107–134.

———— 1998. A comparison between children's and adults' ability to detect conceptual information conveyed through representational gestures. *Child Development, 69,* 85–93.

Kelly, S. D., Singer, M., Hicks, J., and Goldin-Meadow, S. 2002. A helping hand in assessing children's knowledge: Instructing adults to attend to gesture. *Cognition and Instruction, 20,* 1–26.

Kendon, A. 1980. Gesticulation and speech: Two aspects of the process of utterance. In *Relationship of verbal and nonverbal communication,* ed. M. R. Key, 207–228. The Hague: Mouton.

———— 1985. Some uses of gesture. In *Perspectives on silence,* ed. D. Tannen and M. Saville-Troike, 215–234. Norwood, N.J.: Ablex.

———— 1988. *Sign languages of Aboriginal Australia.* New York: Cambridge University Press.

———— 1990. Signs in the cloister and elsewhere. *Semiotica, 79,* 307–329.

———— 1992. Some recent work from Italy on quotable gestures ('emblems'). *Journal of Linguistic Anthropology, 2,* 72–93.

———— 1994. Do gestures communicate?: A review. *Research on Language and Social Interaction, 27,* 175–200.

———— 1995. Gestures as illocutionary and discourse structure markers in Southern Italian conversation. *Journal of Pragmatics, 23,* 247–279.

Kieran, C. 1980. The interpretation of the equal sign: Symbol for an equivalence relation vs. an operator symbol. *Proceedings of the Fourth International Conference for the Psychology of Mathematics Education,* 163–169.

Kita, S. 1993. Language and thought interface: A study of spontaneous gestures and Japanese mimetics. Ph.D. dissertation, University of Chicago.

———— 2000. How representational gestures help speaking. In *Language and gesture,* ed. D. McNeill, 162–185. New York: Cambridge University Press.

Kita, S., and Özyürek, A. 2003. What does cross-linguistic variation in semantic coordination of speech and gesture reveal?: Evidence for an interface representation of spatial thinking and speaking. *Journal of Memory and Language, 48,* 16–32.

Klahr, D. 1984. Transition processes in quantitative development. In *Mechanisms of cognitive development,* ed. R. J. Sternberg, 101–140. New York: W. H. Freeman and Co.

Klima, E., and Bellugi, U. 1979. *The signs of language.* Cambridge: Harvard University Press.

Knapp, M. L. 1978. *Nonverbal communication in human interaction.* 2d ed. New York: Holt, Rinehart and Winston.

Kohlberg, L. 1969. Stage and sequence: The cognitive-developmental approach to socialization. In *Handbook of socialization theory and research,* ed. S. Goslin, pp. 347–480. Chicago: Rand McNally.

Kotovsky, K., Hayes, J. R., and Simon, H. A. 1985. Why are some problems hard? Evidence from the Tower of Hanoi. *Cognitive Psychology, 17,* 248–294.

Krauss, R. M., Chen, Y., and Gottesman, R. F. 2000. Lexical gestures and lexical access: A process model. In *Language and gesture,* ed. D. McNeill, 261–283. New York: Cambridge University Press.

Krauss, R. M., Dushay, R. A., Chen, Y., and Rauscher, F. 1995. The communicative value of conversational hand gestures. *Journal of Experimental Social Psychology, 31,* 533–553.

Krauss, R. M., Morrel-Samuels, P., and Colasante, C. 1991. Do conversational hand gestures communicate? *Journal of Personality and Social Psychology, 61,* 743–754.

Kuhn, D., and Pearsall, S. 1998. Relations between metastrategic knowledge and strategic performance. *Cognitive Development, 13,* 227–247.

Lakoff, G., and Johnson, M. 1980. *Metaphors we live by.* Chicago: University of Chicago Press.

Lane, H., Boyes-Braem, P., and Bellugi, U. 1976. Preliminaries to a distinctive feature analysis of handshapes in American Sign Language. *Cognitive Psychology, 8,* 263–289.

Lane, H., and Grosjean, F. 1980. *Recent perspectives on American Sign Language.* Hillsdale, N.J.: Erlbaum.

Lang, J. W. 1976. Amphibious behavior of *Alligator mississippiensis:* Roles of a circadian rhythm and light. *Science, 191,* 575–577.

Langer, J. 1969. Disequilibrium as a source of development. In *Trends and issues in developmental psychology,* ed. P. Mussen, J. Langer, and M. Covington, 22–37. New York: Holt, Rinehart and Winston.

Lee, V., and Beattie, G. 1998. The rhetorical organization of verbal and nonverbal behavior in emotion talk. *Semiotica, 120,* 39–92.

Lempers, J., Flavell, E., and Flavell, J. 1976. The development in very young children of tacit knowledge concerning visual perception. *Genetic Psychology Monographs, 4.*

Lenneberg, E. H. 1964. Capacity for language acquisition. In *The structure of language: Readings in the philosophy of language,* ed. J. A. Fodor and J. J. Katz, 579–603. Englewood Cliffs, N.J.: Prentice-Hall.

Leung, E., and Rheingold, H. 1981. Development of pointing as a social gesture. *Developmental Psychology, 17,* 215–220.

Lickiss, K. P., and Wellens, A. R. 1978. Effects of visual accessibility and hand restraint on fluency of gesticulator and effectiveness of message. *Perceptual and Motor Skills, 46,* 925–926.

Liddell, S. K. 1980. *American Sign Language syntax.* The Hague: Mouton.

——— 1984. "Think" and "believe": Sequentiality in American Sign Language. *Language, 60,* 372–399.

——— 2000. Indicating verbs and pronouns: Pointing away from agreement. In *The signs of language revisited: An anthology to honor Ursula Bellugi and Edward Klima,* ed. K. Emmorey and H. Lane, 303–320. Mahway, N.J.: Erlbaum.

Liddell, S. K., and Johnson, R. 1986. American Sign Language compound formation processes, lexicalization, and phonological remnants. *Natural Language and Linguistic Theory, 4,* 445–513.

———— 1989. American Sign Language: The phonological base. *Sign Language Studies, 64,* 195–277.

Liddell, S. K., and Metzger, M. 1998. Gesture in sign language discourse. *Journal of Pragmatics, 30,* 657–697.

Lillo-Martin, D. 1986. Two kinds of null arguments in American Sign Language. *Natural Language and Linguistic Theory, 4,* 415–444.

———— 1999. Modality effects and modularity in language acquisition: The acquisition of American Sign Language. In *Handbook of Child Language Acquisition,* ed. W. C. Ritchie and T. K. Bhatia, 531–567. New York: Academic Press.

Lillo-Martin, D., and Klima, E. 1990. Pointing out differences: ASL pronouns in syntactic theory. In *Theoretical issues in sign language research I: Linguistics,* ed. S. Fischer and P. Siple, 191–210. Chicago: University of Chicago Press.

Livingston, S. 1983. Levels of development in the language of deaf children. *Sign Language Studies, 40,* 193–286.

Logan, G. D. 1979. On the use of a concurrent memory load to measure attention and automaticity. *Journal of Experimental Psychology: Human Perception and Performance, 5,* 189–207.

Lou, M. W.-P. 1988. The history of language use in education of the Deaf. In *Language learning and deafness,* ed. M. Strong, 75–98. Cambridge: Cambridge University Press.

Lucy, J. A. 1993. Reflexive language and the human disciplines. In *Reflexive language: Reported speech and metapragmatics,* ed. J. Lucy, 9–32. New York: Cambridge University Press.

Machida, S. 1986. Teacher accuracy in decoding non-verbal indicants of comprehension and noncomprehension in Anglo- and Mexican-American children. *Journal of Educational Psychology, 6,* 454–464.

Macnamara, J. 1977. From sign to language. In *Language learning and thought,* ed. J. Macnamara. New York: Academic Press.

Mallery, G. [1881] 1972. *Sign language among the North American Indians compared with that of other peoples and deaf mutes.* The Hague: Mouton.

Marcos, L. R. 1979. Hand movements and nondominant fluency in bilinguals. *Perceptual and Motor Skills, 48,* 207–214.

Marmor, G., and Petitto, L. 1979. Simultaneous communication in the classroom: How well is English grammar represented? *Sign Language Studies, 23,* 99–136.

Marschark, M. 1994. Gesture and sign. *Applied Psycholinguistics, 15,* 209–236.

Mayberry, R. I. 1992. The cognitive development of deaf children: Recent insights. In *Child Neuropsychology,* ed. S. Segalowitz and I. Rapin, 51–68. Handbook of Neuropsychology, ed. F. Boller and J. Graffman, vol. 7. Amsterdam: Elsevier.

Mayberry, R. I., and Jaques, J. 2000. Gesture production during stuttered speech: Insights into the nature of gesture-speech integration. In *Language and gesture,* ed. D. McNeill, 199–214. New York: Cambridge University Press.

Mayer, R. E., and Anderson, R. B. 1991. Animations need narrations: An experimental test of a dual-coding hypothesis. *Journal of Educational Psychology, 83,* 484–490.

McDonald, B. 1982. Aspects of the American Sign Language predicate system. Ph.D. dissertation, University of Buffalo.

McNeill, D. 1985. So you think gestures are nonverbal? *Psychological Review, 92,* 350–371.

——— 1987. *Psycholinguistics: A new approach.* New York: Harper & Row.

——— 1989. A straight path to where? Reply to Butterworth and Hadar. *Psychological Review, 96,* 175–179.

——— 1992. *Hand and mind: What gestures reveal about thought.* Chicago: University of Chicago Press.

McNeill, D., Cassell, J., and McCullough, K.-E. 1994. Communicative effects of speech-mismatched gestures. *Research on Language and Social Interaction, 27,* 223–237.

McNeill, D., and Duncan, S. D. 2000. Growth points in thinking-for-speaking. In *Language and gesture,* ed. D. McNeill, 141–161. New York: Cambridge University Press.

Meadow, K. 1968. Early manual communication in relation to the deaf child's intellectual, social, and communicative functioning. *American Annals of the Deaf, 113,* 29–41.

Meissner, M., and Philpott, S. B. 1975. The sign language of sawmill workers in British Columbia. *Sign Language Studies, 9,* 291–308.

Melinger, A., and Kita, S. n.d. Does gesture help processes of speech production? Evidence for conceptual level facilitation. *Proceedings of the Berkeley Linguistic Society.* In press.

Miller, P. J., and Hoogstra, L. 1989. How to represent the native child's point of view: Methodological problems in language socialization. Paper presented at the annual meeting of the American Anthropological Association, Washington, D.C.

Mohay, H. 1982. A preliminary description of the communication systems evolved by two deaf children in the absence of a sign language model. *Sign Language Studies, 34,* 73–90.

Moores, D. F. 1974. Nonvocal systems of verbal behavior. In *Language perspectives: Acquisition, retardation, and intervention,* ed. R. L. Schiefelbusch and L. L. Lloyd. Baltimore: University Park Press.

Morford, J. P., and Goldin-Meadow, S. 1997. From here to there and now to then: The development of displaced reference in homesign and English. *Child Development, 68,* 420–435.

Morford, M., and Goldin-Meadow, S. 1992. Comprehension and production of gesture in combination with speech in one-word speakers. *Journal of Child Language, 19,* 559–580.

Morrel-Samuels, P., and Krauss, R. M. 1992. Word familiarity predicts temporal asynchrony of hand gestures and speech. *Journal of Experimental Psychology: Learning, Memory, and Cognition, 18,* 615–622.

Müller, C. 1998. *Redebegleitende Gesten: Kulturgeschichte, Theorie, Sprachvergleich.* Berlin: Verlag Arno Spitz.

——— 2001. Gesture-space and culture. In *Oralité et gestualité: Interactions et comportements multimodaux dans la communication,* ed. C. Cavé, I. Guaïtella, and S. Santi, 565–571. Paris: L'Harmattan.

Murphy, C. M., and Messer, D. J. 1977. Mothers, infants, and pointing: A study of gesture. In *Studies in mother-infant interaction*, ed. H. R. Schaffer. New York: Academic Press.

Namy, L. L., and Waxman, S. R. 1988. Words and gestures: Infants' interpretations of different forms of symbolic reference. *Child Development, 69,* 295–308.

National Council of Teachers of Mathematics (NCTM). 1989. *Curriculum and evaluation standards for school mathematics.* Reston, Va.: NCTM.

Neill, S. 1991. *Classroom nonverbal communication.* London: Routledge.

Neill, S., and Caswell, C. 1993. *Body language for competent teachers.* London: Routledge.

Newport, E. L. 1981. Constraints on structure: Evidence from American Sign Language and language learning. In *Minnesota Symposium on Child Psychology,* vol. 14, ed. W. A. Collins. Hillsdale, N.J.: Erlbaum.

Newport, E. L., and Meier, R. P. 1985. The acquisition of American Sign Language. In *The cross-linguistic study of language acquisition,* vol. 1: *The data,* ed. D. I. Slobin, 881–938. Hillsdale, N.J.: Erlbaum.

Nicolades, E., Mayberry, R. I., and Genessee, F. 1999. Gesture and early bilingual development. *Developmental Psychology, 35,* 514–526.

Nobe, S. 2000. Where do *most* spontaneous representational gestures actually occur with respect to speech? In *Language and gesture,* ed. D. McNeill, 186–198. New York: Cambridge University Press.

Norman, D. A., and Bobrow, D. G. 1975. On data-limited and resource-limited processes. *Cognitive Psychology, 7,* 44–64.

Nusbaum, H. C., and Schwab, E. C. 1986. The role of attention and active processing in speech perception. In *Pattern recognition by humans and machines,* vol. 1: *Speech Perception,* ed. E. C. Schwab and H. C. Nusbaum. New York: Academic Press.

O'Reilly, R. C., Braver, T. S., and Cohen, J. D. 1999. A biologically based computational model of working memory. In *Models of working memory: Mechanisms of active maintenance and executive control,* ed. A. Miyake and P. Shah, 375–411. New York: Cambridge University Press.

Özyürek, A. 2000. The influence of addressee location on spatial language and representational gestures of direction. In *Language and gesture,* ed. D. McNeill, 64–82. New York: Cambridge University Press.

————— 2002. Do speakers design their co-speech gestures for their addressees?: The effects of addressee location on representational gestures. *Journal of Memory and Language, 46,* 688–704.

Özyürek, A., and Kita, S. 1999. Expressing manner and path in English and Turkish: Differences in speech, gesture, and conceptualization. *Proceedings of the Twenty-First Annual Meeting of the Cognitive Science Society,* 507–512.

Padden, C. 1983. Interaction of morphology and syntax in American Sign Language. Ph.D. dissertation, University of California at San Diego.

————— 1990. Rethinking fingerspelling. *Signpost,* October 2–4. International Linguistics Association, University of Durham.

Perry, M., Berch, D., and Singleton, J. 1995. Constructing shared understanding:

The role of nonverbal input in learning contexts. *Journal of Contemporary Legal Issues, 6*, 213–235.

Perry, M., Church, R. B., and Goldin-Meadow, S. 1988. Transitional knowledge in the acquisition of concepts. *Cognitive Development, 3*, 359–400.

―――― 1992. Is gesture-speech mismatch a general index of transitional knowledge? *Cognitive Development, 7*, 109–122.

Perry, M., and Elder, A. D. 1997. Knowledge in transition: Adults' developing understanding of a principle of physical causality. *Cognitive Development, 12*, 131–157.

Petersen, S. E., Fox, P. T., Posner, M. I., Mintun, M., Raichle, M. E. 1988. Positron emission tomographic studies of the cortical anatomy of single-word processing. *Nature, 331*, 585–589.

Petitto, L. A. 1992. Modularity and constraints in early lexical acquisition: Evidence from children's early language and gesture. In *Minnesota Symposium on Child Psychology*, vol. 25, ed. M. Gunnar, 25–58. Hillsdale, N.J.: Erlbaum.

Philips, S. U. 1985. Interaction structured through talk and interaction structured through 'silence.' In *Perspectives on silence*, ed. D. Tannen and M. Saville-Troike, 205–213. Norwood, N.J.: Ablex Publishing Corporation.

Phillips, S. B., Goldin-Meadow, S., and Miller, P. J. 2001. Enacting stories, seeing worlds: Similarities and differences in the cross-cultural narrative development of linguistically isolated deaf children. *Human Development, 44*, 416–422.

Piaget, J. [1975] 1985. *The equilibration of cognitive structures.* Chicago: University of Chicago Press.

Pimm, D. 1987. *Speaking mathematically: Communication in mathematics classrooms.* London: Routledge and Kegan Paul.

Ramachandran, V. S., and Blakeslee, S. 1998. *Phantoms in the brain: Probing the mysteries of the human mind.* New York: William Morrow and Co.

Rauscher, F. H., Krauss, R. M., and Chen, Y. 1996. Gesture, speech, and lexical access: The role of lexical movements in speech production. *Psychological Science, 7*, 226–231.

Rimé, B. 1982. The elimination of visible behaviour from social interactions: Effects on verbal, nonverbal, and interpersonal variables. *European Journal of Social Psychology, 12*, 113–129.

Rimé, B., Schiaratura, L., Hupet, M., and Ghysselinckx, A. 1984. Effects of relative immobilization on the speaker's nonverbal behavior and on the dialogue imagery level. *Motivation and Emotion, 8*, 311–325.

Riseborough, M. G. 1981. Physiographic gestures as decoding facilitators: Three experiments exploring a neglected facet of communication. *Journal of Nonverbal Behavior, 5*, 172–183.

Rizzolatti, G., and Arbib, M. A. 1998. Language within our grasp. *Trends in Neuroscience, 21*, 188–194.

Rogers, W. T. 1978. The contribution of kinesic illustrators toward the comprehension of verbal behavior within utterances. *Human Communication Research, 5*, 54–62.

Roth, W.-M., and Welzel, M. 2001. From activity to gestures and scientific language. *Journal of Research in Science Teaching, 38*, 103–136.

Sandler, W. 1986. The spreading hand autosegment of American Sign Language. *Sign Language Studies, 50,* 1–28.

―――― 2003. On the complementarity of signed and spoken language. In *Language competence across populations: On the definition of SLI,* ed. Y. Levy and J. Schaeffer, 383–409. Mahwah, N.J.: Erlbaum.

Saussure, F. de. [1916] 1959. *Course in general linguistics.* Trans. W. Baskin. Reprint. New York: Philosophical Library.

Saxe, G. B., and Kaplan, R. 1981. Gesture in early counting: A developmental analysis. *Perceptual and Motor Skills, 53,* 851–854.

Schick, B. S. 1987. The acquisition of classifier predicates in American Sign Language. Ph.D. dissertation, Purdue University.

Schlesinger, H. 1978. The acquisition of bimodal language. In *Sign language of the deaf: Psychological, linguistic, and sociological perspectives,* ed. I. Schlesinger, 57–93. New York: Academic Press.

Schwartz, D. L. 1995. The emergence of abstract representations in dyad problem solving. *Journal of the Learning Sciences, 4,* 321–354.

Schwartz, D. L., and Black, J. B. 1996. Shuttling between depictive models and abstract rules: Induction and fallback. *Cognitive Science, 20,* 457–497.

Senghas, A. 1995. The development of Nicaraguan Sign Language via the language acquisition process. *Proceedings of Boston University Conference on Language Development, 19,* 543–552.

―――― 2000. The development of early spatial morphology in Nicaraguan Sign Language. *Proceedings of Boston University Conference on Language Development, 24,* 696–707.

Senghas, A., Coppola, M., Newport, E. L., and Supalla, T. 1997. Argument structure in Nicaraguan Sign Language: The emergence of grammatical devices. *Proceedings of Boston University Conference on Language Development, 21,* 550–561.

Shatz, M. 1982. On mechanisms of language acquisition: Can features of the communicative environment account for development? In *Language acquisition: The state of the art,* ed. E. Wanner and L. R. Gleitman, 102–127. New York: Cambridge University Press.

Shavelson, R. J., Webb, N. M., Stasz, C., and McArthur, D. 1988. Teaching mathematical problem solving: Insights from teachers and tutors. In *The teaching and assessing of mathematical problem solving,* ed. R. I. Charles and E. A. Silver, 203–231. Reston, Va.: National Council of Teachers of Mathematics.

Shiffrin, R. M., and Schneider, W. 1984. Automatic and controlled processing revisited. *Psychological Review, 84,* 127–190.

Siegler, R. S. 1994. Cognitive variability: A key to understanding cognitive development. *Current Directions in Psychological Science, 3,* 1–5.

―――― 1996. *Emerging minds: The process of change in children's thinking.* New York: Oxford University Press.

―――― 1997. A microgenetic study of self-explanation. Paper presented at the biennial meeting of the Society for Research in Child Development, Washington, D.C. April.

Siegler, R. S., and Chen, Z. 1998. Developmental differences in rule learning: A microgenetic analysis. *Cognitive Psychology, 30,* 273–310.

Siegler, R. S., and Crowley, K. 1991. The microgenetic method: A direct means for studying cognitive development. *American Psychologist, 46(6),* 606–620.

Siegler, R. S., and Jenkins, E. 1989. *How children discover new strategies.* Hillsdale, N.J.: Erlbaum.

Siegler, R. S., and McGilly, K. 1989. Strategy choices in children's time-telling. In *Time and human cognition: A life span perspective,* ed. I. Levin and D. Zakay. Amsterdam: Elsevier.

Siegler, R. S., and Shrager, J. 1984. Strategy choices in addition and subtraction: How do children know what to do? In *The origins of cognitive skills,* ed. C. Sophian. Hillsdale, N.J.: Erlbaum.

Siegler, R., and Stern, E. 1998. Conscious and unconscious strategy discoveries: A microgenetic analysis. *Journal of Experimental Psychology: General, 127,* 377–397.

Singer, M., and Goldin-Meadow, S. n.d. What happens when a teacher's gesture and speech don't overlap? Children learn. In preparation.

Singleton, J. L., Morford, J. P., and Goldin-Meadow, S. 1993. Once is not enough: Standards of well-formedness in manual communication created over three different timespans. *Language, 69,* 683–715.

Slama-Cazacu, T. 1976. Nonverbal components in message sequence: "Mixed syntax." In *Language in man: Anthropological issues,* ed. W. C. McCormack and S. A. Wurm. The Hague: Mouton.

Slobin, D. I. 1996. From "thought and language" to "thinking for speaking." In *Rethinking linguistic relativity,* ed. J. J. Gumperz and S. C. Levinson, 97–114. Cambridge: Cambridge University Press.

Smith, E. E., and Jonides, J. 1995. Working memory in humans: Neuropsychological evidence. In *The Cognitive Neurosciences,* ed. M. Gazzaniga, 1009–1020. Cambridge: MIT Press.

Snyder, S. S., and Feldman, D. H. 1977. Internal and external influences on cognitive developmental change. *Child Development, 48,* 937–943.

Stigler, J. W., and Hiebert, J. 1999. *The teaching gap.* New York: Free Press.

Stokoe, W. C. 1960. *Sign language structure: An outline of the visual communications systems.* Studies in Linguistics, Occasional Papers, 8. Buffalo, N.Y.: Department of Anthropology and Linguistics, University of Buffalo.

Stone, A., Webb, R., and Mahootian, S. 1991. The generality of gesture-speech mismatch as an index of transitional knowledge: Evidence from a control-of-variables task. *Cognitive Development, 6,* 301–313.

Strauss, S. 1972. Inducing cognitive development and learning: A review of short-term training experiments. I. The organismic developmental approach. *Cognition, 1(4),* 329–357.

Strauss, S., and Rimalt, I. 1974. Effects of organizational disequilibrium training on structural elaboration. *Developmental Psychology, 10(4),* 526–533.

Supalla, S. 1991. Manually Coded English: The modality question in signed language development. In *Theoretical issues in sign language research,* vol. 2: *Acquisition,* ed. P. Siple and S. Fischer, 85–109. Chicago: University of Chicago Press.

Supalla, T. 1982. Structure and acquisition of verbs of motion and location in

American Sign Language. Ph.D. dissertation, University of California at San Diego.

Supalla, T., and Newport, E. L. 1978. How many seats in a chear? The derivation of nouns and verbs in American Sign Language. In *Understanding language through sign language research,* ed. P. Siple, 91–132. New York: Academic Press.

Supalla, T., Newport, E. L., Singleton, J. L., Supalla, S., Metlay, D., and Coulter, G. n.d. *Test battery for American Sign Language morphology and syntax.* Burtonsville, Md.: Linstok Press. In press.

Suty, K. A., and Friel-Patti, S. 1982. Looking beyond Signed English to describe the language of two deaf children. *Sign Language Studies, 35,* 153–168.

Tervoort, B. T. 1961. Esoteric symbolism in the communication behavior of young deaf children. *American Annals of the Deaf, 106,* 436–480.

Thal, D., Tobias, S., and Morrison, D. 1991. Language and gesture in late talkers: A one year followup. *Journal of Speech and Hearing Research, 34,* 604–612.

Thelen, E., and Smith, L. B. 1994. *A dynamic systems approach to the development of cognition and action.* Cambridge: MIT Press.

Thompson, L., and Massaro, D. 1986. Evaluation and integration of speech and pointing gestures during referential understanding. *Journal of Experimental Child Psychology, 57,* 327–354.

Turiel, E. 1969. Developmental processes in the child's moral thinking. In *Trends and issues in developmental psychology,* ed. P. Mussen, J. Langer, and M. Covington, 92–133. New York: Holt, Rinehart and Winston.

———— 1974. Conflict and transition in adolescent moral development. *Child Development, 45,* 14–29.

Umiker-Sebeok, J., and Sebeok, T. A., eds. 1987. *Monastic sign languages.* The Hague: Mouton.

Valenzeno, L., Alibali, M. W., and Klatzky, R. L. 2003. Teachers' gestures facilitate students' learning: A lesson in symmetry. *Contemporary Educational Psychology, 28,* 187–204.

Volterra, V., and Iverson, J. M. 1995. When do modality factors affect the course of language acquisition? In *Language, gesture, and space,* ed. K. Emmorey and J. S. Reilly, 371–390. Hillsdale, N.J.: Erlbaum.

Vygotsky, L. S. 1978. *Mind in society: The development of higher psychological processes.* Cambridge: Harvard University Press.

Wagner, S., Nusbaum, H., and Goldin-Meadow, S. n.d. Probing the mental representation of gesture: Is hand-waving spatial? Under review.

Walker, L. J., and Taylor, J. H. 1991. Stage transitions in moral reasoning: A longitudinal study of developmental processes. *Developmental Psychology, 27,* 330–337.

Wang, L., and Goodglass, H. 1992. Pantomime, praxis, and aphasia. *Brain and Language, 42,* 402–418.

Wesp, R., Hesse, J., Keutmann, D., and Wheaton, K. 2001. Gestures maintain spatial imagery. *American Journal of Psychology, 114,* 591–600.

Wickens, C. D. 1984. Processing resources in attention. In *Varieties of attention,* ed. R. Parasuraman and D. R. Davies, 63–102. Orlando, Fla.: Academic Press.

Wilbur, R. 1986. Interaction of linguistic theory and sign language research. In

The real world linguist: Linguistic applications for the 1980's, ed. P. Bjarkman and V. Raskin. Norwood, N.J.: Ablex.

Wilkinson, A. C. 1982. Partial knowledge and self-correction: Developmental studies of a quantitative concept. *Developmental Psychology, 18(6),* 876–893.

Wolff, P., and Gutstein, J. 1972. Effects of induced motor gestures on vocal output. *Journal of Communication, 22,* 277–288.

Wundt, W. [1900] 1973. *The language of gestures.* The Hague: Mouton.

Wynn, K. 1990. Children's understanding of counting. *Cognition, 36,* 155–193.

Zaslavsky, C. [1973] 1999. *Africa counts: Number and pattern in African cultures.* 3d ed. Chicago: Lawrence Hill Books.

Zelazo, P. D., Frye, D., and Rapus, T. 1996. An age-related dissociation between knowing rules and using them. *Cognitive Development, 11,* 37–63.

Zukow-Goldring, P., Romo, L., and Duncan, K. R. 1994. Gestures speak louder than words: Achieving consensus in Latino classrooms. In *Education as cultural construction: Exploration in socio-cultural studies,* vol. 4, ed. A. Alvarez and P. del Rio, 227–239. Madrid: Fundación Infancia y Aprendizaje.

Credits

Figure 5 M. W. Alibali and S. Goldin-Meadow, "Modelling learning using evidence from speech and gesture," *Proceedings of the 15th Annual Conference of the Cognitive Science Society* (1993), 207. © 1993 by the Cognitive Science Society. Reprinted with permission.

Figure 8 Adapted from S. Goldin-Meadow and C. Butcher, "Pointing toward two-word speech in young children." In *Pointing: Where language, culture, and cognition meet,* edited by S. Kita (Hillsdale, N.J.: Erlbaum, 2003), p. 99, fig. 5.3.

Figures 14 and 15 S. Goldin-Meadow and M. A. Singer. "From children's hands to adults' ears: Gesture's role in the learning process," *Developmental Psychology,* 2003, *39*, figs. 2, 3, and 4. © 2003 by the American Psychological Association. Adapted with permission.

Figures 19 and 20 S. Goldin-Meadow, H. Nusbaum, S. Kelly, and S. Wagner, "Explaining math: Gesturing lightens the load." *Psychological Science,* 2001, *12*, 518 (fig. 1) and 520 (fig. 3). © 2001 by the American Psychological Society. Reprinted with permission from Blackwell Publishers.

Figure 21 S. Goldin-Meadow, H. Nusbaum, P. Garber, and R. B. Church, "Transitions in learning: Evidence for simultaneously activated strategies," *Journal of Experimental Psychology: Human Perception and Performance,* 1993, *19*, 100–101, figs. 2 and 3. Copyright © 1993 by the American Psychological Association. Adapted with permission.

Figure 23 P. Garber and S. Goldin-Meadow, "Gesture offers insight into problem-solving in adults and children," *Cognitive Science,* 2002, 826, fig. 3. © 2002 by the Cognitive Science Society. Adapted with permission.

Index